IN THE REIGN OF

ROTHSTEIN

♠ ♥ ♦ ♣

DONALD HENDERSON
CLARKE

IN THE
REIGN
OF
ROTHSTEIN

IN THE REIGN OF
ROTHSTEIN

by

Donald
Henderson
Clarke

New York: 1929
The Vanguard Press

PUBLISHED JANUARY, 1929

To

Dr. and Mrs. Louis H. Clarke

*They have stood for so much from
their son that they probably
can stand for this*

ACKNOWLEDGMENT

The making of this book has been a most happy
one due to the cheerful helpfulness of

Hal Burrows, who designed the jacket,
E. V. Ireland, who drew the end papers,
Howard and Betty Dietz, who read the proofs,
and *The World* for the use of its library.

FOREWORD

As a reader of books I bear a striking resemblance to the late Count Tolstoi—I read the conclusion of a book first. I never read introductions, either, but that doesn't prevent me from writing them. I've written lots of pieces I should hate to have to read.

In the first place, although I knew a good many gamblers, confidence men, badger game workers, pickpockets and murderers in my time, I never was interested in their professions, except as they affected me in my day's work as a newspaper reporter. I knew very well and very favorably two extremely successful murderers who, although arrested, never were convicted. A most pleasant companion—I might say a real friend—was a former dope peddler who has turned bootlegger. As he puts it, "The cops used to be my enemies; they beat me up whenever they met me. Now that I'm in a respectable business they are my pals."

Another chap I liked very much was a pickpocket —one of the best in New York. He must be, because so far as I know he never has been arrested. A friend tried to point out to me one fight night at the old Madison Square Garden how artistically this pickpocket was doing his work. But I didn't look.

I used to tell these friends of mine occasionally,

"You know, I like you, but I could sit in the death house at Sing Sing and see all you lads burned in the chair without batting an eye. If I suddenly were made a dictator, I certainly would make one grand clean-up." But as affairs of society are conducted, there was nothing for me to do. I knew what their different businesses were, but I didn't know it legally. Their businesses were none of my business. District Attorneys and police know these persons' business too—better than anyone. But proving a specific case against them is something else again.

I was in charge of a good many investigations for big newspapers, and looking back at it, I think I was a pretty fair investigator. But my investigations were carried out by ringing front door bells and presenting my card and stating my full name and my occupation and then asking questions.

I carried my feeling about my own conduct pretty far. For instance, I never would meet any one socially who was connected with prohibition enforcement. I never could tolerate grafters who posed as law enforcers. It seemed to me that meeting a burglar who was proud that he was a good burglar, or meeting a pickpocket who took a solemn pride in the fact that he was a good pickpocket, was vastly different from meeting an official who was pretending to be what he wasn't. Just as I couldn't, and didn't want to, prove legally that the crooks (who didn't pretend they were anything else) were guilty of any specific criminal act, on the other hand, I couldn't prove legally my suspicions that a good many public officials were crooks while making loud virtuous noises. I went about among crooks who appeared to me to be intrinsically honest, strange as that may seem, as well as among officials whose honesty to me (and in some cases with extremely good reason) seemed pretty shaky.

Naturally, I was asked many times about my duty as an American citizen. My reply to that always was that my first duty was to keep my own conscience clear—and I have a trick conscience. I know it would act up if I told on any one. I tried it once when I was about six years old. And I've been trying to live down that episode ever since.

I knew a lot of crooks—and I knew, in the course of my work, a lot of law enforcement officials. And I couldn't be either. I couldn't do any of the jobs they both have to do.

Every one who is honest knows the law isn't justice. It's a game. And it's a game at which I always preferred to be merely an onlooker.

This book will make plain how the law worked in the case of Arnold Rothstein—to mention only the chief character—who openly violated our legal code every day of his adult life in the City of New York.

DONALD HENDERSON CLARKE

CONTENTS

CHAPTER ONE

THE MAGIC OF A NAME

Nicky Arnstein surrendered himself most spectacularly to the police in May, 1920, in connection with the $5,000,000 bond thefts in Wall Street. Unsympathetic judges raised his bail from $60,000 to $100,000. This was $40,000 more than had been arranged for by Arnold Rothstein. So Nicky temporarily went to the Tombs.

Fannie Brice, then Nick's loyal wife (she divorced him later), the late William J. Fallon, who was the most amazing criminal lawyer in the history of New York courts, Harold Norris, of the National Surety Company, and the writer, then on the staff of the *New York World*, went to a café within a hop of the Criminal Courts building in New York, to have a drink or two, and consider the situation.

Nicky had made his sensational trip down Fifth Avenue, where he was not recognized, and through Lafayette Street to the District Attorney's office, in a new and shining Cadillac landaulet. The irony of the situation was heightened by the fact that Nicky rode in the rear of a police parade! The *World* knew that jaunt was coming off because Rothstein had told an editor about it; so George Boothby, of the staff, met the party and made the historic trip.

This automobile with nickel plate a-plenty, spark-

1

ling like a bridal gift, was left at the curb in front of the café, and in plain sight of the Criminal Courts building. Once within the back room, Fannie dried her tears and did a few imitations of herself which impressed those of us who were there as being much funnier than any imitations of other persons this most gifted comedienne ever had done on the stage. During a lull in the laughter, some one casually glanced out of the window and observed that the roadster no longer was glittering at the curb. It was gone! ✶

Now, not unknown in that particular oasis in what was supposed to have been an entirely arid New York, was a chap who was known to be a camp follower of one of the powers of Tammany Hall. Fallon and Norris promptly hopped on this individual, called him many picturesque names, and threatened him with several dire fates if he didn't get the automobile back immediately. Their method of approach was distasteful to the chap, whom we will call "Jack" for the sake of ease, although that was not his name. And Jack swore back at them.

After Fallon and Norris had told him what was on their minds, I addressed myself to Jack, whom I had known in the course of business for a considerable time. Jack had an uncanny gift of being able to prophesy disagreements in jury trials in criminal cases; and he continually maintained that he always kept his gun in readiness to shoot. Whether this latter was an alcoholic dream or not, I never took occasion to discover.

Anyway, I went to my friend Jack, and said in effect: "Look here, Jack. Go ahead and be mad at

2

Fallon and Norris. That was not their car that was stolen. The car belongs to Nicky Arnstein. Nicky is a member of your club in good standing—if being charged with being the 'master mind' in a $5,000,000 haul counts for anything in your set—and he is being bailed by Arnold Rothstein. You knew that, didn't you—Arnold Rothstein. And, besides, Fannie Brice has had enough trouble. Listen to her crying back there."

"A. R. is on the bail?" Jack repeated. "Well, I don't mind telling you a mistake was made. The guys that took that car didn't know who it belonged to—see? They thought it was just one of those cars. And they'll be getting busy in about five minutes changing it so its own mother wouldn't recognize it. That is, maybe they will. Wait a minute."

Jack went to a nickel-in-the-slot telephone and called a number in the Orchard exchange. What the number was and what he said I did not hear, and, what is more, did not care anything about hearing. What you don't know never hurts you much in New York's swifter currents.

In a moment or two, Jack turned away from the telephone and walked to the bar for another drink. "It's O. K.," he said. "The car'll be back in a few minutes. It's like I said. Those guys didn't know whose bus it was."

"That must be a great business—stealing cars," was suggested.

"It's a pretty good graft—better than blowing safes, anyway," Jack agreed. "The head guy here in

3

New York used to be the best peterman—safe blower—in the country. That guy's an artist."

Jack told of a few details of the guy's artistry which have slipped from memory (as they did while they were being related), and added that the work of losing the identity of an automobile required no little genius, and several automobiles.

"They switch engines and bodies and everything around so fast it would make your head swim," said Jack. "Remember," he added, "I did this for you, and not for those big bums back there. Fallon thinks he can get away with everything. I like some of you newspaper guys who are regular."

"That's fine, Jack, thank you," I said in reply, thinking at the same time that the man who was bringing back the automobile hadn't been anywhere near that café on that day. But I didn't again mention Rothstein, either to Jack, or to Fallon, or Norris, or Fannie Brice, whom I rejoined immediately. Although I was supposed to be very friendly with Bill Fallon, and in fact had been with him on this occasion night and day for several days, neither Fallon nor Fannie had said anything to me up to that time about Rothstein putting up the bail. And I have always followed a policy of not knowing too much.

It may be mentioned that I felt that this procedure bore luxuriant fruit a few months later when, escorted down to Washington to be asked questions about various matters relating to Arnstein, Rothstein and Fallon by the federal authorities who were prosecuting the Arnstein case, I could truthfully say that I knew nothing of legal import. This writer, frankly, never wanted to *know* anything very definite about Rothstein, who has been called the "Brain," the "Master Mind," the "Wolf," the "Czar," and other high-sounding titles of the underworld. Whatever he was, he certainly was the most amazingly powerful influence in it and the most generally feared. Parenthetically, it may be observed, the police were as gracious to him as they were to a Police Commissioner.

Well, to get back to the café. It wasn't long before the pretty roadster pulled up at the curb, the check for the highballs was paid, the amount was rung up on a cash register that might have been audible in the District Attorney's office, and Fannie Brice, Fallon, Norris, and the writer went out into the street.

There, lined up beside the car, were four men, among them Monk Eastman, who a short time later was to fall beneath a fusillade of revolver bullets in East Fourteenth Street. Eastman, notorious killer, said:

"We're sorry this happened, Mr. Fallon. We didn't know to whom the car belonged. Will you introduce us to the lady?"

"Introduce you blankety-blank blanks to a lady! I should say not," said Fallon.

And, piling into the car, we all headed up town for the lady's apartment, leaving the four lads standing at the curb, looking wistfully after the flash of nickel, the scintillation of plate glass, and the purr of perfect mechanism which was going out of their misunderstood lives forever.

Now this hitherto untold bit showing the manner in which the underworld functions is illustrative of one of the most characteristic attributes of Arnold Rothstein. He honestly could say that the persons who took the automobile were only names to him, and that he was in ignorance of the whole transaction. But such was the power of his name in the latter years of his reign that a mere mention of it was more puissant in many quarters than the actual presence would have been of the entire Police Department and the District Attorney's staff.

The proximity of the District Attorney's office did not prevent Monk Eastman and his followers from stealing the car. Mere mention of Rothstein's name got the car back.

You, Mr. Average Citizen, may wonder where the sway of a man like Arnold Rothstein touched your life. You know that we have lovely laws in this country, aimed at making everything sweet and pretty for you and your family. You probably believe that most of these laws are actually enforced.

You know there are laws against gambling—and yet Rothstein ran, or backed, gambling houses all over the country for years.

You know there are laws against shooting other persons with revolvers—including shooting policemen—and yet two policemen were shot, not seriously, but nevertheless conclusively, in a raid on a crap game in which Rothstein was a participant, and nothing was done about it in the way of convincing

6

any one, but plenty was done in the way of wasting court's time and Grand Jury's time—and taxpayers' money—for months and months. And it was generally believed that Rothstein fired the shots.

You know there are laws against bucketing, and yet Fuller and Company and Dillon and Company failed for millions, impoverishing you and persons like you, who may have no way of knowing whether or not the brokerage house with which you do business is being conducted in a legitimate manner. And Rothstein was the most interesting figure in the legal investigations of these failures. He bailed the five indicted principals and was questioned at great length, but to no useful purpose, about $187,600 in checks that he received between January and November, 1921, from the Fuller firm.

You know there are laws against stealing of all kinds. Yet, except for the short terms that Big Nick Cohen, Nicky Arnstein and three minor figures served in Atlanta, nothing ever has been done in a constructive way about the $5,000,000 bond robberies which agitated the country in 1919. The lawyer for the receiver in bankruptcy for Nicky Arnstein asserted in court, following Rothstein's death by a revolver bullet, on election day morning, 1928, that he believed the $5,000,000 in bonds, or most of them, would be found in Rothstein's effects.

You know there are laws against bribing baseball players to throw baseball games. Yet enough of the White Sox of Chicago were bribed to throw the 1919 World Series to Cincinnati. Rothstein was accused in this deal, but hotly protested his virtue and

7

asserted that he had lost $60,000 betting the wrong way.

You know there are laws against peddling dope in this country. Yet the United States Attorney's office, following Rothstein's death, seized $7,000,000 worth of narcotics—and this hoard was unearthed through clues obtained by studying Rothstein's private memoranda.

You know there are laws against shooting craps. Yet everyone, including the Police Commissioner, the District Attorney, and all the uniformed patrolmen and plain clothes detectives in the New York Police Department, knew that Arnold Rothstein was the greatest, most prodigiously successful crap shooter that ever threw a "natural," or successfully faded an opponent.

You know there are laws against betting on horse races in the state of New York. Yet everybody knew Arnold Rothstein as the biggest bettor on horses that ever lived. He made Pittsburgh Phil, Riley Grannan, and all those old timers look small when it came to placing money on horses. His greatest winning in one race—$800,000 on the good horse Sidereal—was a sensation. Think of it—nearly $1,000,000 (and some reports erroneously placed the winnings at that figure) on one horse in one race. That is a great story in itself, and the inside facts will be told for the first time in these pages.

You know there are laws against selling alcoholic beverages. Yet they are sold. And the traffickers in alcohol need cash—to put over deals and to get bail when they are in trouble. And Arnold Rothstein was the greatest source of ready money in the underworld.

That, in fact, was the secret of the prodigious power Rothstein wielded—millions in money. It was millions in "easy money," accumulated by outsmarting the world; gathered in by those white, womanish hands, which in turn were guided by the smartest unsocial mind of his time.

The influence of this money was so enormous that the probability is that even Rothstein himself couldn't really grasp the extent of his power. The American Federation of Labor made the charge, June 11, 1927, that, "It is said that nearly ten days before the beginning of the present reign of terror [in the fur strike] one Arnold Rothstein, said to be a famous or infamous gambler, had been the means of fixing the police in behalf of the Communists."

Now this writer's sources of information are pretty good. And he never did believe that Rothstein had anything to do with "fixing" that situation with the police. What he may have done was lend the Left Wing some money. Money with the Rothstein label on it was marvellous money to use in New York and its environs in Arnold Rothstein's time.

Rothstein was a great money lender. Those closest to him admit that the money he handled was "dirty," but they don't believe that Rothstein himself ever arranged the details of any criminal racket. He would finance persons, of whose ability to repay he was certain, and his power and prestige went with the backing.

He knew practically everybody—judges, lawyers,

newspaper editors, politicians, brokers, lights of the "400," and luminaries of the underworld. They were all one to Arnold Rothstein, and he would use his friends to the limit, when the occasion demanded. And he wasn't above preparing for the occasion by letting certain indebtednesses carry over indefinitely.

It is interesting, perhaps, to realize that policemen can get as hard up for cash as any other citizens trying to live on small salaries. There is one traffic policeman whom Rothstein pointed out as having borrowed $2,300 from him, to be repaid at $30 a month, without interest.

Rothstein told this story to a close friend as an example of his own love of his fellow men.

"He has paid me regularly $30 a month right on the dot," Rothstein said. "And do you know, it would be a tragedy to me now if that man should miss a payment? I have sized him up as a man of character."

If one policeman borrowed money of Arnold Rothstein, what was to prevent other policemen from borrowing money from him? It is no crime to borrow money. Arnold Rothstein never was convicted of a crime in his life. He died with a spotless record so far as convictions are concerned. Any one could borrow from him. And thousands did.

The Easy Money flowed to Rothstein in a golden torrent, and trickled out again, and poured back in an augmented flood. He was "kidding" the world. He was the Prince of Outlaws, the supreme manifestation that it is possible to become a millionaire without labor.

I have just learned, for instance, that Rothstein bet $1,600,000 on the 1928 elections.

That story is not germane to this situation except that it serves to illustrate one point in Rothstein's successful gambling operations. That is, that all the big bettors in New York—and they are many—knew that they could place a bet on anything at any time with Rothstein. His motto was that the man who wanted to bet usually was wrong.

As the centre of a vast avalanche of bets, Rothstein was able to manipulate the odds, betting both ways at different prices, so that no matter which way the situation turned out, he won.

No one, it is agreed, not even the late Richard Canfield, understood percentages as well as Rothstein.

"I am 100 per cent right," was a favorite expression of Rothstein's.

One other point: on that trip to Washington, mentioned above, the writer was asked who was the "Master Mind," the guiding genius, back of the successful and diversified frustrations of the law in New York. Sol Myers, of the National Surety Company, and John B. Dooling, an assistant in the New York District Attorney's Office, were the only questioners whose names are recalled.

Rothstein's name was mentioned by the questioners. Myers wanted to know if a big newspaper couldn't be interested in getting on the trail of the Mysterious Influence. The writer said:

"It seems to me that if, as you say, there is jury fixing and general disorganization of the machinery for enforcing the laws in New York, it is up to the Government to clean it up."

Myers said that they might just as well have talked to the writer over the long distance telephone as have summoned him to Washington.

Developments through the years have indicated that they might just as well have looked for the $5,000,000 in stolen bonds over the long distance telephone, as looked for them the way they have.

All the forces of Law and Order were out after Arnold Rothstein's scalp for years. And he made them look foolish.

All the forces of Law and Order—the District Attorney's office, the Bar Association, the United States Attorney's office, and the Appellate Division of the Supreme Court—were gunning for the late William J. Fallon. And, cruising jauntily through the courtrooms, with admitted crooks and shady characters in his retinue, he made them look silly.

Mention is made of Fallon and Rothstein together, because one was the keenest criminal-legal brain power, and the other, the biggest money power that ever represented the interests of the underworld. And Fallon's story is part of Rothstein's story.

Money is needed to combat money; and brains are required to combat brains.

Sicking a fifty-dollar-a-week detective onto a hundred-thousand-dollar-a-day crook isn't fair to the crook. It's belittling him.

And Bill Fallon showed them what happens when you pit political office-holding minds against real brains.

12

CHAPTER TWO

MOSTLY OF EARLY DAYS

A RNOLD ROTHSTEIN used to dismiss his youth rather summarily.

"I didn't go to school much," he said, "but I used to gamble a lot and lose. I started as a salesman for my father, who was in the wholesale cotton goods business. I landed in Chicago one time and got into a game of pinochle. After I had lost all my own money, I lost my expense money. And then I lost my samples.

"When I got back to New York I looked up a job as a cigar salesman. This took me into pool-rooms (racetrack gambling rooms) and at first I lost money on the horses. Gradually, however, it dawned on me that if any one was going to make money out of gambling he had better be on the right side of the fence. I was on the wrong end of the game.

"I went to work in a poolroom, and from then on I was a winner."

A bookmaker of the present day who worked with Rothstein in the same old-time poolroom, has told his Broadway friends—he has spoken freely only since Rothstein kept his fatal appointment with a bullet in the Park Central Hotel on November 4, 1928—that Rothstein was a "chiseler," even as a young man. A "chiseler," to Broadway, is a chap given to sharp practices even with those who trust him. This bookmaker said:

"I caught Rothstein taking bets for himself after the races were won. When I called him down for it, he said:

" 'It's easy money. You're in on it too.'

" 'I told him to go to Hell, that I didn't make my money that way.' "

It is interesting that the bookmaker who refused to share in Rothstein's scheme for getting money from his employers didn't inform his employers of his discovery. That would have been "squealing," and a "squealer" is the lowest form of animal life on Broadway. No crook who squeals is respected by any one.

By 1909, when Rothstein was twenty-six years old, he was recognized among the élite of Broadway as a most promising young man. He had learned to shoot craps in the property room in the rear of the old Victoria Theatre, which stood on the site of the present Rialto Theatre; he knew all that was necessary for any one to know about decks of cards; he was remarkably dexterous with a pool cue; he would bet on everything and anything, from a horse race to whether or not the next automobile to pass would have odd or even numbers on its license plates.

The property or "prop" room of the Victoria was a splendid preparatory school of its kind. That famous amusement place, owned by the late Oscar Hammerstein and managed by his astute relative, Willie, had a Monday matinée clientele which probably never has been surpassed for sheer toughness

14

anywhere at any time. This did not happen because the Hammersteins wanted it to be that way. It happened because the tough youths developed the habit of gathering there on a Monday afternoon. And as they all were creatures of habit, this one was broken only by the expedient of getting rid of Hammerstein's Victoria. That ended the games in the "prop" room.

This gathering was tough, in a sense. But Arnold Rothstein did not have then, and did not have at the time of his long anticipated exit from life on the wings of a bullet, any habits ordinarily classed as "bad." Rothstein never smoked tobacco, and he never drank alcohol. To any one who knew him it must seem ridiculously unnecessary to state that he never used drugs. But even that is included for the sake of the record.

In fact, so far as Rothstein's personal conduct was concerned in his early and in his later years, he would have graced (when he was on his good behavior) any pious gathering. His voice was mild and pleasing; his manner was graceful; his grammar was not perfect, but it would do. And his wit was amazing.

This natural fund of humor, and his ability to draw it with the lightning speed generally credited to those obsolete and crude ruffians of the effete old West in hauling out their Colt forty-fives, enabled Rothstein to get himself gracefully out of many serious discussions, not to say serious impending combats, in the Victoria days and also right through his career up to the time of his death.

This year—1909—was a red letter year for Rothstein. His wit was winning him a respected place among the chaps who admitted that they were the shining figures in the gay life of that time. These charming and lovable characters included T. A. Dorgan ("Tad"), the cartoonist, who has invented more slang phrases than any other living human; William (Billy) Mizner, who used to say that his father left him the world for his plaything, and whose *bons mots* still are current wherever stories are told and who now is writing motion picture plays for large sums of money on the West Coast; Frank Ward O'Malley, one of the finest and sweetest gentlemen who ever wrote entertaining stories for the old *New York Sun;* the late "Spanish" O'Brien, who was a handsome, irresponsible Irishman, born in Paris, and who worked at editing newspapers as a sideline to his vocation of indulging in Homeric conversations with his friends; Jack Francis, who always has been credited with knowing more about Broadway than any other man; Vernie Barton, gambler and bon vivant; Ben De Casseres, who used to balance a seidel of Pilsner on his head and take the solar system by the oratorical tail and whirl it around the room to the dazzled delight of all and sundry; and Hype Igoe, of *The World*, who used to lug his famous ukelele to the gatherings which generally took place in Jim Moran's "big white room" at Jack's Restaurant on Sixth Avenue.

These wits of Broadway were in no way connected with the underworld. They knew Arnold Rothstein merely as a most entertaining companion, who always gambled, who ran a gambling house or two,

16

who would bet on anything at any time, and whose favorite diversion during lulls in the conversation at table was to haul out a roll of bills and play poker hands with Vernie Barton and others, calling the hands from the serial numbers on each bill.

Rothstein, for example, would take a roll from his pocket and someone else would take a roll from his. Rothstein would read off, "B61298333B" from a fifty dollar bill. That would be three "3's" in poker parlance. His opponent would read off "Y86318226D." That hand holds three pairs—two "8's," two "6's" and two "2's." There only can be five cards in a poker hand, so only two pairs are possible. The "8's" and "6's," however, would be beaten by any three of a kind. So Arnold Rothstein would win this imaginary hand, just as he won most of the real hands.

Since Rothstein played this little game a great deal in his idle moments, and since his hobby always was to tote about huge sums of money in crinkling, snapping notes fresh from factory, one might be pardoned for wondering if he ever took the trouble to look over the possible poker hands on his bills before he drew them from his bank. No available record exists, however, to prove that this depressing thought ever occurred to any of the gay spirits who jousted at this form of poker with the irrepressibly cheerful Rothstein.

The truth is, however, that in those days at Jack's, Rothstein had his best times when he, Mizner, Barton and O'Malley, got hold of what they called among themselves a "chump." A "chump," more than likely, was merely an unknowing fellow who thought he knew a great deal about the ways of the world, and who, having been introduced all around to every one at the table by false names, was led on to discuss the individuals at the table as if he knew them. It is surprising on how many occasions this very situation was developed, and how well the "chump," being slightly "oiled" as they used to say —and may still say for that matter—of a person who had taken on an alcoholic cargo to the point of submerging the Plimsoll mark, turned out to know "O'Malley, the star reporter of *The Sun*," "Arnold Rothstein, the big gambler," or "Tad, the cartoonist."

In 1909, however—which, if not the exact year, is approximately the period during which Rothstein was developing the social side of his character—Rothstein had yet to become a figure in the news. He had not then moved to the first of his beautiful homes in the city, a private house in the Seventies, with a marble front and an interior most richly and tastefully decorated—a single, beautiful oil painting here, a water color there, and rugs to make a collector's mouth water.

However, he was known in old Rector's, with its big lion hanging outside on Broadway just south of Forty-fourth Street, with its red-carpeted diningroom, and its reputation for a hot bird and a cold bottle, and in the Waldorf-Astoria, whose Peacock Alley at that time was the gathering place for men of money and women of beauty from the far places of the world.

18

And it was about this time that he went into gambling seriously by opening a small basement place in West Forty-fifth Street.

When he first appeared in the news, Rothstein was a slim, young man of twenty-six, with dark hair, a complexion remarkable for its smooth pallor—as if he never had to worry about razors—white, skilful hands, and amazingly vital, sparkling, dark brown eyes.

The Rothstein eyes were features above all others that those who met him recalled most faithfully— those laughing, brilliant, restless eyes glowing in the pale but very expressive face.

He laughed a great deal; he looked worried when it suited him to appear worried. A casual observer might have said that Rothstein's face was an open book. It certainly was far from the ordinary concept of a "poker" face. In the course of an evening at table, or at play, it ran the whole gamut of expressions. But, mostly, it was a smiling, a laughing face.

Until about fifteen years ago Rothstein was not noted, as he was later, for his beautiful, white, even teeth. In 1909, he still had his own teeth. In later years, somewhere about the time of the murder of Herman Rosenthal and the conviction and execution of the four gunmen and Lieut. Charlie Becker, Rothstein parted from his own teeth, and replaced them with a set that made many professional beauties —Rothstein preferred blondes for scenery—extremely jealous.

He was about five feet seven inches tall, slim of figure, most meticulously garbed, not in the garish style of Broadway, but in the more subdued method of Fifth Avenue, and was extremely quick in his movements. In his later years, although most abstemious in eating, he gained weight, but he never lost anything of that pantherish quickness, which was more like the catlike suavity of muscular coördination that is Jack Dempsey's than anything else.

It was at this time, too, that he formed the habit of walking home by devious routes in the gray dawns after hot gambling nights, and of buying a box of figs from an all-night street stand on the way. He never gave up his fondness for figs, nor his belief that they were about the only medicine that a man who watched his diet, and was fairly successful in getting his sleep, even if by daylight, really required.

Of that remarkable muscular quickness that has been mentioned, it might be said here that not so long before the end, the lights went out suddenly in the restaurant in which he was sitting late one night. They flashed on again in an instant, and disclosed Rothstein seated easily twenty feet from his original position. He moved like a ray of light, whether it was to take one of the innumerable telephone calls which poured in on him wherever he was, or whether it was merely to rise and greet a friend.

When he walked along the street he was "like a horse;" he saw on both sides as well as in front. From his earliest years he never walked into a room without knowing exactly how many persons were there, where they were sitting or standing, and where every article of furniture was placed.

In those lightning glances of his, he also was forming his estimates of character. He prided himself inordinately on his ability to read character. It was a matter of habit with him to size up persons, mentally, physically, emotionally and financially.

He walked along the curb lines on the street, mostly with a casual friend. No person or vehicle on the street escaped his nervous attention.

In his terrifically exciting life, these habits were to save him from disaster time without number.

Arnold Rothstein loved to associate with newspaper men, who like to call themselves trained observers. He always could excel these trained observers. With him the power of observation was not a game—it was a matter of life and death.

But, though Rothstein had not yet made a name for himself in the newspapers, this was to come in November, 1909, from his fondness for pool, a fondness that lasted through his life. He always was willing to bet any amount of money on his prowess with a cue—that is, except against recognized professional champions in that field.

On Thursday, November 18, of this year, Rothstein and a number of friends dined at Rector's. With them was Jack Conaway, a young broker of Philadelphia, a noted whip and cross-country rider, and known in the sporting world as a "blood" of the first water.

Jack Conaway was the champion pool player of the Philadelphia Racquet Club, and enjoyed a tremendous reputation in his home town, where it was believed that he had no real rivals outside of professional pool playing ranks.

21

Knowing Rothstein's pride in his pool, friends of Conaway told Rothstein that he wasn't so much of a pool player as he thought he was, and that they had money to back their opinion that Conaway could beat him.

Rothstein, laughing as usual, said he thought he could beat Conaway any time or any place, so a match was arranged right there. As every one in the party was interested in the match, and as it was apparent that no single string of points would ever settle this debate, Rothstein and Conaway went to McGraw's billiard rooms, near the old *New York Herald* building. They arrived there at 8 o'clock in the evening, with a score of followers. The reason they had selected McGraw's was that club tables usually closed at midnight—and Rothstein and his friends were well known in McGraw's. In fact, many of those who knew him at that time had an impression that Rothstein was interested in the place.

The first match was for fifty points, and Conaway won. The second game was for 100 points, and Rothstein won this one.

By the time this second game had been won by the margin of a ball by spectacular sort of shooting on the part of Rothstein, against just as adroit cue manipulation by Conaway, the air was full of hundred, fifty and twenty dollar bills. Every one was betting, including the players.

The excitement continued until 2 o'clock Friday morning, which was the usual hour for closing the rooms. Conaway, then nearly a thousand dollars in debt to Rothstein, said he didn't believe that Rothstein had won so much from good playing as from good luck, and said he would like to keep on and prove he had the right view of the situation.

This is interesting in retrospect, because all through the intervening years which saw Rothstein running his fortune up into the millions, those who lost to him insisted that it was not skill but good luck that won for Arnold Rothstein. This was true particularly, of "Nick the Greek," the greatest gambler in America, outside of Rothstein; a great, tall, handsome, dashing citizen of Chicago, who popped up in New York every so often with bank rolls of two and three hundred thousand dollars, to roll the dice against the master of them all—only to go back to dig up another roll.

Rothstein was perfectly willing to let Conaway think it was luck that was breaking against him in the pool match, so he gladly agreed to keep right on shooting. Conaway promised every attendant who would stay a $25 tip, and the game continued.

All during Friday morning Conaway and Rothstein chalked their cues and pocketed the balls, with Conaway losing most of the matches. He would win occasionally, but when they were playing "doubles" or "quits" to give Conaway a chance to wipe out his indebtedness, Rothstein had a streak of luck.

Friday afternoon, just after Rothstein had swept all the balls on the table into the pockets, and was nibbling a sandwich while the attendant re-set the pyramid, some one asked him how he felt:

"Pretty woozy," he said.

23

Both he and Conaway were dipping their heads in bowls of cold water at intervals during the afternoon and evening. In the afternoon Conaway was about $4,000 in the hole, but at 8 o'clock, after twenty-four hours of continuous play, he had gotten his losses down to about $2,000. After that he couldn't prevail at all against Rothstein, although they kept right on, first one and the other drawing applause for an adroit shot, or for clearing the table on the break.

By midnight Friday, a large throng that had heard about the game on Broadway and its environs, crammed the billiard rooms to capacity. Marathon dancing wasn't known in those days, but apparently this made a fairly good substitute. The two players staggered like drunken men around the table, focussing glassy eyes on the multi-colored balls, but pushed their cues with a precision born of desperation and long practice.

At 2 o'clock Saturday morning McGraw told them that they would have to stop.

"I'll have you dead on my hands," he said. "And if you don't want to sleep, some of the rest of us do."

Conaway and Rothstein asked for "just one more" string, as the agreed-on number of points in pool or billiards is termed, and they still were playing the "one more string" at 4 o'clock in the morning, when McGraw told the attendants not to rack the balls any more, and said to the players:

"You'd better get to a Turkish bath—the two of you. You can continue your little game some other time."

Rothstein was around $4,000 ahead when the game was thus broken up for him and Conaway. That wasn't much money looked upon in the light of later accomplishments in his life. But it wasn't such an insignificant sum at that for a young man of twenty-six to win over a friendly little game of pool.

The fact that the game had lasted for thirty-two hours without a break caused it to be accepted up and down Broadway as the world's record pool game of all time, and ultimately led to an account of it being printed in the newspapers of that day. The description of Rothstein was "Arnold Rothstein, the son of a wealthy business man." And that is the last time that Rothstein ever was described that way in his life.

On their way in an automobile to the Turkish bath, Rothstein and Conaway arranged for another pool match to be played in Philadelphia, for $5,000 a side. Available statistics and friends of Rothstein are silent on the point of this second game, although some friends have an idea that the game duly was played, and that Rothstein won.

However, pool merely was a side issue with the talented Rothstein. His serious business at this time was his gambling house, which he moved soon from West Forty-fifth Street to West Forty-sixth Street. It was in this house that the late Charles G. Gates, son of "Betcher-million" John W. Gates—who, by the way, never compared with Rothstein as a plunger —dropped $40,000, one night early in November of 1910.

The tale of that evening is one of the illuminating

lights that is shed now and then on the quality of divine faith in one another that prevails among the gambling fraternity—and for that matter among all who follow their devious paths in the shadowy purlieus of the underworld.

Charlie Gates, who it will be recalled was the despair of his multi-millionaire sire, had been operated on for appendicitis in July of that year. Extraction of the appendix also appeared to have removed from the youthful Gates' system for a time some of his penchant for doing big things in a big way. But his period of inanimation was not long.

Vernie Barton and Charlie Gates met at Jack's, whither Gates had sojourned after dinner in Rector's. Gates was living at the Plaza at that time.

The dinner was not a dry meal. Prohibition did not prevail in those halcyon days; and champagne was the most important item of the repast. Champagne also prevailed at Jack's.

Gates mentioned during the evening that he had been pretty quiet, and recalled that his last plunge into the whirlpools of chance, of any account, had been in Los Angeles a year before, when he won $29,000 from the bookmakers in an afternoon, and bought a prize bulldog for $8,000 as a souvenir of the happy occasion. He was out of the stock market, in which his experiences had been eminently disastrous, and was devoting himself with outward seriousness to Texas Oil, which was supposed to be his business.

"I wouldn't mind having a little play to-night," Gates said.

"That's just what I was thinking myself," Vernie said.

Gates's friends tried to stop him from leaving the party, but Gates insisted on going with Barton. And it was to Rothstein's house they went. That is, the place was known as Rothstein's, but Rothstein had a partner, who is most important to this story, one William Shea, who had been a foreman in the Department of Water Supply, Gas and Electricity, until he found that there were sources of revenue far superior to the city payroll, and put his discovery to account.

Gates bought a stack of chips for $100, and lost it immediately. That was at the "wheel," as roulette is termed. After buying more chips and losing them too, Charlie tried his luck at faro. His luck was just the same—very bad.

After such a very short time that Gates hadn't even begun to get warmed up, Rothstein stopped the play. Gates had lost $40,000. It had been a long time since any such pleasantly easy money had walked into his gambling house, and he didn't want to take any chances with it.

Gates, who had many admirable qualities, was noted as a good loser. With perfect equanimity he dashed off a check for $40,000. He smiled acquiescence when he was told the fun was over, and he grinned cheerfully when he handed over the check.

Rothstein laughed pleasantly too when he handed the check to Shea. But it was the last laughing, so far as is known, that he ever did over that particular check.

For various reasons, Shea elected to go to the bank with Gates, who was just as accommodating about that detail, as he was about all the others. From the bank, Gates went home to his hotel, and Shea did not go back to his and Rothstein's gambling house in Forty-sixth Street.

Shea just whiled away the time, here and there, and while he whiled it he explained to his friends that for a long time he had been under a strong impression that his friend and partner, Rothstein, had not been on the square.

"I've been convinced for some time," Shea said, "that Arnold has been tossing the bank roll to his friends. I don't mind a guy being nice to his friends but when he fixes it up so that his friends can get away with my money in our gambling house, I don't care so much for it.

"Take Arnold's friend, George Young Bauchle, the eminent lawyer, for instance. When Mr. Bauchle has been playing in our house, Arnold always let him bet as much as he wanted to, and as often as he wanted to on the last turn out of the box. And Mr. Bauchle has been pretty lucky at calling the turns, and our bank roll has been pretty well nicked. I figure that this $40,000 just about squares Arnold and me."

It might be mentioned that "last turn out of the box" in faro bank, refers to a privilege which may be accorded a bank player when only three cards remain in the box. If he can call the order in which the three cards will come out he can collect his bets at the odds of four to one—or could in those days, and in that house, anyway.

Meanwhile, Rothstein wasn't whiling any time away. He was burning up the streets in pursuit of Shea. But he found time to tell his version of the affair, which was that his partner had left him with the check for $40,000, and hadn't come back, which didn't seem exactly right to him.

Finally, on Friday afternoon, Rothstein located Shea in the Hotel Knickerbocker, which was the first oasis on Broadway to charge 20 cents for a drink of whiskey, and it isn't ethical to mention this hotel without referring to the picture of Old King Cole which adorned the wall back of the bar.

"Where's my share of that money?" Rothstein wanted to know.

Shea wasn't at all embarrassed. He told Rothstein exactly what he had been telling his many friends.

"And I'm going to keep it all because I figure it makes us square," were Shea's final words.

Rothstein saw that discussion with Shea would get him nowhere, so, in a rage, he returned to his gambling house, dissolved the partnership, and continued alone after that. It would be interesting to be able to record here that Rothstein used his famous phrase for persons who he thought might not fulfill their obligations:

"God help you, if you don't."

Unfortunately, however, there is no evidence that Rothstein had begun to use that expression at that period of his life, a strictly formative period in which he slowly was gathering his powers for the greater accomplishments of the future. And there is no surface indication that Rothstein ever squared this account with Shea, although it is a known and accepted fact that Rothstein always was regarded as the most dangerous individual to cross in New York.

Bauchle, the lawyer, a man of wealth and social standing, and also known about New York at that time as one of its pleasant living figures, laughed heartily when the story told by Shea reached him.

"You can say for me," he told a newspaper man, "that I have not been in Rothstein's house since last September. Prior to that I played there a few times, but if I had any privileges that other players didn't have I didn't know it."

The gambling world's view of Shea's action in this affair is not uninteresting. Opinion at the time was about equally divided. A goodly percentage of the élite among the high stakes players inclined to the view that Shea had turned a mighty smart trick. Others were emphatic in saying that he had done wrong. Shea said himself that if he hadn't been absolutely certain that Rothstein had tricked him he wouldn't have dreamed of keeping the $40,000.

Rothstein kept out of the public eye for the next seven years, except that, with other gambling house owners, his name was mentioned in connection with the shooting of Herman Rosenthal in 1912, after Rosenthal had made an affidavit accusing the police, and particularly Lieut. Charles Becker, head of the so-called "Strong Arm" Squad, of having been grafting systematically on gamblers.

Rothstein kept his houses running, for the most part, however, and, smiling, and unruffled as ever, continued to be one of the wits at Jack's.

One of the dramatic moments that still lingers in the minds of that little coterie in the white room at Jack's was the night of the execution of Becker in the electric chair at Sing Sing. They all sat around their famous table—Rothstein among them—with their watches in their hands, and estimated the lethal moment, which one of their number, O'Malley, was observing in the interests of his newspaper. And Rothstein always considered that one of the greatest expressions that O'Malley ever fathered in his long career as a newspaper reporter was his line to the effect that "the Negro showed the Czar of the Tenderloin how to die," this in connection with the fact that Becker was frightened at the prospect of death, and the Negro who had to sit in the chair on the same occasion, was perfectly self-possessed.

During the racing season at Saratoga, in that red letter year, 1909, Rothstein had married Caroline Green, who had been in James T. Powers's production, "Havana."

At that time a very beautiful girl, Mrs. Rothstein is a beautiful woman now. Every one who has known her has admired her for her character and charm, and loved her for her very human qualities. As this passage will end references to Mrs. Rothstein, so far as this narrative is concerned, it must be taken for granted that during the years to come she saw very little of her husband at night, and not so very much of him days.

31

As Rothstein grew more and more famous, or infamous, whichever way you look at it, Mrs. Rothstein's closest friends found it more and more difficult socially to be with her.

Finally, about a year before the end, Mrs. Rothstein, for about the one thousandeth time, said to her husband:

"We cannot go on like this. You have more money now than we need. Why don't you retire—get out of the life you have been living, and let us enjoy ourselves together?"

"It's too late. I can't do it," was the reply. "You know there is no one I love except you, and that you always have been the only woman in the world, but I've gotten into it, and I can't get out of it. Why, every one would think I was a welsher if I quit now that I've got a few millions."

Mrs. Rothstein told him then that she was through. She said they would have to have a divorce, or a separation.

"I can't stand this any longer," she said.

Rothstein regarded her soberly. Perhaps he was recalling what had in past years been one of his favorite stories—that on their honeymoon she had lent him all her jewelry in order to pay some bets he had lost during one of the occasional bad breaks that even he ran into now and then at the track—or perhaps thinking of other times, when in a thousand ways she had shown her loyalty and devotion to him. But he was adamant.

"All right," he said, "you go ahead and do whatever you think will make you happy. I'll give you twenty-five grand (a grand is $1,000) a year unless you marry again. If you marry I'll give you fifteen grand as long as you live with your husband. If he dies, or you leave him, I'll make it twenty-five grand again. But I wish you wouldn't leave me after all these years."

Mrs. Rothstein saw little or nothing of her husband after that. And it was following that break in their lives that Rothstein met Inez Norton, the blonde, for whom he provided liberally in his disputed will.

CHAPTER THREE

WARMING UP

THE second phase of Rothstein's career as a public figure opened with a raid by gunmen on a historic crap game, held on the second floor of the Hotel St. Francis, 124 West Forty-seventh Street, New York, on the evening of May 15, and the early morning of May 16, 1917.

This was one of those notable "travelling" games, of which Rothstein was a sponsor, and which the underworld and amateur gamblers alike considered strictly on the level.

(It is a shame to bring up such a thought in this connection, but the late Richard Canfield's best remembered mot is: "There isn't any such person as an honest gambler.")

These "travelling" games were introduced after the murder of Rosenthal in 1912, and have been continued ever since. The prospective player goes to a designated restaurant, or hotel, and there is told by a watcher where the game will be that night. Games have been known to move several times in a night, due to tips that either the police or gunmen are on the warpath.

In connection with the "on the level" games it may be added that there are also plainly dishonest games run by almost openly dishonest gamblers. Their

34

trick is to steer the prospective customer for the honest game to their own game, which he is led to believe is the honest game he is seeking. Once there, they take his roll as painlessly and as rapidly as circumstances permit.

An excellent account of this St. Francis affair was printed in *The World*, of May 17, 1917. The only reason that this account is not followed in its entirety is because, like many other stories about the "King of the Gamblers," all the facts were not included. And in this instance, the most dramatic incident was not brought out. It should be borne in mind, however, that this is no adverse criticism of the man who got and wrote the story. He did a remarkably fine job from all angles. The additional facts, as related here, were known in *The World* office afterwards.

Fifteen men, who included Arnold Rothstein, Eddie Katz, of Cleveland, then stopping at the Hotel Knickerbocker, several actors, a member of the Stock Exchange, and other prominent citizens whose names were known at the time, but who denied they were participants in the festivities, were rolling the bones.

Men "in the know," had been coming and going about the game all evening. Newcomers would enter the lobby of the hotel, glance inquisitively at a stout, able-looking citizen in an armchair near the elevator shaft; the stout citizen would lift an eyebrow to the colored elevator boy, and the elevator would shoot to the second floor. That is all there was to that.

But at 3 o'clock in the morning, while the night clerk was making up his records, five men entered the lobby and walked straight for the elevator. After one look at them, the stout citizen shook his head emphatically and excitedly at the elevator lad.

But these men didn't mind head shakes. Three of them stepped quickly and quietly into the car, and one of them pressed a hard, large, pulse-stimulating SOMETHING against the spot that the elevator boy had just been thinking of embellishing with an egg sandwich and a cup of coffee.

"Just go right ahead, Sonny," whispered a Voice.

The elevator boy said afterwards that the elevator just naturally seemed to raise itself right up to the second floor and stop there by its own volition.

Then the three men went into the room. And the elevator boy waited right there. He knew that the other two men were downstairs. He didn't move.

In the room the three men, who had stopped a moment to put on masks, pointed revolvers at the crap players. And one of them said:

"Now, all of you stand up against the wall, hold your hands up in the air, and don't make a peep."

In the second that the gunmen had taken to come through the door, Rothstein had dropped a huge roll of bills to the floor, and kicked it under the rug. Reports at the time were that this roll contained $20,000. It was known later, however, that the roll really contained $60,000.

But that quick action by the master gambler wasn't really the dramatic feature that illustrates, as well as any other single act of his career, the absolute calm courage, and calculating nerve of the man.

As he shot the roll under the rug, he fixed his eyes

36

on the face of the underworld character, who, he believed then, and believed all his life, furnished the information that brought the gunmen on their errand. While the gunmen were taking jewelry and money from the other players, several thousands of dollars in cash, and several thousands of dollars in jewelry, including a stickpin of Rothstein's that he valued highly, Rothstein never took his gaze from the face of the man he was sure was the betrayer. He knew if he did so, that individual could signal to his confederates that the $60,000 was under the rug.

Now, it takes courage in an emergency like that to seize the fraction of a second available to hide the most valuable of one's possessions in the best available spot; and it takes a rare presence of mind and a deal of self-possession, with revolvers poking at one, to conclude on a course of action and stick to it, displaying meanwhile utter disregard of the revolvers and their holders.

In this case, one of the holders was known as a "killer" all through the underworld. But Rothstein took the main chance, and won out. He always chuckled merrily over that story.

But that was far from ending this incident. Two of the gunmen laid aside their weapons, and went through the gamblers' pockets, while their comrade covered them. The whole procedure was quiet and orderly, as if it had been rehearsed. Finally, the gunmen doffed their masks, and became sociable.

One of them said to Eddie Katz:

"Haven't I seen you in Cleveland?"

"I guess so," said Eddie.

37

"Well," the gunman said, "when you get back give my best regards to your friends, and tell 'em how well I'm making out."

The gunman lifted Eddie's stickpin from his tie.

"Hey, won't you leave me that. I'd rather give you twice as much money as it's worth, and keep it," said Eddie.

"Don't worry, I'll send you the pawn ticket," was the reply. "What's your address?"

The second collecting gunman examined Rothstein's pin.

"How much is that worth?" he asked.

"Thirty-five hundred," Rothstein said.

"I'll take it," the gunman said.

As it turned out, that gunman might just as well have left his calling card with his name and address on it as walk off with that particular stickpin in that casual fashion. That made Arnold Rothstein angry.

He stayed angry while the three gunmen went out of the room, dropped back to the ground floor in the elevator, rejoined their two friends, and quietly and unostentatiously disappeared, not being bothered by the stout individual who still was sitting in his armchair, or by the night clerk, who was so busy with his books that he couldn't believe any hold-up had happened, or even that a big crap game had been in progress on the second floor.

Still angry the next day, Rothstein told who the gunmen were. One glance had been enough for him. A friend—a newspaper man—asked him, if he were going to be "yellow," and not report the raid to the police.

38

"I'm not yellow, and I never report anything to the police," was Rothstein's answer.

"Well, if you don't do something about this, Arnold, you'll be a mark for thugs after this," his friend told him. "They'll think you're yellow, whether you are or not."

"One of those guys is a killer," he observed, meditatively.

He went to the police soon after that, the first and last time there is any record of Rothstein taking any such action. During his lifetime he was held up dozens of times, but always preferred to handle his own private affairs in his own private way. On this occasion it may have been that stickpin.

Anyhow, on Rothstein's complaint, the police showed remarkable speed, and soon had two prisoners, Albert Johnson, twenty-eight, and Eugene F. Price, thirty-five.

After that, Arthur Wood, then Police Commissioner, and the newspaper friend of Rothstein above referred to were dining together. Commissioner Wood said:

"Well, I guess your friend, Arnold Rothstein, is yellow after all. I thought he was going through against those thugs that held him up. If he doesn't identify them, the police won't have any case."

This conversation was relayed to Rothstein, and he went right down to Police Headquarters and identified the two gunmen. On August 23, 1917, they were convicted of robbery from the person by a jury before Judge McIntyre.

Rothstein, as complaining witness in that case, repeated in court that there was only $20,000 in the roll. But he always told intimates it was $60,000, which may be explained by the fact that Rothstein never was eager to have generally known the really enormous sums in cash that he at times carried with him. There were numerous other occasions when for public consumption he made the sum of money he had smaller than it really was.

This year of 1917 was a hard luck year for the "Big Shot." He was robbed of $28,000 in another floating crap game in Harlem before it was over.

It wasn't until January, 19, 1919, however, that the most significant crap game raid in Rothstein's career occurred. This was not a raid by gunmen. It was an organized sortie by the police led by Inspector Dominick Henry. Most interesting developments grew out of it.

Inspector Henry got word that this particular mobile crap game at this particular moment was pausing momentarily in an apartment on the fourth floor of 301 West Fifty-seventh Street. With eight detectives, who included John Walsh, John McLaughlin and Frank Oliver, he went to that address. McLaughlin, Walsh and Oliver ascended to the fourth floor, while their comrades watchfully stood about below.

An underworld version of the affair was that the police had been informed that players in this game were all ready to "stand for a pinch." The truth of the matter was that the floating game had been again and again a mark for gunmen, that Rothstein himself had lost another $11,000—a trifle to his pocketbook but a blow to his vanity—to gunmen only two weeks before, and he and the other regular players were rather feverish about it. This particular game, in fact, already had floated down from a house in West Ninety-eighth Street, where it had begun the day before, but whence it had flitted on the word that gunmen were on the trail.

Anyhow, McLaughlin rapped on the door of the apartment. The door opened part way on a chain, and McLaughlin called:

"Open up in there!"

With the words, three bullets hopped through the door—Wham! Wham! Wham!—just like that. The first pellet tickled McLaughlin's shoulder; the second one burned Walsh's right arm, and the third made a neat hole in Oliver's left sleeve. It was just good fortune that death rode on none of the missiles.

Even as the three detectives crashed their weight into the door as one person—and let it be said right here, once and for all, that no one who has known him could ever question in the slightest the courage of the New York policeman—McLaughlin showed the rare quality of presence of mind.

"Go easy now," he panted to Oliver and Walsh. "It's the police!" he called to the gamblers.

No more shots were fired. Twenty men stood about the room, in which dice and money in large, yellow lumps were visible. Abe Attell, the former featherweight champion, and later a personal attendant to Rothstein, who was to be mixed up with his employer in the charges growing out of the "Black

41

Sox" baseball scandal, was visible. Rothstein, however, was absent.

Shouts from below caused Detective McLaughlin to stick his head from a window, and pointing fingers from the street indicated the figure of a man on the platform of the fire escape at the second floor. No ladder extended from that platform to the street. And the street was dotted with detectives and soldiers in uniform who had been attracted by the shots and shouts. The figure on the platform was Arnold Rothstein, the King of the Underworld. His throne always was a hard one. It certainly was not comfortable that dawn.

Accounts the next day were that Rothstein had fired the three shots. A revolver, which he had a permit to carry, was identified as his. Those shots were going to cause a deal of pother, a long sitting of an extraordinary Grand Jury, bickerings back and forth among very prominent personages indeed, conviction of Inspector Henry on a charge of perjury, reversal by a higher court, and full reinstatement and establishment of the innocence of Henry—an innocence apparent from the first to all who studied the case.

The situation that morning was that Magistrate Mancuso held each of the twenty-one prisoners under bail of $1,000 on "suspicion of felonious assault."

A newspaper account said:

"The prisoners had little difficulty in raising the $1,000 bail."

Yes. They had very little trouble—no more

trouble than it required to stand by while Arnold Rothstein peeled $21,000 from a roll and handed it to the clerk.

The police said, by the way, that some of the dice they picked up at this game were loaded, although the gamblers always denied this. The police story also had it that one of their number said to Attell, when it was learned he had lost $1,000:

"Didn't you know the dice were loaded, Abe?"

And that Attell shook his head sadly, and replied:

"It's happened to me before."

But Abe's fellow gamblers always insisted that it was Abe's hard luck, and not trick dice that caused Abe's impoverishment.

The trick in this crap game, however, was not in the dice. It was in who fired the shots that singed the policemen. Those "in the know" showed no hesitation at first in saying, perhaps not in these exact words, but to this general effect:

"Arnold fired the shots because he thought someone was crashing the game. He'd gotten pretty mad over being held up all the time, and he had a permit to carry a revolver. So, when he heard those guys at the door, he just naturally turned loose. When he found out it was the police, he didn't shoot any more. Arnold didn't want to shoot any cops."

At least one newspaper account of the affair mentioned that the shots were fired by Rothstein.

Be that as it may, the situation so far as the surface indications are concerned is best described perhaps by skipping ahead to February 13, and taking a look at the District Attorney's office, which Edward

Swann then was conducting along what might be termed promisory lines.

On that day Swann, his assistant Jim Smith, and "Honest Dan" Costigan, who had just been relieved of an Inspectorship by Police Commissioner Richard E. Enright, had one of those chats which go in the records as "conferences." This was a four-hour chat.

At the close of it Dan Costigan bustled off about his business, and Swann told newspaper men that Inspector Dominick Henry, a captain, and ten policemen from the West Sixty-eighth Street station would be subpœnaed to appear before the Grand Jury in a gambling inquiry.

That's the way a District Attorney makes an "announcement," by the way. He receives the representatives of the press in the sacred precincts of his own office, and tells them as much as he considers proper about some subject. If the gentlemen, and others, of the press think what he has said is of sufficient importance, it is an "announcement." If a newspaper isn't friendly with the District Attorney, or other official, it may be "admission" instead of "announcement," which would make it appear as if a newspaper reporter was the person with the bright idea, and the official—nothing but a "Yes" man. If newspapers don't think it merits space, what the District Attorney or any one else says is not printed at all.

"I directed Jim Smith to start this investigation. There was a raid made by Inspector Henry's men on January 19 on an alleged crap game (the word 'alleged' here is interesting as it is proof that it even

44

was never legally established that a crap game had been in progress) in a fourth floor apartment at 301 West Forty-seventh Street. Two detectives were wounded by bullets and twenty men were arrested, among them Arnold Rothstein. Nineteen of the alleged gamblers were dismissed by Magistrate McQuade. Rothstein was held for a hearing on a charge of felonious assault:

"We want every one present at the raid to tell the Grand Jury who shot the detectives. We want to know what happened after the detectives were shot. They were taken to a hospital. You gentlemen know whose car took them there I suppose?"

The District Attorney paused and looked meaningly at his audience. The audience had heard, as most persons who hear about events of interest in the life of New York had heard, that Rothstein had taken the detectives to the hospital. Everybody had heard that. It just naturally was taken for granted —just as it was taken for granted that it was a crap game that the detectives had been raiding.

Some bold spirit answered the District Attorney's query by saying:

"Was it Rothstein's car?"

The District Attorney smiled again, and said:

"I wonder?"

The District Attorney then was asked if the inquiry would be confined to the Rothstein case:

"Gambling will be inquired into in general," was his reply. "We are particularly anxious to know about the Rothstein matter. Men who witnessed the shooting will be given ample opportunity to refresh their memories. Those who elect to testify falsely before the Grand Jury will have to stand the consequences. The penalty for perjury, if I am not mistaken, is still seven years in State prison."

Through many painful years this writer has become impressed by the fact that there is a large slice of false front over all our institutions. He has had a leading jurist, noted for his stand as a "dry," serve him liquor in his home, and ask him if he thought the jurist's bootlegger was treating him fairly. He has heard district attorneys say importantly many times what they were going to do, feeling at the same time that he and the district attorneys were merely playing a game—the game not only of fooling the public, but of fooling themselves.

Suppose for instance that several persons, including policemen, had said casually right after the shooting of the policemen that Rothstein had done it. When they talked, they knew no one had been hurt very much; they knew the police knew all about Rothstein being a gambler—hadn't he always run gambling houses, and wasn't he always betting? They thought, innocently enough, that it was just a joke on the policemen, and that since Arnold had a revolver permit, and no one was hurt much, and he was perfectly willing and glad to pay for his fun, that this would be all there was to it.

Suddenly, however, the complexion of the affair changed. It appeared that shooting policemen in the performance of their duty isn't considered humorous by the law. It also suddenly was developed that a

46

prison sentence hung over any one who might be proved to have pulled the trigger.

So every one forgot. No one had seen Rothstein with a revolver. No one saw him pull a trigger. The police didn't know. The "alleged" gamblers didn't know. Reporters stopped writing stories that Rothstein had done the shooting, and the Grand Jury got busy. On June 5, 1919, it handed up two indictments against Arnold Rothstein, each charging him with felonious assault in the first degree and assault in the second degree upon Detectives John McLaughlin and John J. Walsh.

Following the Grand Jury's action, Judge Crain promptly issued a bench warrant for Rothstein's arrest, and detectives started for his home and for Belmont Park, where racing was then in progress, looking for him. After District Attorney Swann's pronunciamento, and the February Grand Jury's four months' labors in the matter, one might have been pardoned for the belief that some progress had been made in the effort to determine who had shot the cock robins of the Police Department.

As the *Evening World* stated:

"The affair [the shooting] created much comment at the time, but there appeared to be some police indifference about who did the shooting, and it was continual and persistent work on the part of Assistant District Attorney James Smith, which brought evidence from nineteen witnesses upon which the indictments were based."

Well, after all this gargantuan labor on the part of Smith and the Grand Jury, when the case came up in court it was on July 25, 1919, before Judge John F. McIntyre, in General Sessions, in the form of a motion by former Magistrate Emil Fuchs, attorney for Rothstein, that the indictments be dismissed. Judge McIntyre said for the record on that occasion:

"This is a motion to dismiss an indictment lodged by the Grand Jury of this county against the defendant, Arnold Rothstein.

"The indictment, among other things, charges the defendant with having committed a felonious assault. It appears that the Grand Jury was engaged in conducting a John Doe proceeding covering a period of over five months, in the course of which the Grand Jury saw fit to direct the lodgement of an indictment against the defendant.

"The record is barren of any evidence tending directly or indirectly to connect the defendant with the commission of any crime. Much time was spent and doubtless public money expended in an effort made to fasten the crime upon the defendant, and I might add that in the Court's judgment the time was uselessly spent. Not a word of evidence appears in the Grand Jury minutes showing that the defendant committed an assault upon anybody. All that is disclosed is as follows:

" 'Q.   Do you know who did the shooting?'

" 'A.   No.'

" 'Q.   Did you see Rothstein have a gun, or did you see him do the shooting?'

" 'A.   No.'

" 'Q.   Well, who in your opinion did the shooting?   Give us your best opinion.'

" 'A. From reading the papers my opinion is that it was Rothstein.'

"This appears to be the only evidence which in any wise relates to Rothstein.

"Under our system of jurisprudence, fortunately, a surmise, a conjecture or a guess can have no place as evidentiary of the commission of a crime. Why the Grand Jury ordered an indictment in this case is incomprehensible. It should not have been voted. It was idle to do so. The motion to dismiss is granted."

Jim Smith, who presented the case to the Grand Jury, was on his vacation when Judge McIntyre threw it out of court.

Blasé Broadway grinned cheerfully over this dénouement. It hadn't expected anything else. Rightly or wrongly, Broadway—whose habitués are fond of referring to it as "the boulevard,"—always figured that Rothstein knew too many persons of influence, and had too much money, to get into any really serious difficulties. "The Brain," as they were wont to refer to the master, might have his little ups and downs, like being robbed of a few thousand dollars now and then, or being called to court, as he said himself in court on occasion, "to give you people a little publicity," but nothing really serious could happen to him—unless, of course, he should "get his" some day, from a bullet. That was the underworld view of Rothstein; and it was a view that was shared by many others.

Of course, it may have been a wrong view. But when Rothstein finally was "bumped off," he had a clear record so far as convictions of any kind were concerned. Officially, he had been suspected of being the head of the International Dope Ring, the "fixer" of the Chicago White Sox, the receiver of the loot in the $5,000,000 bond thefts of which more will be said later, the manipulator of deals at race tracks and, in fact, the great overshadowing menace back of most of the sculduggery which was befuddling the courts, making a joke of the law and diverting uncounted millions of dollars into underworld channels. But he denied it all. And no one during his lifetime proved that he committed a single illegal act except in connection with running gambling houses and betting. And Rothstein testified under oath that he ran gambling houses, and made huge bets. But nothing was done about that, either.

And, the normal, average citizen, who knows nothing of this sort of thing except what he reads in the newspapers, and is inclined to write off a goodly percentage of what he reads as "newspaper talk," and who probably doesn't believe it's true that one can hire a murder done just as one arranges for any other bit of off-color business, can have no conception of the fear with which Rothstein was regarded. Get in bad with a Police Commissioner, or a District Attorney, or a Governor, or any one like that and you could figure out with a fair degree of certainty what might happen to you on the basis of what you had done. Get in bad with Arnold Rothstein, and all the figuring in the world wouldn't get you anywhere. It's true that nothing might happen to you but Fear. But that's an awful calamity to come upon any man.

Offhand, the two most terrifying flights in literature that come to mind are the flight out of Paris in "The Tale of Two Cities," and the flight of the ship in "The Ancient Mariner." No one was chasing the wildly flying carriage in Dickens's book, and no one was in the wake of Coleridge's ship's crew. But Fear was shrieking at their heels.

Or your Fear might have a tangible foundation. For instance many residents in the underworld assert to this day that the late Charles Becker had nothing directly to do with the murder of Herman Rosenthal. They said:

"These other guys thought Becker would appreciate it if a 'squealer' was bumped off; so they bumped him off. They just did it to oblige Becker. He didn't have to order anybody to do anything."

Members of the old Hesper Club, of which Rosenthal was a graduate, and which was one of the most famous colleges for gamblers in the "good old days" in New York, often have told this writer their certainty of Becker's innocence, just as they have agreed that the four gunmen were guilty. Their view of the gunmen, by the way, is that they were more to be censured for their stupidity than anything else.

Well, there might be some good natured, and rather stupid chaps who might like to please Arnold Rothstein at your expense. Perhaps you can see how it might be.

They would get together with a few bottles of alcoholic beverage, and a little heroin, and get themselves into a state where shooting a guy in the back

51

looked like a most praiseworthy and noble act to their distorted viewpoints.

A fairly large number of citizens had that thought in the back of their heads; and there was just as large a number who believed the tales—of which there were legion—of what fates from plain beatings up, on through the list, had befallen those who had offended A. R.

It was natural for those who entertained the idea that Rothstein was the biggest figure in the life of New York, that he overshadowed the police and the courts, not to be surprised because a Grand Jury hadn't pinned on him a little pistol practice with policemen as targets.

It was just as natural, also, for these persons to nod understandingly when a story began making the rounds, just about the time that Swann was prophesying Grand Jury proceedings in the shooting matter, that Rothstein had arranged everything very sweetly for himself by laying out $32,000 where it would do the most good.

Unknown to the public at that time, Mayor Hylan wrote a letter to Police Commissioner Enright in which he mentioned that rumor. The Mayor went further. He mentioned Herbert Bayard Swope, of the editorial staff of *The World*, by name; and mentioned two other men by implication, as persons who had been chiefly instrumental in seeing that the case against Rothstein got nowhere.

Now, this was a bad break for law and order. The Mayor didn't know what he was talking about. He was so angry at Swope because of *The World's* attitude towards his administration, that if some one had told him that Swope wore horns and had sprouted a tail over night, Hylan would have been glad to believe it.

Swope, who recently resigned as Executive Editor of *The World*, was a great newspaper man and, since his taste ran to horses and that sort of thing, and since he was by way of being one of the characters of New York, he knew Rothstein. He knew thousands of persons—kings, peddlers, princes, waiters, presidents, diplomats, office boys and masters of finance. If of any one person it could be said that "he knew everybody," that person certainly was Herbert Bayard Swope.

Swope knew Rothstein very well. Hylan took advantage of that. And he named Swope as one of the persons who had helped make things sweet and pretty for Rothstein. Of course, it was easy to prove how absurd his charges were—Swope was actually in Paris at the time of the shooting. However, there were lengthy Grand Jury proceedings which dragged on until March 31, 1920.

It should not be difficult by this time to perceive that a tremendous ado grew out of those revolver shots which some one fired at the two policemen in the raid on the "alleged" crap game. It should be equally easy to see that the Law had spent nearly a year of its time for the general purpose of establishing the blamelessness of the characters of Swope and two other men, whose characters always had been considered excellent, but that so far as the Law was concerned the crap game hadn't even existed.

But every one knew some one had shot a couple of policemen, whose names had been forgotten in the shuffle by this time.

And the shuffle wasn't over by a long shot. More pother and oratory and solemn getting nowhere in a big way was about to be instituted. Dominick Henry was duly indicted and tried and convicted before a jury of perjury—he had submitted affidavits to Commissioner Enright reflecting on the character of Assistant District Attorney Jim Smith.

And then the Appellate Division unanimously threw out the verdict of perjury as not being warranted in any way by the evidence, and Dominick Henry, always most highly respected by every one who ever came in contact with him, went back to his job of inspector in the Police Department. And, getting the overlordship of traffic, he added to his already fine reputation by instituting many improvements that still are in use in New York.

A Grand Jury for Dominick Henry, and a jury trial, and a review of his case in a higher court, and then the suit that Henry brought against the City to compel it to pay the costs of his legal defense against an indictment that wouldn't hold water; and reviews of that case.

Those shots at the "alleged" crap game may not have been of the variety that are heard around the world, but they certainly were mighty costly shots to the taxpayers of New York City.

54

CHAPTER FOUR

EASY MONEY

In following the ripples made by those pestiferous revolver bullets, this narrative sped right past the baseball scandals of 1919. The charges and counter-charges of that scandal are not of any great importance here. The fact, however, that both Rothstein, and his lieutenant, Abe Attell, were "mentioned" in connection with the bribing of the players, is significant. Also, the fact that the late William J. Fallon, most brilliant of all the brilliant lawyers who fought the causes of the underworld in the New York courts, was counsel for Attell in these proceedings is most interesting.

Back of Fallon, and the baseball scandal, and the bucketshop failures, and Nicky Arnstein, and the $5,000,000 bond robberies, was the sinister figure of Rothstein, tantalizing to the forces of law and order, brilliant and mockingly glamorous to the cohorts of crime.

While Bill Fallon, his bright head thrown back, his handsome face flushed with power, and his tall, graceful body instinct with a native force that dissipation for a time seemed to leave unscathed, went riding roughshod over prosecutors, marching at the head of a triumphant company of characters well known in Broadway, conspicuous among whom was the towering, athletic figure and regular profile of "Dapper Don" Collins, badger game expert, bootlegger, confidence man and all around trimmer—while Fallon went from triumphs in state court to victories before federal tribunals, law violation took on a semblance of glamor; ordinary decency for a space looked stupid and commonplace.

Back of Bill Fallon was the glitter and stale perfume and the hectic gayety of Broadway. Such was the real power of his intellect at the task of defending accused clients before the bar of justice, so-called, that in many minds the issues became confused. Such was the spurious reputation of Arnold Rothstein in many quarters that one might have been pardoned for regarding him as a sort of glorified knight riding a tilting match against a gluttonous plutocracy, taking from the unethically rich with adroit fingers, to reward the deserving poor with large-hearted benevolence. After Rothstein's death a multitude of words were sent rushing through newspaper columns to assail the public eye with the rare benevolence of Arnold Rothstein.

This writer gladly admits to having had a tremendous admiration for Bill Fallon. His talents may have been misdirected (he was told so often enough, anyway by me); but they nevertheless were superlative talents.

Rothstein and Fallon! What a combination! To the unthinking eye they looked unbeatable during their brief day in the sun. But now they are gone, one by a revolver bullet which, fired from behind, penetrated the intestines and caused an unromantically fatal infection; and the other from an illness brought on by Broadway nights. Fallon went at forty-one; Rothstein went at forty-six.

Fallon, like Rothstein, came from a family of impeccable character, in excellent circumstances. It was natural for both men to know, and be liked by, persons in all walks of life.

The strange case of Nicky Arnstein had been attracting more attention in 1919 and the early part of 1920 than the activities of Arnold Rothstein ever did. Fallon was lawyer for Arnstein. Rothstein furnished the $100,000 bail for Arnstein. He was to furnish other bail for clients of Fallon—in the multi-million dollar bucket shop failures, and in other matters, in which he also appeared as a figure —the authorities said a figure of chief importance, but this they never were able to prove.

This writer first really got to know Fallon in connection with the trial of Peter F. ("Kid") Regan, alias Joe Ryan, who had two trials in the summer of 1919 before the late Judge John F. McIntyre, on indictments of grand larceny growing out of a coin matching game.

The World had been interested in this case, which had been submitted to it by Leonard Wallstein, of the Citizens' Union. A young man, from a Western city, had met the "Kid," and the "Kid" had suggested that by prearranged signals they match coins to win from a third man. The young chap from the West, like so many other young, and old, men from everywhere, never had heard of the coin matching game, and didn't suspect that his newly discovered friend, the "Kid," was an old friend of the other man.

On the chance that the reader may not be familiar with this artifice of the professional trimmer of suckers, it might be explained that the operator ingratiates himself with the intended victim, and then proposes to him that they match coins with a third man, a supposed stranger to them both. The operator and the victim arrange a set of signals so that their coins will never agree, and as the odd man wins by the rules of the game, it looks like a sure thing to any one who is willing to get money that way.

It might be mentioned at this point, that most of the crooked tricks to separate suckers from their money are based on the fact that the sucker isn't any more honest, from the crook's point of view, than the crook himself. A man is mighty hard to "trim" if he isn't looking for something for nothing. In fact, in a long experience around police and courts and crooks, this writer cannot recall a single instance of a "sucker" being trimmed when, in the writer's opinion, the "sucker" wasn't looking for a trimming.

If a man doesn't play cards with strangers, and doesn't roll dice with strangers, and doesn't play faro with someone's else bank, and doesn't figure that he can beat roulette, or win at the races, and doesn't grab at what look like brilliant chances to make a pile of money without any work, and doesn't trust strangers with money, and doesn't carry much money with him, and doesn't play the stock market, or any game he doesn't know all about and with persons he knows all about, he can't lose very much.

If a man doesn't think the beautiful woman who smiled at him in the hotel dining-room, or at the cigar counter, or in the corridor in which his room in the hotel is located, really hasn't become hopelessly enamoured of his manly beauty, he isn't likely to be alone with her any place where the badger game can be worked on him.

If a man minds his own business—"keeps his nose clean" in gangster argot—he can go through life very sweetly. Crooks respect a man that isn't trying to outwit another man at his own game. They should, anyhow. Because the way they lose their own money is by trying to beat someone's else game. The bookmaker bucks the wheel; and the wheel owner bucks the horses; the bookmaker bucks Wall Street; and the Wall Street broker bucks the wheel. Any time one of them sticks to his own knitting, he leaves a tidy fortune with which his heirs can make up for his neglect.

To come back to that Regan case, which illustrates two or three other interesting points in the Fallon character and method of legal procedure. I had known of Fallon before that. But I hadn't come in contact with him. *The World* was interested in convicting the "Kid," and Fallon naturally was interested in turning him loose.

The World and the Citizens' Union were so deeply interested because they thought they saw a connection between the Police Department and the Underworld, since Police Lieutenant "Marty"

Regan (one of the outstanding heroic gentlemen of the Department, by the way) was the "Kid's" brother, and was accused by the victim of having figured in trying to protect the "Kid's" interests in the case.

This conclusion never impressed me, but it was part of my job to go through with the case as thoroughly as possible. The District Attorney's Office was 100 per cent coöperative. It grew to be 1,000 per cent coöperative as soon as it was discovered that Bill Fallon had been retained to do the defending. How they hated Bill in that office!

If I had known what I now know I would have enjoyed much more the two trials of the "Kid," both of which ended in disagreements. As it was, I came to have a great admiration for Fallon's talents, and a sincere regard for him personally. This attitude never would have prevented me from fighting Fallon in the open, if the occasion ever had arisen. It was entirely apart from the professional angle.

In the first place, I know now that just before the trial Fallon said to friends:

"The only way I can win this case, or get a break in it, is to ride the judge. Just watch me do it."

Fallon did "ride" Judge McIntyre, in both trials. And in the second session he had the Judge beside himself. Jim Smith had taken upon himself the prosecution of this second trial with the promise that he would beat Fallon to a frazzle.

In the first place, at the beginning of this second trial, a witness for the District Attorney's office, who was a clerk in a big store which had cashed one of the checks the complainant asserted he had lost in the coin matching game, went to Fallon and said:

"Mr. Fallon, I am a great admirer of yours, and it made me feel bad to have you make such a fool of me on the witness stand in the last trial. I never have heard the last of it at the store. And the credit manager [also a witness] has told every one how good he was as a witness and how bad I was. And it would be a great favor to me, Mr. Fallon," this ingenuous youth concluded, "if you would lay off me in this trial, and apply yourself to our credit manager."

"I am glad you came to me," Fallon said. "I am glad you have shown some faith in me. I certainly will help you out with your friends in the store, and arrange everything most pleasantly with your credit manager."

Perhaps that credit manager, if he still is alive, will learn here why he went through such a terrible ordeal on the witness stand in the second trial of the Regan case, and why the clerk, who had made such a pathetic spectacle of himself in the first trial, loomed like a paragon among witnesses in the second. Well, that is why. The clerk merely asked Fallon to do him the favor, and Fallon took a deal of pleasure in doing it.

To understand this next little story in connection with this trial, Fallon's promise to "ride" the judge should be kept in mind, as well as the fact that Judge McIntyre at the beginning of the session had said to Fallon:

"If I have the same difficulties in this trial as I did

61

in the last trial, I warn you I will make a summary commitment."

This was the Court's way of telling counsel that he would be clapped in jail for contempt if he didn't behave. There were more such threats from the bench until Smith and Fallon had summed up, and the judge had charged the jury. Then, in making the usual requests for additional charges to be made to the jurors, Fallon referred to Judge McIntyre's charge as "an animated summing up for the prosecution."

Judge McIntyre turned purple and pounded his gavel on the bench. Then, restraining himself with great difficulty, he adjourned proceedings until the court stenographer could make an immediate transcript of Fallon's remarks. A casual observer might have been excused for believing that at least a firing squad was in order for Fallon.

Finally, after several minutes wait, word came that the transcript had been made. Fallon, and his then partner, Eugene F. McGee, came in the court room laughing. Then filed in, in frock coats, an important, and solemn appearing coterie of prosecutors headed by District Attorney Swann, and his assistant, Alfred Talley, later a judge of General Sessions.

Just after Judge McIntyre had taken his seat, and while a funeral silence prevailed, Fallon glanced over at Talley, who was turning the leaves of a legal appearing book, and said:

"What are you doing, Talley, looking up some law? What is it? Maybe I can save you the trouble."

This frightful lèse majesté was drowned in the thunder of Judge McIntyre's voice as he told why the jury had been retired, and why this gathering had been assembled. Then the stenographer read what Fallon had said.

"What have you to say to that?" the Judge demanded, leaning forward, and fixing Fallon with glowing eyes.

"Nothing," said Fallon, rising easily to his feet, "except that I believe the Court was unfair, consciously or unconsciously. I ask your Honor to read your own charge, and see if, consciously or unconsciously, your Honor did not do as I said."

For some reason, the tension relaxed. I failed to understand the reason why then, and I fail to see it now. Judge McIntyre merely said he would read the record as Fallon suggested. And that was that.

This is one of the pictures of Fallon that stick in the memory. The cause he was trying wasn't a great one, but he tried it for all there was in it. And he certainly didn't come out second best in his tilts with the Court.

Frankly, judges and prosecutors wanted no part of Bill Fallon when he was at the height of his fame. Ugly rumors of jury fixing were spread about him early, and he was to make his most spectacular case the defense of himself on a charge of bribing a juror, with the juror he was charged with bribing already convicted of perjury, and in the witness stand testifying against him, and he was going to win that amazing case too.

Later Alfred Talley said from the bench, in dismissing this juror, that he believed the charge against Fallon, despite the fact he had been acquitted. All I would like to say about that, and I would like to say it so that it can be heard, is that it's a wonder they didn't charge Bill with having bought up a juror when he was fighting for his own liberty.

This is no defense of Bill Fallon. There isn't the least doubt that he made a frightful mess of his life, and that he kept a flock of persons out of jail who richly deserved to be in jail, and that his way of life was not the right way of life. I told him that several times, and since I want to be fair about it, he told me the same thing about myself.

My way of life wasn't the right way, may be, but my way had nothing to do with defending any criminals, or trying to keep criminals from getting their just deserts.

And, it wasn't because I hadn't been told that I could make money more easily than I was making it. That suggestion came two or three times—if I only "would get wise to myself."

I considered that I was wise enough to keep clean hands. I never had any temptation to have any other kind. I absorbed a good many highballs in those days, and rather enjoyed doing it. Now, I couldn't enjoy doing it.

This reminds me that Nicky Arnstein in the story of his life, which has just been published, was kind enough to protect me by saying that "a star reporter" of *The World* was supposed to ride to Police Headquarters with him on the day of his famous surrender, but that the "star reporter" had had too much to drink, and didn't keep the appointment. That morning wasn't the only morning in those days that I failed to keep an appointment for that reason, either. However, it is necessary to correct Nicky on one detail. Rothstein, and not Fallon, arranged this audacious trip and gave *The World* advance information about it.

Personally, I'd be interested to know how many thousands of dollars Bill Fallon spent on the days and nights before Nicky's appearance. I spent about a thousand, and I only was tipping a waiter occasionally, or feeing a hat boy. Oh yes, I also bought a silk shirt for Bill, who had to interrupt the party one morning to drop down to General Sessions to sum up for another lawyer in a malpractice case. Bill had slept on the floor of a flat in West Forty-fifth Street a couple of hours that morning, preparing himself for the summing up in this case which he hadn't been near, so far as I know.

He had a dish of black coffee; I bought the shirt in a shop on Sixth Avenue on the way downtown in a taxicab, and Bill put it right on.

While Bill was summing up, a deputy assistant district attorney, whom I had known for years, came in and sat down beside me. I said to him:

"It sounds to me as if Bill is going to win this case, too. What do you think?"

"Sure he will," said the other. "It isn't often you can hear a summation like that. There's no one in his class in this building."

Everybody knew that, but few of them were saying it.

I remember, when we hurried from court after Bill's summing up we were pursued by a very lovely girl in a Stutz roadster, who was trying to overtake Bill. We finally got back to Broadway, and the next night we walked into a Place, and a man came up to Bill, and said:

"Congratulations, Mr. Fallon. That was a great piece of work."

"What was?" Fallon asked.

"Why, winning that case for that doctor downtown."

"Oh, was he acquitted?" said Bill, and we went on our way.

Prohibition hadn't yet closed the bar rooms, and in the back room of this Place, at that time, used to come occasionally Fannie Brice, Ann Pennington, and many girls from the "Follies." They used to laugh and talk, and have a drink or two perhaps, and then go their ways.

I recall another incident, trivial in itself, but interesting to me, which took place after the enactment of the Volstead Act. Two policemen went into this Place one day, and began to take whiskey, gin, brandy and everything drinkable they could lay their hands on out to a taxicab. Bill Fallon came in while they were in the midst of this pleasing pastime.

"What are you doing?" Fallon asked in no uncertain tone.

"We are taking this booze to the station house," one of the policemen said. "Who are you anyway?"

"Well," Bill said, "it doesn't matter who I am if

66

you have a search warrant, but if you haven't, it may matter a lot. Have you a search warrant?"

They hadn't a search warrant.

"On whose authority are you acting?" Fallon wanted to know.

They decided it was on their captain's authority.

"Well, call him up," said Fallon, "and find out. I want to know who is responsible for this outrage."

One of them got the captain on the telephone, and reported that the captain wasn't taking the responsibility either.

"All right," Bill said, "then go right out to the taxicab and bring that booze back and put it where you got it from, and get out of here, and don't come back.

"Now give us a drink, Tom," he added comfortably to the bartender, who had been standing silently and nervously by with the rest of the patrons until then. "Give everybody a drink—except those cops."

And everybody had a drink while the policemen restored to their proper places the illegal beverages.

The only policemen and detectives I ever saw around Fallon treated him with exaggerated respect. He defended many of them, and successfully, when they were up on charges.

Of course, no policeman would be a match in wits in a debate with a man that was making a great name by thwarting justice in the courts. Fallon knew his law, and could think like chain lightning on his feet.

Another memory of Fallon is in connection with a case in the Bronx, in which a man named Fritz, an owner of taxicabs, was indicted of murder. A young woman had been found dead in Fritz's car. The prosecution intended to prove that Fritz had caused the injuries which resulted in death.

Now a public official for whom I not only had a great personal liking, but also a deep respect, Dr. Charles Norris, Chief Medical Examiner of New York City, was going to be one of the expert witnesses for the People. I told Fallon of my regard for Dr. Norris, and of the splendid type of public servant I deemed him. I asked Fallon what he thought of the case.

"Well," he said, "it'll be rather easy. I got $10,-000 for defending this man, and it'll be one of the easiest $10,000 I ever earned. He never should have been indicted of first degree murder in the first place, and he wouldn't have been if they had known their criminal law; in the second place, I'll have experts who are just as good as the State's experts, and in the third place, I wouldn't have to be as good a lawyer as I am to be a better trial lawyer than Francis Martin. (Then District Attorney in the Bronx; now a Supreme Court Justice.)

Fallon got the acquittal all right, and Dr. Norris was forewarned all right. But the interesting feature was that Fallon asked his hypothetical question without ever having prepared a hypothetical question.

I don't know just how many words were contained in this hypothetical question to his expert. But there were thousands. That sort of question always is most carefully conceived. In fact, it is not unusual in an important case to call in an expert at such matters to write the question.

In this case, Fallon asked for an adjournment till next day in order to finish his question, and said outside of Court that he was tired, and wanted a drink. He arrived in Court next morning without any manuscript, but he got up in his usual confident manner, and started to pretend to read the question, and he kept right on pretending that he was reading until he was through with a hypothetical question that must have been good enough for all practical purposes, because the jury acquitted his client.

Fallon's association with "Dapper Don" Collins, as the latter was called in the newspapers here and abroad, and as he probably will be referred to again, was a subject of conversation every now and then between Fallon and me. "Dapper Don's" name in the underworld is "Ratsy" Tourbillon. His real name is Robert Arthur Tourbillon. Quite a bit more will be written about him in this book, because he is one of the underworld figures about whom a great deal of glamor has been cast, enthusiastic writers even having gone so far as to refer to him as the "King of the Criminal Empire."

So far as my information goes, "Ratsy" got his real start on Broadway by stealing coins from telephone pay stations. He would place a pretty, innocent looking girl—and "Ratsy," as handsome a racketeer as ever racketed, always seemed to be able to get plenty of those—in front of the booth, while he went in, ostensibly to telephone, but really to save the telephone company the trouble of toting home the money in the coin box.

Bill Fallon got "Ratsy" out of lots of legal difficulties. It would be possible to trace back many of them, but dates and details aren't important at the moment. They will be mentioned later. The point is that Bill became rather disgusted with "Ratsy" on one occasion because, he asserted, "Ratsy" had taken one of the letterheads from the offices of Fallon & McGee, and used it to blackmail a Chicago man out of $5,000.

And all the girl got was a "kick in the pants," is the only added detail that Fallon contributed.

While Fallon was in this mood I read in a newspaper that a jury in one of the courts finally had convicted "Ratsy" of some dereliction or other. Shortly afterwards I met Fallon at a favorite rendezvous of his, and said:

"Well, I'm glad to see that your old friend, 'Ratsy' Tourbillon will be where he won't cause any trouble for a while."

Bill grinned.

"Oh, no," he said. "I stopped in on the way uptown just now and got a writ of reasonable doubt in that case. Why, Arthur never should have been convicted on that evidence. It's an easy case to beat."

"For Heaven's sake, why do you want to spend your time keeping that bird loose?" was asked.

"Ah," was the reply, "Arthur's such a handsome fellow. He's so decorative. There are so many frightful looking human beings around that I believe

70

in doing all I can to preserve the ones who are easy to look at."

That's how simply Bill Fallon turned loose a convicted crook—just "dropped in," and said a few words to a judge, and the job was done. The secret was that "Bill" knew the few words to say better— so far as my experience and my information goes— than any other criminal lawyer of modern times.

And, by the way, here is one of Bill Fallon's oft repeated rules for cross-examination. He said that a lawyer never should bring out all the points where a witness had varied from the facts in cross questioning. That would give a witness an opportunity to correct himself before the jury. But wait until the summation, Fallon said, and then you could prove to the jury the witness was a liar, and the witness wouldn't have a chance to set himself straight.

A friend of mine, who defended himself in one case, rather than have any other lawyer when Fallon was not available, due to work in another court, used this rule in his own cross-examination—along with some other recipes of Fallon. He said that it took a deal of restraint not to bring out discrepancies in a witness's testimony, but he stuck heroically at his task, in order to have that heavy artillery for his summation. Then, suddenly, he tried a wrinkle of his own, and didn't sum up at all.

The jury acquitted him in short order, but he said afterwards that he lived about fifty years trying to figure out whether he hadn't carried restraint too far in that case.

"I certainly was aching to make that speech," he said.

CHAPTER FIVE

HEYDAY OF THE KING

THE war bred income taxes, Liberty Bonds, Prohibition and over-night millionaires. It was another case of Pandora prying the lid from the crate and releasing a thousand ills to prey upon the world.

One set of individuals set out to cheat on income taxes in a large way; another went into the business of stealing bonds; another, and far larger set, began to get rich by trafficking in alcohol; and still another set applied itself industriously to the task of separating the suddenly rich from their riches.

The clean-up, following the murder of Rosenthal in 1912, had driven the gamblers from quasi-public safety into hiding. Street-walkers had been driven from the streets; little children no longer wondered where father was to-night—they could see him getting stewed with mother and their friends; the corner saloon had gone, and twenty drinking places had erupted in its place.

Majority opinion in New York was that absorbing alcoholic refreshment is an innocent pastime: history proves that no law can alter majority opinion.

Policemen drank like every one else. After all, a blue uniform and a brass button or two doesn't change a human being into another species. Bootleggers, operating in violation, not only of the law, but also of the Constitution of the United States, made no secret of their business.

Policemen knew the bootleggers better than any one else. It is a patrolman's job to know everybody on his beat; and he does. A policeman once showed me several oases in the neighborhood in which I was living that I never had suspected; and I knew several myself. One of these oases was in the apartment house in which I lived.

Police officials, and city officials, and state and national officials, and the judiciary and members of the legal profession all kept right on imbibing cocktails and gin and whiskey just the same as ever, if not more so.

I'm not making any case for or against Prohibition here. I'm merely setting down the facts as I know them. And these aren't facts any one told me: they are facts right out of my own personal experience.

Now, if law enforcement officials—men who have taken an oath not only to obey the law, but to see that others obey it too—just naturally don't see any harm in violating one of the most wide-sweeping and generally violated laws on the books, the moral effect on them can't be very beneficial.

By the very nature of their work, Federal Prohibition enforcement agents are drinkers. Perhaps some persons believe they drink only as a matter of duty. These persons should have seen them, as I have, spending their off moments, and large sums of money, drinking at bars. Maybe they were only keeping in training for their jobs. I don't know. Maybe it was their expense money they were spend-

73

ing. I believe their salaries are somewhere around $6 a day. Probably diamond stickpins, and diamond rings, which I've seen on them, and dashing automobiles in which I've seen them riding, and homes which they own, were left to them by rich uncles. I don't know.

I've seen them raid several speakeasies several times, and the speakeasies still are running, and the Prohibition agents still are working hard at their job of absorbing evidence.

Broadway never was a prim thoroughfare, but its atmosphere to this observer, at least, has grown more and more lax, from war times till now. This change was not outward: it was inward.

Outwardly, Broadway looked pretty virtuous. To a stranger in the city, or the average resident, who goes from his home to his office and back again daily —maybe in a subway train buried under a mass of sweating humanity—Broadway was groping towards higher things.

But the underworld of Broadway wasn't groping towards higher things: it was attaining them.

To the professional moralist a bad omen was the first appearance of a chorus with bare legs, which was at the Winter Garden somewhere around the beginning of the World War. Vyvyan Doner, a lovely young woman, of artistic ability, told me that she designed those first bare-legged outfits, all by herself, when she was about fifteen years old. I haven't seen Vyvyan for several years but I assume she still is carrying on in an artistic way, and she should be sweeter and lovelier than ever right now,

74

and be growing lovelier through the years. She impressed me as that sort of girl, both physically and spiritually.

I've heard it said that silk stockings are more seductive than no silk stockings at all. But that isn't the point here. The point I am trying to make is that it seems to me the professional moralist, and sumptuary law maker—the reformer—looks too much at the surface; too hard at the epidermis, and too little at the soul.

The moralist will howl about bare legs, and one-piece bathing suits (both of which I believe are healthful symptoms) and will close his eyes to the fact that he is promulgating laws to help and not to hinder the criminal; or that he is aiding in the enactment of reforms that result only in driving human behaviour, or misbehaviour, from the sunshine into the dark.

A saloon into which one can see from the street, and that is open to every one at any time, seems to my perverted mind to be preferable to a saloon which is run upstairs behind locked and barred doors.

As we all might just as well understand the viewpoint from which this is being written, I will say that I believe it is better to have every social ill right out in public than it is to drive those ills back into the interior workings of the social body. By the same token, I'd rather have my disease, if I must have it, where the doctor or surgeon can see it plainly, than have it buried somewhere in the mysteries of my lights, or my gizzard.

75

If the State ran gambling houses an Arnold Rothstein wouldn't be possible.

However, we are getting a trifle ahead of ourselves.

Rothstein, Fallon and Arnstein—and "Ratsy" Tourbillon—to take four outstanding figures of this epoch, accomplished all their master strokes after Prohibition, after Liberty Bonds were issued, after folk suddenly had been made rich by the war.

Liberty Bonds were lugged about by mere boys in large bales, and they were easy to steal and to market. Bootlegging poured an enormous golden flood of easy money into underworld channels. And Rothstein not only backed bootleggers, but he also won unbelievable sums in bootlegging money. What he won at the fascinating game of chemin-de-fer from the get-rich-quick millionaires of the war never will be known definitely.

"Ratsy" Tourbillon turned for the moment, at least, from his earlier pursuits of blackmail and badgering, to bootlegging, where, gossip has it, he is at present a notable figure. Whether he qualifies as a "baron" or a "duke" in that particular feudal system, I don't know.

Bill Fallon came upon this scene from his home in Westchester County and found it good. There was money in the underworld. The underworld needed a good lawyer, and Bill figured he was the man.

I often have speculated about the psychologies of Rothstein and Fallon and Tourbillon and Arnstein. I've wondered if Rothstein wasn't a bit of a megalo-

76

maniac, as was Napoleon; if Fallon hadn't a touch of the inferiority complex, shown in part by his derisive attitude towards authority and his penchant for punishing himself by keeping himself always broke and in trouble, and by his morbid affairs with many women. Fallon ruined himself just as surely as if he had set about the job deliberately.

Tourbillon I always considered an interesting case of arrested development. While he has been given credit for the intellect of a Machiavelli, my impression from several meetings, and not a little knowledge of his activities, always was that he had the mischievous mind of a lad of about twelve or thirteen—with all the lad's cunning and cruelty.

The three, I would say, were cases for a psychiatrist. A man with Rothstein's abilities could have lived a life of great usefulness in the community. Fallon could have made a name for himself in the law that would have gone blazing down through the pages of history. What might have been done with Tourbillon I don't know.

"Dapper Don" is in another category. He is entirely beyond me, unless, as I say, he merely stopped growing mentally, as well as emotionally, at an early age, and just went along to grow up on the physical side into the amazingly handsome racketeer that he was when he and I were patrons of the same speakeasies, callers at the same law offices, and spectators in the same courtrooms.

Nicky Arnstein often told me that he was a successful contractor before he took up card playing as a business and made a reputation as an international

card sharp and all-around crook of the first water.
I don't like to say this about Nicky because I always
liked him. However, he made his reputation for
himself. No one else did, despite the fact that he
would have it appear that way.

I recall in 1920, when W. G. McAdoo was a can-
didate for the Democratic presidential nomination, I
was at McAdoo's home in Huntington, L. I., for *The
New York Times*. Nicky had invited another newspaper reporter and me to call on him at his country
place, which also was in Huntington.

We motored over there one afternoon, and drank
some very excellent wine. And we praised the Arnstein children, and admired particularly a folding
partition which Nicky said he had designed.

He was more proud of Fannie Brice, his wife, and
the children, and that folding partition than of anything else, so far as I ever was able to observe.

Nicky just wasn't oriented right, I guess.

In the story of this fascinating and interesting
period of New York's history, the names of several
beautiful and brilliant women are indissolubly inter-
woven.

Of course, Fannie Brice figured rather largely in
the bond theft scandals as the wife of the chief public figure in them, which was Nicky Arnstein.

She went to Rothstein and got the bail for her
husband; and she was in court as a witness, and she
was a notable figure about the town.

Peggy Hopkins Joyce appears several times in the
public records of this period, not only because of her
own sensational weddings and divorces and her thea-

trical enterprises, but also because she was a witness in cases in which Fallon was a lawyer, and Rothstein was a prominent figure. Peggy Joyce was a close friend and client of Fallon, and a friend of Rothstein.

Perhaps the best job that Peggy did in her life was to get a receipt from a representative of that nauseous publication, *Broadway Brevities*, on one occasion when she paid over some money. In the trial, prosecution, and conviction of Stephen Clow, publisher of the vicious periodical, Peggy Joyce's receipt was one obstacle that could not be circumvented. Peggy and Bill were arraigned on opposite sides in this case. Bill was defending the *Brevities'* crew, and Peggy was in the vanguard of the attack.

Gertrude Vanderbilt is another charming and talented woman whose name is inextricably mixed up with the situation, and whose appearance helped to lend a little of beauty and romance to what otherwise might have been nothing but a sordid account of millions looted from the public.

Miss Vanderbilt's name also appeared in the records of the bucketshop trials, not in any criminal or legally reprehensible way, but in a manner that would indicate clearly her association with Bill Fallon.

Louise Groody, another charming figure of the stage, flits across the scene. She was the wife of W. Frank McGee, the convicted bucketeer. It was asserted that she and Florence Ely, the actress wife of Edward M. Fuller, tossed gold around in scoopfuls and enjoyed high jinks here and in Paris, on the

79

millions that poured into the bottomless hole that was Fuller & Co. Their denial of these assertions appears elsewhere.

It may be gathered that one who looks back on the period of the reign of Rothstein in its entirety—gazes down at it as a highflying eagle might regard the patchwork landscape below—sees it in pattern form.

The underworld doesn't stick out sharply from the great world of affairs; the textures merge and run into each other. Always the underworld is pushing into and receding from the real world. Rothstein's family is eminently of the upper world. A brother is married into the Social Register.

Fallon's family was eminently respectable, and is yet. Fallon's wife has re-married, and is living a happy and helpful life.

Arnstein's parents were well-to-do, and most upright members of the community.

"Ratsy" Tourbillon came from one of those grand old blue-blooded Southern families, according to his tale, which has partly been verified.

Not the faintest breath of suspicion of any violation of any laws ever touched Peggy Hopkins Joyce, Fannie Brice, Louise Groody or Gertrude Vanderbilt.

But they are down there in that shifting patchwork, brightening it up in retrospect, lending it zest and color.

And there are those beautiful blondes of Rothstein's fancy—Inez Norton, the last and luckiest, apparently.

It would be fatuous to say that easy money did

not flow under the stimulating influence of feminine beauty and charm. A banker will work a little harder to get a pearl necklace for his wife or his sweetheart. It would be odd if a gambler or a racketeer wouldn't increase his energies to the same purpose.

And how the thousands—and the millions—can flow and run and melt away under the warmth that spreads from tender glances experienced and from the hopes of sweeter caresses to follow.

Scotch at twenty-five dollars the bottle in night clubs: rye at thirty-five dollars. Six or eight persons at table. Champagne any price, from twenty-five dollars up. Cover charges two and five dollars a person. A half-dozen night clubs in a night. A bit of jewelry at two, or three, or four or five thousand dollars the bit, now and then. An automobile here; a bill paid for gowns there.

Without the feminine influence life would lose its thrill. This reign of Rothstein, in the memory of the person fairly familiar with some of its aspects, doesn't have the appearance of dry-as-dust court proceedings, or of important dates strung along in a row; it is a medley of impressions. . . .

Rothstein quietly going about his business of gambling, and lending, and backing friends and acquaintances; Arnstein playing cards, and rolling dice, and making merry at gay parties, and planning big things in a big way; Fannie Brice keeping them roaring with laughter at the "Midnight Frolic," or in the "Follies," Louise Groody and Gertrude Vanderbilt earning thousands of dollars by their ability to charm theatre audiences, and taking part in the gay night life of the city afterwards; Peggy Joyce flitting gaily from New York to Europe and back again, selecting and discarding husbands, and gowns and bracelets, and ideas—and then suddenly, a big failure on Wall Street, and one or two of them in the public eye for a moment as they are questioned about this check or that check, or this expenditure or that. Then they go back to their lives again. The curtain has been drawn aside for a moment: a tantalizing glimpse has been had behind the scenes of Easy Money.

A kaleidoscopic, shifting, hectic existence, of which probably no one who forms his conclusions merely from reading newspapers ever begins to visualize correctly.

My picture of Rothstein physically is simply of a quiet, medium-sized man, inconspicuously dressed, in this restaurant or that, or in this court room or that, or strolling on a sidewalk with a friend, frequently reaching down to snap the garter on his sock, his ready laughter revealing those white, even, artificial teeth, hardly whiter than his pallid skin, which was like a woman's.

To the police, and the District Attorney's Office, and the United States Attorney's Office Rothstein was the big centralized power in the underworld. He was back of the bond robberies, and he was back of the bucketshop frauds, and he was back of organized gangs, and he was an engineer in the "international dope ring," and no matter if the Cook County Grand Jury had given him a clean bill of health in the matter, he really had "fixed" those infamous world series.

I pitied Rothstein because, if these suspicions weren't true, they were a frightful burden for any man to bear. And I pitied him if they were true because something was going to happen to him somehow, some day, if he kept on tempting fate. By "pity," I don't mean my heart bled for him, or anything like that. I refer to a more general feeling of regret that any human being should be on the wrong track, when there is so much happiness to be gotten out of this life by sticking to the right track.

And, contrary to common belief, the underworld is inhabited exclusively by human beings. Members of it don't act any differently in their ordinary relations with their fellow human beings from a deacon in the Baptist Church back home—except, perhaps, the denizen of the underworld may be a brighter, more entertaining companion.

You might, for instance, have known Nicky rather well without suspecting that he was anything worse than a light-hearted man-about-town. I recall particularly a long chat I had with him in a speakeasy during the period when the genius of Bill Fallon, and the bail money furnished by Arnold Rothstein was keeping him out of jail.

Nicky had gone into the place early in the morning after having been up all night playing cards. Nicky is one of the most noted of the transatlantic card manipulators. But none of Nicky's real friends miss an opportunity to play a friendly game with him, because he is a delightful companion in his real character. This was a friendly, and not a business game in which he had been engaged.

Well, during the discussion of a "coffee royal," which is black coffee with brandy or whiskey added, Nicky discoursed not on cards, or horses, or women (the writer never heard him discuss women other than to say how very fond he was of his wife) but on the love of beauty that is in every man's soul.

Recollection of the details of the conversation now is dim, but it included a rather poetic diatribe on thoughts engendered by sight of a little bird in a park in London one early morning—a bright-eyed, hopeful little bird, busily pecking at the odds and ends which birds peck at, when it was not shooting what Nicky was convinced was a warmly and friendly, not to say fraternal, glance at him.

"Where do you think that beautiful little bird was bound for?" Nicky wanted to know. "That bird didn't know any more than I did, sitting there on my bench, what really is life; what we really are here for, where we all are going. The bird was there then: he would be gone in a moment—like you and me, and all the rest of us. He was making me happier to watch him. I thought if I made some one happy, if even for a moment, some time, I hadn't done so badly."

There was a lot more of rather sentimental philosophy about the bird, and its eyes, and its wise little ways, which probably concealed an appalling lack of wisdom—of philosophy, that is.

"But it was wise in the way of birds," Nicky said.

No story about individuals can be any good unless the reader can know them from their human side—from the side presented to their friends and acquaintances—no matter how far from the true moral or ethical worth of the characters this view may have led the observers.

The same formula holds true of the surroundings of these individuals. For instance, Jack's Restaurant was anathema to many persons. In its prime no chap in the Social Register was apt to go into Jack's unless he had lost all his sense of values through too copious libations. It was not a place in which "one should be seen."

But many were seen there—the most interesting persons in New York. One may visualize again the plain interior, with the white linen-covered tables, and the Irish waiters. There was no music, and that is why Jack Dunstan, the striking-looking, old white-haired proprietor could keep open all night when other restaurants were closed.

Perhaps it is after midnight. The place is jammed to the doors. Broiled lobsters, thick steaks, lobster fat on toast, Welsh rarebits, scrambled eggs and Irish bacon, broiled pigs feet with deviled sauce —champagne, highballs, Pilsner beer, straight whiskey, pousse cafés, absinthe, cocktails, and more champagne and more beer—women painted and unpainted, women laughing hysterically, or smiling amusedly, or smiling hopefully—college boys, politicians, business men, De Wolf Hopper proclaiming he was the best bad actor in America; Ben De Casseres at the famous round table spouting philosophic theories, while the late Jack London made mental notes to use in a novel later; Hype Igoe tinkling his ukelele; Frank O'Malley telling a story; Arnold Rothstein and "Spanish" O'Brien kidding one another—a commotion as the famous "flying wedge" of husky waiters, with trained muscles and strategy made perfect by much practice, toss a bothersome customer so far out into the street, that he's lucky if he stops going before he hits the building on the opposite side.

Every one that is known in the night life of New York used to go to Jack's. And Arnold Rothstein was certainly known to the night life. After Jack's was forced to close at 1 o'clock in the morning, Rothstein went to Child's Restaurant, at Columbus Circle —wheat cakes, coffee, butter cakes, lady-like young men, actors, newspaper men again—many of the faces once familiar in Jack's. Prohibition had struck. Drinking was in speakeasies. Not only Jack's, but Rector's, Delmonico's, Shanley's, Mouquin's, Bustanoby's—all were doomed.

After Child's became too uninteresting Rothstein removed to a noted delicatessen-restaurant in Broadway in the Seventies. But he was asked to move from there. This place also had a typical midnight clientele—respectability rubbing shoulders with the underworld, but Rothstein was not wanted.

His final headquarters was at Lindy's restaurant. It was from Lindy's that he walked to his death.

In these restaurants Rothstein transacted an enormous amount of mysterious business. The telephone constantly was calling him; softspoken, mysterious individuals, who called him "A.R.," continually were sidling in and carrying on whispered conversations.

But, during it all, it should be remembered that

Rothstein merely seemed to those friends of his who were engaged in legitimate enterprises, to be a person of many affairs which didn't concern them, and which apparently had to be looked after outside regular office hours, and which, obviously, could be conducted outside a regular office.

The stories which have been spread that he was afraid to sit anywhere, except in a booth, or facing a door, are pure poppycock. Up to the end, he was just as likely as not to be sitting in Lindy's at a table in the middle aisle with his back turned to the door.

But even Rothstein's closest friends, who refused to believe the current rumors about his association with dark affairs, have admitted that they had the feeling, when they stop to think about it, that Rothstein always was protected.

He always was looked after in Jack's. The flying wedge would have flown extra fast if Rothstein had needed it—no doubt about that.

A friend who walked home from Jack's with Rothstein on many mornings said that this was proof that Rothstein never had a bodyguard in those days.

"Well, maybe he thought you were enough," was suggested.

A sporting editor was telling this writer how he frequently rode home from the Empire Track in Yonkers with Rothstein in his automobile. Said this chap:

"And every time he had a fairly large roll, and counted it on the way to town. One day it was eighteen thousand and something. Another it was twenty-two thousand, and the last day I rode with him it was a lot more than that.

"I noticed he never stopped to let me off until he had gone into a bank and made a deposit. And suddenly I thought that maybe he was just having me ride home with him so that I would be some sort of protection. He knew that the underworld knew that if I were killed my paper would move heaven and earth to catch and punish the murderer. I never rode with him after that."

Now, the man that told the writer this story, after Rothstein's death, was extremely indignant because Rothstein's character had been assailed. He had known Rothstein at the race tracks for years, and no one could tell him that Arnold Rothstein was any more than the most terrific bettor in the history of the world.

But, curiously enough, while he stoutly defended Rothstein, he became indignant when he told how Rothstein had made bets for him on different races until he had run $50 up to $800, Rothstein always keeping the money. Then one day, despite this chap's objections, Rothstein bet the $800 on a single race and lost it.

However, as Rothstein was successfully outwitting the world it isn't surprising that he should bamboozle a few isolated individuals along the way.

Yet it was difficult to be around Rothstein in his natural environment and not be impressed. In the days of Jim Moran's room in Jack's restaurant, for instance, it was obvious that he was always "protected." That is, those who foregathered there with him always knew that in case of serious argument the person opposed to Rothstein would get the worst of it, and without Rothstein raising a hand. The best such a rash person could get would be the ungentle ministrations of the "flying wedge."

This sense of power gave Rothstein poise and assurance. His vanity was overwhelming, but since he had real abilities upon which to rest it, his outward aspect merely was that of a man entirely sure of himself. The truth is, of course, that persons who violate laws aren't necessarily repulsive. They can be quite charming, as a matter of fact; and in many instances their charm and their ability to entertain are their chief stock in trade.

They are also like other business and professional men in that they are not always talking shop. A surgeon doesn't discuss the intricate details of operations when he chats with a lawyer, or a banker. A crook is the same way. Like Nicky Arnstein he may like to discuss art, or philosophy, or interior decoration, or something on that line. A good many of those men have had plenty of time to do some extensive reading at the State's expense.

Another point might be borne in mind, and this is that there was more than one facet to Rothstein's character. I have told how generously he treated his wife when they separated. Yet a woman who worked in a confidential capacity for Rothstein asserts that he left it to her to answer Mrs. Rothstein's cables or telegrams. She said Rothstein would toss over a message from Mrs. Rothstein, and say:

"You know how to answer that—the usual junk."

Perhaps the same flaw in the Rothstein mechanism which prevented him from yielding to his wife's plea to sever his connections with the underworld was responsible for this brusque treatment of her. The only other mistake which he seems to have made was in not sharing the firm belief of a number of not particularly myopic individuals, both in the underworld and out of it, that somewhere was a bullet on which his name was written.

CHAPTER SIX

ON THE NOSE

THE greatest and most spectacular coup on the American track was made by Arnold Rothstein on July 4, 1921, at Aqueduct, when he won $800,000 on Sidereal, a colt appropriately named, by Star Shoot out of Milky Way.

I know little about horse racing, but I've always loved to look at them when I've had a chance, and I myself never have enjoyed any stories more than the tales of big moments at the track as told by old timers who have lived through so many times the breath-catching, nerve-ripping, heart-stopping moments when those glorious creatures with the blood of a thousand chivalrous ancestors in their pounding arteries come roaring down to the judges.

This story, of the real way that coup was worked on that blazing July afternoon never has been told anywhere. It's one of the epic tales of the turf, and of Rothstein. But after all, Sidereal—by Star Shoot out of Milky Way—(what names those race horses have!) is the hero of the story.

He ran in the silks of Max Hirsch, whose brother-in-law, Willie Booth, was Rothstein's trainer, but to the turf world he meant Rothstein. Hirsch had been nursing Sidereal along as if he were a doting mother and the horse his only child—only more so.

91

Sidereal was primed for a killing, but not that day. Hirsch had entered Sidereal for the race he won, but he had no intention of starting him in it. He had picked out for the colt what is termed an "easier spot"—an overnight event to be run a few days later. Word to this effect had spread around the track, and everyone present who gave the matter a thought believed that Sidereal would be scratched. As a matter of fact, there wasn't any public interest in Sidereal. He was a maiden, and had never won, and his fast trials had been hidden so well, that even the rail birds and clockers knew nothing good about him. Besides, there were twenty other starters although seven scratches left only thirteen finally in the race, and to the students of the game it looked like anything but a place to make a killing.

As a matter of fact, Hirsch was on his way to the secretary's office at an early hour to withdraw the horse when he met Rothstein. It was two hours before the race was scheduled to be run, yet the track was crowded. Rothstein said:

"What a great day for an old time killing! Those bums on the lawn won't know what they are doing when this crowd begins to push and shove them around."

The bums he referred to were the oralists, memory brokers, or commissioners, or any one of a dozen other fancy names of the men who accept legal oral wages in these days. They used to be called bookmakers when money was passed.

"Gee, I'd like to have that colt ready, to do his best to-day," Rothstein continued. "A fellow could win a million dollars and it wouldn't be noticed in this mob."

Hirsch listened, hesitated for a second, and turned away from the secretary's office, and replied:

"Sidereal is ready. The question is, are you ready to make your killing if I can get Sidereal here from Belmont Park on time?"

Rothstein replied in a characteristic way. He said simply:

"I'm always ready to win a bet."

"O.K.," said Hirsch.

Hirsch who had been perspiring a bit anyhow from the normal warmth of the day, had begun to perspire more when he made up his mind so suddenly to try to get Sidereal from Belmont Park, at least three miles away, to the track before scratch time. He began to sweat in earnest when Rothstein hurried off to make arrangements, as Hirsch knew, for an extraordinary betting campaign. And the water began to pour out of him when he was unable to get any response over the telephone from Belmont Park.

He then called his wife, who lived half a mile away from the stable at Belmont, and asked her to race in an auto to the park, ask the foreman to change Sidereal's plates, slip the colt into a van, and get him to Aqueduct in time for the race, if she ever wanted to see her husband again.

That done, Hirsch stood around, and did a deal more of sweating. And he had good cause. In the first place, if the horse wasn't in the paddock thirty minutes before post time the trainer would be fined and the horse automatically scratched. In the second place, Rothstein was running a Napoleonic campaign.

He had gone right to three of the biggest players on the tracks—men whose resources ran up in the millions—and he had borrowed their betting commissioners. Now this might not seem very significant to the uninitiated, but to any one who understands the ins and outs of betting on horses in a large, free way it should mean a lot. It meant in effect that Rothstein, in borrowing the commissioners, not only had gotten a small company of expert bettors to work for him, with no chance of his identity being revealed, but also it meant that he had borrowed the unimpeachable and enormous credit of his three wealthy friends.

Rothstein's orders to the commissioners were simple. They merely were to go out and bet all the money they could as long as they could get any takers. The odds on Sidereal opened at thirty to one.

Such a big price made the commissioners hesitate about following instructions. They knew that to get that price strategy must be resorted to. So they called around them some lesser lights of the betting world, and instructed them to go forth and nibble at that long price on Sidereal, and keep their mouths shut.

These orders were followed, and the sub-commissioners returned with the information that they had placed a few hundred dollars each at thirty to one, and that there was no more of that price left.

Another group was then called together, and sent

out to do some more nibbling at twenty to one. As in the previous instance, this was a success. Each agent had wagered several hundred dollars at twenty to one, and had seen the odds on Sidereal gradually recede to twelve and fifteen to one.

Then came the deluge. The original commissioners went to work. Some went to the clubhouse, and others to the lawn. It wasn't hundreds being bet now. It was "grands," as the gamblers call their thousands. They accepted fifteen to one, twelve to one, ten to one and eight to one. It precipitated the nearest thing to a betting panic known on the American turf.

The oralists, surrounded, and pushed and shoved by hundreds of holiday visitors, literally didn't know what they were doing. They were receiving and accepting wagers on Sidereal in the clubhouse at odds of six and five and four to one while their outside men were telling them that several big layers on the lawn were holding this horse at eight to one. So great was the number of bets poked at the clubhouse oralists by the skilled commissioners that they became bewildered and stopped business to verify the reports they were receiving from the lawn by their outside men.

They got verification, and quickly too. They sent these outside men running to the lawn with orders to bet thousands of dollars at that eight to one. To their surprise they got it. But they knew something was wrong and for the next few minutes worked cautiously. They didn't accept all the bets.

As the bugle blew, and the horses began their

parade to the post, there came an avalanche of wagers. Bets were coming from everywhere. It was a tornado, a howling blizzard of bets. Under it, as under a wild Texas Norther, the oralists crumpled. That was in the clubhouse.

And now it was the same on the lawn. The bottom had fallen from the market out there. There was no more eight to one. There was no six. There was no four. Bettors, clerks, commissioners, handicappers and plain ordinary race-goers joined in the rush to get their bets down on the sure thing Hirsch was sending to the post. When the market broke on the lawn the cat was out of the bag. There was only one man in the world of sport who could pull a coup of those proportions. That was Arnold Rothstein, and every one knew it. And thousands wanted to be in on the kill.

So great was the crush around the different memory brokers, thousands eager to follow the noted plunger's lead, that before the horses reached the post, betting had ceased on the race track. The men laying the odds had been overloaded on the good thing, and had no chance to "lay it off" because practically every one of them was in the same boat. Each stood to lose thousands, and none would take a chance of losing any more, even to oblige regular customers.

Meanwhile, a frantic man, with a bald head, hat in hand, paced restlessly up and down the street leading to the back entrance of the course near which the paddock is situated. Hirsch was waiting for the van, which was bringing Sidereal from Belmont Park.

His watch was ticking, in his opinion, five hundred seconds to the minute. The time to report the horse was getting short. Three minutes to spare, and no sight of the van. Two minutes, and still it was not in sight. A few seconds more and the most spectacular coup in history was a dud. Then, as he took a last despairing glance up the road, he saw the big motor truck.

Waving wildly for the driver to hurry, he sped through the gate, and shouted to the late Jimmy Mc-Laughlin, the patrol and paddock judge:

"My horse is here!"

Then he ran up the street, met the van, and escorted it on the double quick to the receiving paddock, giving the horse a quick superficial examination to see that he was sound and properly shod. He ordered his boy to rush the colt to the regular paddock while he hurried ahead and told McLaughlin:

"Here he comes!"

McLaughlin looked at the horse, glanced at his watch, and remarked:

"You had a close shave, but it's O. K. You beat the deadline by a couple of seconds."

Even though the horse was not actually in the regular paddock on time, he was eligible to start if he were reported at the track, and seen by the paddock judge, for it often happens that a contestant is warmed up on the track before he is taken to the saddling grounds.

The colt was saddled in time, and went out in the parade with his opponents. He was as frisky as any youngster in the race, and with the possible exception

of John Sanford's Slieveconard he was the best looking horse in the race.

With his golden chestnut coat glistening in the sun,
and his noble head swinging and tossing in the air,
he looked a picture horse in that parade, and caused
thousands of casual race goers to admire his beauty,
and hundreds of students of the game to pronounce
him a noble looking horse and one who looked, at
least, like a real runner.

When Mars Cassidy lifted the barrier the thirteen
youngsters went away to an almost perfect start.
The veteran Bill Kelsay was on Sidereal. Sidereal
had some early foot but in the first dash for positions he was out-run by Charles E. Stoneham's Ultimo, Thomas Fortune Ryan's Northcliffe and Harry
Payne Whitney's Brainstorm.

Sidereal raced along in fourth place close to the
leaders until nearing the eighth pole. There Kelsay
called on him and he responded courageously. He
sprang forward when touched with the whip, quickly
sped past the leaders and flashed by the judges a
length and a half in front of Ultimo, who beat Northcliffe by a scant margin for the second end of the
purse.

Brainstorm finished fourth, the Quincy Stable's
Yankee Star fifth and John Sanford's Slieveconard,
the favorite, sixth.

Slieveconard lacked early speed and met with repeated interference. When straightened out in the
homestretch and with clear sailing ahead he finished
resolutely and made up a lot of ground but he could
not get within striking distance of Sidereal.

The race was at five furlongs and Sidereal covered that distance in the fast time of 59 2-5 seconds.

It is an unwritten rule of the American and British turf that a horse has no form, so called, until he has finished in the money. Therefore, it was no reversal when Sidereal won, even though he had been beaten in his three previous races. And horses in which Rothstein was interested were not in the habit of throwing form somersaults. Like the thoroughbreds belonging to all professional gamblers they ran consistently—much more so than those owned by such noted sportsmen as Harry Payne Whitney, the late August Belmont, and Joseph E. Widener, of whom, of course, there couldn't be the slightest suspicion of sharp practice.

From time immemorial the gamblers' horses have run true to form. There is a reason, perhaps, for the owners know full well that the eyes of the Jockey Club always are focussed on their actions and horses, and that a glaring reversal probably would call for an explanation, suspension, or worse. With the sportsman, it is different. The turf world knows that the Whitneys, and the Wideners and the Belmonts always send their horses in to do their best, and when their representatives are inconsistent, all know it is the horse, and not the owner, who is responsible.

There was nothing wrong with the race, so far as Sidereal, Rothstein, Hirsch and Kelsay, the jockey who rode him, was concerned. It should be safe to conclude by this time that this is no brief for Rothstein, but there is nothing anywhere, in the opinion of persons who knew him well in his racing activities, to support the assertions made in many quarters that Rothstein always bet only on "fixed" races—races that were "in the bag."

Rothstein's biggest loss on a single race at the track was on Sporting Blood, one of the best horses in his stable. That was in the last race of the last day at Aqueduct one season. The "Big Shot" tossed away $300,000 of his own money, and $30,000 of Hirsch's money, and about $1,000 of another friend's bankroll in that gamble, which was in a three horse race. His horse was a 1 to 4 shot; a champion matched against two platers.

To an inexpert observer it would seem that a three horse race would be easier to rig for a killing than a twenty horse race. And, if Rothstein was such a marvellous arranger at the track, the question naturally would arise, "Why didn't he fix this one?" or at least, "Why did he bet if he couldn't fix it?"

Hirsch didn't want to bet $30,000 on this race, and the friend didn't want to bet, either. But, it was a peculiarity of Rothstein's that he kept his friends' money, and bet it where he listed. In this case he bet their money and lost it for them, despite their arguments.

Now, a situation is reached that is interesting. If Rothstein didn't bet the money, but only pretended to, that would be something else again. But Hirsch, and the friend, knew well enough that the money had been bet. They knew only too well that Arnold could lose just as well as he could win.

It should be said, before closing this incident, that

100

Sporting Blood lost only to Joseph E. Davis' filly Dough Girl, by three-quarters of a length. It was an exceptionally slow race, as it took Dough Girl one minute and fifteen seconds to travel three-quarters of a mile on a fast track. Sporting Blood was several seconds faster than that normally. He won several important stakes afterward, and is a good sire to-day.

Rothstein's second biggest winning was at Saratoga Springs. He said to Hirsch one day:

"I've been losing a lot of money, and I'm in a bad way. Have you got a horse I can win a bet on?"

"I've got a horse we can win a bet with," Hirsch replied, "but I wanted to win the Hopeful Stakes (a $50,000 race) with him."

Rothstein said:

"I want to win the Hopeful Stakes. I've got a certain amount of pride in my horses and in my stable. That race is a classic, more or less, and it would be fine to win it. But I'd rather win a bet right now than win the Hopeful Stakes later. Maybe we can do both. We can start him in a claiming race."

And by way of illustrating how little Rothstein knew about his horses, and how much he relied on his trainer, he added:

"What's the name of the horse?"

Its one of the rules of a claiming race, that the winner can be claimed by anyone except the owner. That's why stake horses aren't risked in claiming races.

But Rothstein insisted on this horse being entered

101

in a claiming race. And he was. And he won. And Rothstein, who had backed the horse down from 15 to 1 to 6 to 1, made a great killing. But he lost the horse.

Commander J. K. L. Ross, a great figure on the turf for years, and then worth millions of dollars, claimed the horse from Rothstein for about a quarter of his value. And Rothstein had to let him go. That had been part of the risk he had run.

It is the custom when a horse changes owners for the first owner to turn over with the horse the engagements he has made for the horse to race. It was important in this case to Ross to have this horse's engagement for the Hopeful Stakes. But Hirsch, who was extremely upset over the whole business, wouldn't part with the engagement. He said he would sell it for $20,000, but that was the best he would do. Ross, through Bedwell, his trainer, tried in every way to make Hirsch change his mind. But he never did.

Rothstein did the same sort of thing with a horse named Gladiator who had won the Toboggan Handicap at 8 to 1, and who would have been one of the greatest sprinters of all time—a second Roseben, not a few contended—if he hadn't suffered from a wind affliction. He was what is called a roarer.

One day at Aqueduct Rothstein popped Gladiator into a selling race. He had selected, with his usual acumen, an excellent time to do it, because Gladiator had run far back in a previous race. Despite the fact the field in this sprint was rather ordinary, Gladiator's recent bad showing was reflected in the betting,

102

where he was quoted at even money. Rothstein bet $120,000 on his nose, and Gladiator galloped home the winner.

After the race Gladiator was bid up $15,000 over his selling price, which is a record bid-up in the history of the American turf. The previous record was when the late Mike Dwyer, the most spectacular plunger of the early days, entered one of his stake horses in a selling race for the sake of winning a wager at a short price.

There are life-long followers of the turf who will tell you that no stable ever was run so truly to form as was the Redstone Stable of Arnold Rothstein. There are other persons who will tell you differently. But whatever was the case with the horses, there is no doubt that Rothstein had good ones, and that they ran, and that he bet the family prayers on them when they looked good.

Stories calculated to show that Rothstein was crooked in all of his racing bets are told. There is a certain type of person who believes that everything is crooked. That sort of individual would not know the inside tale of a race like that of Sidereal, and wouldn't believe it even if he heard it.

Rothstein lost as well as won money at the race track. He probably lost more than he won. At the time of his death he still owed a large amount of money to bookmakers from disastrous wagers.

On Memorial Day, preceding his death, Rothstein visited Belmont Park. On his arrival he told his friends he wasn't going to bet, that he had gone for a day's sport, and that the most he would do would be to place a few piker bets on horses he doped out himself. But before the bugle brought the first field to the post the old gambling spirit took a strangle hold. He bet $2,000 on the favorite, and lost. Friends joshed him for being unable to restrain himself, but he laughed and replied:

"That's only a piking bet. I'll win that back in the next race, and then bet fives and tens for the remainder of the day."

But his choice in the second race went the same way as that in the opening event. It was beaten off. He was now a loser of several thousand dollars, and his gambling blood was stirred to a high pitch. He was avaricious; he wanted his money back with interest.

He forgot his intention of placing only a few small bets, and went after the oralists in earnest. He lost bet after bet, and at the end of the day his program showed he had picked six straight losers, and had lost $130,000.

This money, or at least most of it, had not been paid when he was shot. Several of the men to whom he had lost bets called on him for payments time and again, but to no avail. Strange as it may seem, these men did not become angry when the "Big Shot" told them that he was unable to pay. He told them he was not a welsher, that he would pay a hundred cents on the dollar, but that they would have to be patient.

"I am far from broke," he said. "I have collateral worth millions of dollars, but I am short of cash, and if I should attempt to liquidate those squawkers, Fuller and McGee and Uncle Sam would pounce down on me."

They had known him as a gambler who was slow pay, but they considered him sure, and when they learned his legal difficulties they left him, resigned to wait.

There was a period when stories were going the rounds that Rothstein had been ruled off the tracks, or that he had been requested to reduce his bets. The truth is he was never ruled off. What happened was this.

After the baseball scandal of 1919, the members of the Jockey Club decided that Rothstein was not an asset to the turf. Because his losses had run consistently, and because to their knowledge he had violated none of the rules of racing, there were no grounds for ruling him off.

The late Major Belmont, however, who was chairman of the Jockey Club, and had a pretty free hand on rules and regulations pertaining to the turf, had made up his mind that Rothstein, as an owner, plunger, and regular, must go.

He called Rothstein before him and issued an ultimatum. It was:

"Sell your horses: stop your spectacular betting: stop coming to the tracks regularly, or we will rule you off."

Rothstein didn't like that. He squirmed and pleaded that he had done no wrong, that he liked the turf and the thoroughbred, and that he had any number of prominent business and political giants who would vouch for his honesty and sportsmanship.

105

Major Belmont agreed that everything he said might be true, but stuck to his guns. Rothstein had to go.

"If you want to visit the track with, or without your family or friends occasionally—a Saturday or a holiday, or any day if you don't make it too often—we will not object," Major Belmont said. "But under no circumstances will we tolerate any more plunging and spectacular betting by you. The first thing you must do is to fire all of those betting commissioners you have in your employ, and we don't want you to engage new ones if, and when, you decide to accept our terms and make an occasional visit."

Rothstein knew the Major was in earnest, and after protesting a few minutes longer he finally said he would accept the first part of the ultimatum, and left the Major's office with a polite "Thank you."

On at least one previous occasion Rothstein had been barred from the clubhouse at Jamaica, and this ruling, if it had remained in effect, would have denied him the privileges of the clubhouse at every track in the Metropolitan District, which includes Belmont Park, Aqueduct, Empire City, Saratoga and Jamaica. Together with several other professional gamblers, he was informed by the police at Jamaica that his presence was undesirable. But this ban was lifted in a surprisingly short time. It was said that he brought pressure to bear through several very influential channels.

While other gamblers on the turf refuse to say he was crooked or a welsher, they are practically unanimous in declaring that he was slow pay. After losing bets he refused to pay according to the gamblers'

106

unwritten rule of play and pay the next day, on the grounds that he was too busy to straighten out his accounts and draw checks. As excuses he used to give the most remarkable reasons ever heard on a race track. Instead of paying on his arrival following a losing day, he would resume betting in an effort to win back his losses by the pyramid system, contending that he must win a bet some time, and that when he did get over a winner, he would be clear.

Rothstein's crookedness outside of the track had nothing to do with his straightness on the track. The Jockey Club couldn't get anything on him, and they tried hard enough.

Incidentally, so far as I know, the Jockey Club is the first powerful organization to recognize the danger which lies in the concentration of millions of dollars of easy money in the hands of bootleggers, and to take concerted action against them.

Until now it has not been printed anywhere that the Jockey Club prepared during the late fall and early winter of 1928 to keep the bootleggers out of racing by the adroit expedient of examining all trainers who apply for licenses as to the qualifications of their employers. If a trainer can't give an employer a clean bill of health the trainer won't get a license.

The Jockey Club understands better than most the political and economic power of the bootleggers. The gentlemen who run the metropolitan tracks at a loss every year for the pure sport of seeing noble horses run know the underworld as one foeman knows another. They realize that political influence will be brought to bear, but they are going to wage the campaign relentlessly.

Having no axes to grind, they do not shut their eyes to the facts. They don't have to be told that when a bootlegger like the late Frankie Yale dies of hot bullets, and upwards of 65,000 persons either attend his funeral, or send floral testimonials of respect, there is power and influence in bootleg money.

They don't have to be told that one bootlegging New York political boss in the 1928 elections turned in his whole district clean for the Democratic ticket. That chap gives away so much coal in the winter and ice in the summer, and clothing and provisions and easy cash at all times, that he truly is an overlord in his own domain. He is above the law in the ordinary sense of the word. Police and district attorneys don't want any of his medicine.

Why, the tale of bootleg money is incredible. There is one man whom we will call Sam, because that is not his name. Sam had had millions out of the bootlegging racket, but he met with hard luck, and one night found himself broke. He had only $1,700 in his pocket.

Two foreigners approached him in a café and told him of a plan to smuggle grain alcohol here from Belgium. He wouldn't listen to them. After they had left, he changed his mind, and traced them to one of the popular chop houses in mid-town New York, where the cocktails, ale and wines are as good as they ever were.

When Sam finished his talk with the two men, they had $1,000 of his money as an evidence of his good faith, and he was United States agent for their smuggling enterprise, his share to be one-half the profits. My recollection is that the price for the alcohol in Belgium was 40 cents, and the price laid down in New York was $5.20. Those figures may be off a few cents either way, but not more than a few cents.

Within three months Sam had $900,000 in cash in his bank. He had been lucky, and had gotten through four shipments of the alcohol. And they prattle brightly of "diverting industrial alcohol," or of this or that. The bootleggers don't even laugh about it; they just take it for granted that a Prohibitionist is either a fanatic, or a grafter. They don't give him credit for any common sense.

One bootlegger had gone broke betting on the horses. His partner became disgusted and stopped him from handling money, which comes in batches of hundreds of thousands of dollars when it comes. Now the bootlegger who was broke is a millionaire again. When he gets through his day's work he goes home; his wife gets out the carpet slippers; one of the children twists a knob on the radio, and the wife says:

"Now dear, isn't it much better to be nice and clean and respectable like this?"

He doesn't bet on the horses any more, or drink so much of his own rum.

One of the biggest bootleggers in New York, a man who ran a fleet of ships, and still does, so far as I know, was asked to lend money to further a "white goods" shipment, as narcotic drugs are called in the underworld. The bootlegger knocked the "white goods" merchant down, and his followers beat the "white goods" merchant up. As respectable business men they were insulted.

Word in the inner circle of Broadway shortly after that was that the merchant had gone to the "Big Jew uptown," and had gotten fixed up. The "Big Jew uptown" was one way in which reference was made to Arnold Rothstein by persons who were extremely chary of using names.

It may look as if this chapter on racing had wandered far afield, but it still is right on the track. The Jockey Club doesn't want the bootleg money in its precincts. And it seriously is concerned over keeping it out. It will be the big battle of 1929—Jockey Club against Bootleggers.

The Jockey Club has killed off "boat races," as crooked races are termed. Where twenty bad races were run on the various tracks in 1927, only one was run in 1928, and that instantly was detected and the guilty ones punished.

Easy money is bad money, dangerous money. Men who have earned their millions by regular business methods know that. Henry Ford said to me once:

"I could give you a million dollars, and never know that it was gone. But one of the first pieces of advice I was given when the money began to come in great quantities was to be careful about giving away my money, because of the danger to character and morals involved."

It takes moral stamina to keep millions from doing

harm. What is going to be the influence of the multi-millionaire bootleggers?

There is a real economic and political problem in the United States to-day. My solution would be to have the Government control the alcohol business and derive the income from it. I don't believe a successful fight can be waged against the embattled bootleg millionaires.

The Jockey Club is out to have a try.

CHAPTER SEVEN

THE RAZZLE-DAZZLE IN STOCKS

ONE way of looking at the failure of E. M. Fuller & Co., in June, 1922, is that it represented a loss to the speculating and investing public of about $4,000,000. Another way of looking at it might be that this same public paid about $4,000,000 for the privilege of getting the best close-up view of Arnold Rothstein it ever was afforded·during the years of his suzerainty.

Rothstein's name appeared on the books of the company in many transactions, most of which never were explained to the satisfaction of the investigators. Edward N. Fuller and Edward F. McGee cheerfully asserted under oath that Fuller had lost $331,000 betting with Rothstein.

The "Big Shot," therefore, became a target at once for the lawyers for the creditors, and many times was a witness in the inquiry which followed the failure. The attempt was made to go into the world series scandal of 1919; the bribing of Charles W. Rendigs, a juror in one of the trials of Fuller and McGee; a loan of a large sum by Charles A. Stoneham, president of the New York Giants through former Sheriff Tom Foley, of Tammany Hall, to the bucketeers just before they failed, and other matters.

More will be said in its proper place about the ·

Rendigs incident. Rendigs was convicted of perjury as a prospective juror in the Fuller case. Then he turned state's evidence, and testified that Bill Fallon had bribed him when he was a juror in the Durell-Gregory trial, and Bill, in the most sensational and brilliant defense in his remarkable chain of sensational and brilliant defenses, got himself acquitted.

To get back to our knitting. A good insight into the impression that prevailed regarding Rothstein and the baseball scandal in particular, and Rothstein and other matters in general, and of Rothstein's methods of combating attack may be had by considering his appearance before Referee in Bankruptcy Coffin, in a Fuller bankruptcy hearing on October 8, 1923.

On this occasion William M. Chadbourne, lawyer for the creditors went at the "Mind" with everything he had, to find out just what Rothstein knew about the baseball scandals.

Word battles were the order of the day. Chadbourne had told the referee that he was going to try to find out how much Rothstein knew about the arrangement by which the Chicago White Sox tossed the series to the Cincinnati Reds. This, Chadbourne submitted, was pertinent to the proceedings because it had been testified previously that Rothstein had won $22,500 from Fuller on the series.

If it could be shown that Rothstein had anything to do with "fixing" the series, Chadbourne successfully had argued, Rothstein would be liable to the creditors of the Fuller company for having obtained money under false pretenses.

113

Rothstein's comment on this was:

"Absolutely, I would be liable. I know that."

Rothstein said frequently to Chadbourne, during the questioning:

"This is no place to ask this kind of question, and you ought to be ashamed of it. Your questions are absolutely outrageous."

On one occasion when Rothstein made this remark, Carl J. Austrian, lawyer for the trustee in the Fuller litigation, interrupted to say to Rothstein:

"Nothing is more outrageous than what we believed happened, and the conduct of witnesses in this proceeding."

"This baseball thing has been the sore spot in my career," Rothstein exclaimed. "I faced the Cook County Grand Jury in Chicago and got vindication."

"Do you know a man in Boston named William J. Kelly?" Chadbourne asked.

"What's that got to do with this case?" Rothstein demanded.

Reminded by the referee that it was not for him to decide what bearing a question might have on the bankruptcy proceedings, he said:

"Do I know him? Yes, I know him."

"He's an attorney, isn't he?"

"I know him as something different. I think he's a blackmailer, to tell you the facts."

"Did you engage W. J. Kelly to represent you in the Grand Jury proceedings over the world series in 1919?"

"You ought to be ashamed to ask me that. This is no place to ask that kind of question. You ought be ashamed. Before I'd be a tool like you are I'd jump into the Hudson River."

This comment was ruled from the record and the question was re-read by the stenographer, whereupon Rothstein said:

"You know it isn't fair."

"You should have thought of that before you took out of Fuller the money you did," Chadbourne said. "Did you have any conversation with W. J. Kelly with respect to the Chicago-Cincinnati series in 1919?" he added.

"I never had any conversation with Mr. Kelly regarding those games. I never spoke to him but once in my life. That ought to stop all your silly questioning."

Rothstein then explained, in response to questions, that Kelly had called him on the phone and that he was introduced to him in Chicago in 1921 as he was about to take a train for New York. He was positive he had never seen or talked with him except on those two occasions. He also denied ever having written any letters to Kelly.

"I am just answering those questions to please you," added Rothstein when he was requested by Referee Coffin to refrain from further comments.

"How can a man refrain?" he asked Mr. Coffin. "It's an absolute outrage."

Q. Did Fuller place any bets with you on the world's series in 1919? A. I don't remember whether he did or not.

Q. Do you know Abe Attell? (Attell was former featherweight boxing champion, a constant com-

115

panion of Rothstein, and one of his bodyguards.)
A. Yes, I know him.

Q. And do you know J. J. Sullivan of Boston, commonly called "Sport" Sullivan? A. Yes, I know him too.

Q. Now don't you know you had a conversation with Kelly about representing you and Attell and Sullivan during the Chicago investigation? A. Absolutely not.

Q. Did you have any conversation with William J. Fallon regarding his representing Sullivan, Attell and yourself? A. Absolutely not, I'm not going to answer any more such questions.

Q. Isn't it a fact that you paid William J. Fallon $26,000 to represent you in those proceedings? A. No, positively no.

Q. Sullivan is known as one of the great handicappers in racing circles in this country, is he not? A. He wants me to tell him something, is that it? (Rothstein made this remark to the Referee, who ruled out questions about whether or not Sullivan was a handicapper.)

Q. You actually did place bets, including one with Fuller, didn't you? A. That hasn't anything to do with this case, and I refuse to answer it.

Q. What do you know about a handicapper? A. I'm not going to answer. I don't know anything about it. I'm in the insurance business. I'm not a gambler.

"You seem pretty well informed," Chadbourne suggested.

"Yes, and you do too," Rothstein snapped.

116

"I've been following your career pretty closely," Chadbourne said.

"And I've been following yours, too," Rothstein said.

Q. Do you not know that Sullivan doped out percentages on races, crap games, etc.? A. I refuse to answer. What has that to do with this case?

Q. Did you bet with Fuller on the result of the world series in 1919? A. Yes, I had one bet, and Fuller won that.

Q. (By Coffin): Did he get his money? A. Sure he did. I always pay my bets.

Q. (By Chadbourne): Didn't you consult Sullivan regarding the world's series of 1919 with respect to the various games so as to be in a position to determine what odds should be placed? A. I don't remember. That's too far back. It's a silly question.

Q. You refuse to answer? A. Yes, on the ground that it has no bearing on the case.

Q. Didn't you consult "Sport" Sullivan as to the way bets should be placed on the world series? A. You don't know what you're talking about. What's that got to do with the case of Fuller assets whether I consulted him or not?

Q. As a matter of fact, you were represented at the hearing (the Cook County Grand Jury investigation into the baseball scandal) by William J. Fallon and Kelly? A. I have no attorney.

Q. Isn't it a fact that you had a conversation with Sullivan prior to the series of 1919 with respect to that series? (Referee Coffin ordered Rothstein to

117

answer simply, "Yes" or "No.") A. I wouldn't answer at all, as it has no bearing on the case.

Q. Did you have a talk with Attell about seeing Sullivan regarding the series of 1919? A. No.

Q. Did Attell report to you any conversation he had with Sullivan regarding that series? A. Absolutely not. I really shouldn't answer those questions and only do it to please you, Mr. Chadbourne.

Q. I want to be fair with you. A. You don't want to be fair with me. That's the last thing in your mind. You wouldn't know how to be fair if you tried.

Rothstein denied that he had been in Boston during the years 1919 or 1921. He said that the last time he was there was ten or twelve years before.

Q. Didn't Attell report to you that because of the nation-wide interest in that series the results could be determined and millions might be made? A. (Hotly) I'm not going to say "yes," or "no." This has got to be a joke.

Then Referee Coffin ordered him to answer, and he refused on the ground that it had no bearing on the case.

Q. Did Abe Attell in 1919, prior to the world's series, repeat any conversation with Sullivan? A. No sir.

Q. Did you know Bill Burns, a former ball player? A. He introduced himself to me one night and I insulted him by telling him I did not want to know him, if you call that knowing him. I'd like to know who's paying you to ask me these questions.

Q. Do you recall another meeting in the Hotel

118

Astor in 1919 with Abe Attell and Sullivan to discuss the world's series with you? A. I'm not going to answer that either because it hasn't anything to do with the case.

Q. Isn't it a fact that at that conference proper percentages on bets on the world series were doped out? A. I'm not going to answer because it has no bearing on the case.

Q. Isn't it a fact that at that conference the question of fixing the White Sox was discussed? A. I don't remember. I wouldn't discuss such a thing. There wasn't any such conference, so how could I discuss it?

Q. Then I understand you never had such a conference? A. I'm not accountable for what you understand.

Q. Did you have a conference anywhere else in New York? A. I don't want to discuss that. There never was such a conference.

(Rothstein here denied that he had any conferences with Attell or Sullivan anywhere at any time regarding the world's series of 1919.)

Q. Did you meet Attell at any time in New York in 1919? A. I'll answer all of these questions at the proper time.

The referee then ordered an answer, but Rothstein wouldn't give it. He said that his examination involving Fuller bets on the White Sox was for the purpose of embarrassing him and Charles A. Stoneham, president of the Giants organization, suspected then, but exonerated later of being a "dummy" partner of E. M. Fuller & Co.

119

"Rothstein won $22,500 from Fuller," Chadbourne said during one passage.

"No, he won from me," Rothstein said.

To a series of questions asked in an attempt to show that Rothstein knew the White Sox games were "fixed" and that he "double-crossed" Fuller on bets, Rothstein said:

"I won't answer."

Q. Did you ever have a conference with "Sport" Sullivan after the series for a division of the winnings? A. I refuse to answer.

Q. Didn't "Sport" Sullivan accuse you of welshing? A. I never welshed in my life.

Q. Don't you know the White Sox players were to get $100,000 bribes? A. No, I don't know that.

Q. Don't you know the White Sox players made the charge they'd been double-crossed, and didn't get the money after they had thrown the first game? A. I never promised them any money. I don't even talk to ball players.

Q. Did you have any connection with William J. Fallon as to getting the Chicago Grand Jury minutes? A. No. (The minutes of the Grand Jury proceedings had disappeared. Fallon was defense lawyer in the Fuller case, and openly was lawyer for Attell in the baseball scandal.)

Q. Don't you know that Fallon got those minutes? A. No, did he?

Q. Do you know a lawyer in Chicago named Leo Spitz? A. Yes, very well.

Q. Did you have Spitz send a man named Sammy

120

Pass here about the extradition of Abe Attell? A. No, I dòn't remember.

Q. Are you prepared to testify you didn't ask Sammy Pass to come here to testify in the proceedings against Attell? A. Yes. Did he?

Q. Didn't you pay Pass $1,000 to come here? A. No.

Q. Did you make him a loan? A. Yes, if it's any of your business. I loaned him $1,000, and he paid me back $500. He'll return the other $500. He's a nice little boy.

Q. Did he ever say he didn't consider that a loan? A. No, he's a nice boy and wouldn't say such a thing.

Q. Do you know Charles W. Rendigs? A. I believe I do.

Q. He's the man indicted in the Fuller case in connection with bribery. Didn't you have a conversation with Rendigs while he was a juror in the Fuller trial? A. Oh, behave. I refuse to answer.

Q. Did you have a conversation with Fuller about Rendigs at the third trial? A. No.

More questions about Rendig's caused Rothstein to say:

"The next thing, you'll be blaming the Japanese earthquake on me. There must be something the matter with those cough drops you're eating."

One of the hearings in which Rothstein was a principal witness before Coffin as referee was on July 27, of this same year, 1923. The lawyers for the creditors were trying to find traces of concealed assets, and they did not find any.

They tried in vain to make Rothstein admit that he had paid the legal fees of Fallon and McGee as attorneys for Fuller and McGee. (Eugene F. McGee was Fallon's law partner at that time, and had no other relationship, except a legal one, with William F. McGee, the broker.) Their question made it plain that, besides discovering assets for the creditors through Rothstein, they were hopeful that they could show that the "Brain" had introduced the indicted brokers to their lawyers, and had directed their defense.

Rothstein couldn't remember anything helpful to the inquiry, and his "I don't remembers," "I don't know what you means;" his "What has that got to do with the cases?" and his "I refuse to answer on the ground that it might tend to incriminate or degrade mes," did not illuminate beclouded questions —much. When he was taken to task for his methods of replying Rothstein said:

"I'm only trying to help you all I can. I could save time by refusing to answer, and have it over with."

Francis M. Fallon, an attorney for some of the creditors said to this:

"Maybe we could find a nice place for you to spend your time in."

"That's all right," was the reply. "Any place would be better than here. This is no fun for me."

He admitted he had lent money to Fallon & McGee, but first refused to mention and then said he couldn't remember the amount, or that he had cancelled an indebtedness of William J. Fallon to be applied on fees for the brokers.

"Did you ever lend Fallon and McGee money for the account of Fuller?" Referee Coffin asked.

"I don't remember," Rothstein said.

He said later it was "absolutely impossible" that he had sent Fallon & McGee checks for $1,250 and $750 in August or September, 1922, as part of the bankrupts' fees.

When Chadbourne asked Rothstein if he had received approximately $385,000 from Fuller personally "in connection with certain transactions between you," Rothstein said he didn't understand. Then Chadbourne asked if Fuller had bet with him, and Rothstein refused to answer.

"That would be a misdemeanor, wouldn't it?" he asked, adding: "I don't recall any such amount as $385,000."

Austrian finally said:

"It is apparent the only things he can remember are those in respect to which we show him documentary proof."

Now that something has been shown of the purpose behind the questioning of Rothstein, and his method of facing the enemy in court, a peep at some of the information on which the questions were based might not be amiss. In order to get this data from court records, a jump ahead may be permissible to May 23, 1924, when those fetchingly clad, smiling and opulent-looking individuals Fuller and McGee, were witnesses.

Fuller and McGee at this time had been convicted and sentenced to serve from fifteen months to four years in Sing Sing. They were out on deferred sentences. They had gone in apparent high humor to the office of Lloyd Church, 5 Nassau Street, who was acting as referee before trial in the action brought by creditors of Fuller & Co., against Rothstein to recover $371,768, which it was asserted the partners lost to the "Big Shot" at gambling.

Fuller and McGee looked healthy, happy, well fed and carefree that day. McGee was toting a smart stick, and his straw hat was a model of the mode. Both wore suits that would have made a Fifth Avenue tailor's dummy jealous. The only apparent difference was that McGee's outfit was dark gray, and Fuller's was brown.

Chadbourne did the questioning; and George Z. Medalie, a most excellent and highly esteemed lawyer of New York, represented Rothstein's interests. Of Fuller, who was the first witness, Chadbourne asked:

"Between the time you first met him and the failure of E. M. Fuller & Co., in June, 1922, did you see Arnold Rothstein frequently?"

"I did," was the reply.

"Did you make any bets with Arnold Rothstein?"

"A great many."

Asked to describe the nature of events on which bets were made, he said he had bet with Rothstein on baseball and football games, horse races and boxing matches.

"On the balance were you winner or loser?"

"I was a loser as a result of those wagers."

Fuller then said, in response to further questions:

"Rothstein never told me that any other person had an interest in our wagers except himself. My custom was to pay my bets the next day in the form of checks made out to Rothstein. I never had any other personal business transactions with Rothstein, and we never lent each other money, except, we might have lent each other $10, $20 or $50 to tide over a check some night when we were in a café."

"Did you ever play cards with Rothstein?" "Oh yes."

"Did you ever lose, playing cards with Rothstein for money?"

"I don't think so."

He could recall very few specific wagers he had made with Rothstein but remembered that he had won "the year Sir Barton won the Kentucky derby."

"I also recall," he added, "a wager made in 1921 that Cleveland would beat the Yankees and that Pittsburgh would beat the Giants. I bet $15,000 on each wager."

"Did you win or lose?"

"I lost both of them."

"Were the losses to be paid to Rothstein?"

"Yes. McGee returned from Europe in September, 1921, and three of us, McGee, Rothstein and I met in an apartment, McGee and I had in Delmonico's. Cleveland was behind the Yankees then, and Pittsburgh about seven or eight games ahead of the Giants, so that it seemed about an even thing. Later I asked McGee if he wanted to take half of

125

those wagers. He agreed, and when we lost we sent the check for $30,000 to Rothstein."

"My recollection is it was a firm check," he continued, "and one-half of it was charged against my personal account and one-half against McGee's.

"There was hardly a day during those years when I didn't see Rothstein some place, in Delmonico's or the Waldorf. We usually had a wager on something every day or nearly every day."

Chadbourne grinned, and looking at Medalie said: "I hope Rothstein doesn't bet with his counsel."

"I don't bet," said Medalie, "not even on the outcome of a lawsuit."

"You would have bet that Ruth would be convicted, wouldn't you?" asked McGee, laughing. (He was referring to Ruth Snyder.)

About fifty checks, made out to cash or Arnold Rothstein, and indorsed by Rothstein, or stamped "for deposit, Arnold Rothstein," were shown to Fuller. He identified his own signature and Rothstein's. The checks covered a period from August 1916, to September 1921, and, according to Chadbourne, totalled about $331,000.

"What was the nature of the transactions in which these checks were given by you to Arnold Rothstein?" Chadbourne asked.

Medalie noted an objection, and Fuller answered, "For bets."

"Of what nature?"

"On baseball games, football games, horse races or prize fights," was the answer.

Fuller could not remember the specific wager or

contest each check represented, but repeated that each had been paid in connection with a bet on some game or race. He said Rothstein never had a general brokerage account with his firm, but said the firm's money frequently was lent to Rothstein.

"Several times," he explained, "Rothstein called us up and asked us to hold a check several days or a week and give him a check he could use at the minute. We had plenty of cash at that time."

He said the checks, which were given to Rothstein in exchange for checks signed by him and dated several days ahead, always were signed by McGee or himself. Rothstein's checks always were good.

McGee smilingly said he bet very little himself but often heard Fuller and Rothstein say to each other:

"I'll meet you at the track."

Regarding his share in Fuller's bet on the Cleveland and Pittsburgh baseball teams he said with good natured sarcasm: "In a moment of generosity Mr. Fuller offered me half the bets and I fell for it."

After examining the fifty odd checks Fuller had made out to Rothstein, McGee said they were not firm checks. Then, he turned to Fuller and added:

"You had some good bets."

Since Rothstein had no Boswell—who, by the way, was greatly maligned when I went to school, for he was the first great reporter, and far greater than Samuel Johnson who is remembered only through his biographer—these dips into the hearings in the Fuller case reveal not only the view of Rothstein held by the investigators and his view of them, but

127

also give the only authentic records of his conversation at any length.

On October 29, 1923, Chadbourne and Austrian had another go at Rothstein before Coffin. The lawyers tried, first without success, to get Rothstein to admit that his secretary, Miss Freda Rosenberg, once was secretary for William J. Fallon. Asked if he had won many bets from Fuller and McGee, he said he had not. He had won a few, perhaps, he said, but had kept only a mental record of them, and that appeared to be a trifle hazy.

"Have you been getting rid of your securities?" Chadbourne asked.

"No," was the reply. "I am solvent. If I owe Fuller & Co. anything, I'll pay it. I handled so much money during the latter part of 1921, and for the first part of 1922, I kept no track of it. But Fuller was no baby. He didn't need a guardian."

"Did you receive as much as $375,000 from Fuller?"

"I don't want to answer that."

"Did you get as much as $100,000 from McGee the year before the failure?"

"No," was the answer.

Rothstein had said at a hearing on October 24 that Fuller and McGee had wanted him "to take an interest in their firm or lend them money."

"I didn't do either," he explained, "because I didn't think they were going to pull through. They were the only ones who believed they could pull through if they got enough money."

"How much did they want?" Referee Coffin asked.

128

"As much as they could get," said Rothstein.

When the question of his gambling with Fuller and McGee was brought up again, he said:

"I never said I gambled with them, or that Fuller is my friend. I was his friend, but he never was mine."

On December 8, 1923, Chadbourne tried to find out from Rothstein where he had secured the collateral which he had testified previously he had put up for a loan of $172,358 from Fuller and McGee. Rothstein said he refused to answer on the ground that it might tend to incriminate and degrade him.

"There's some double meaning in that question," he said to the Referee. "I don't want to answer it. Mr. Chadbourne has an ulterior motive that I get but you don't. I can't compete against Mr. Chadbourne. He's a lawyer. He's too full of tricks, and he's trying to force me to tell untruths."

He described his method of not answering questions by saying:

"I answered that way to keep from going into details."

And he explained:

"I don't mean that for the record."

Referee Coffin said:

"Put that in the record."

But what good putting anything that Rothstein said in the record, so far as the creditors of Fuller & Co. were concerned, hadn't been visible up to the time of Rothstein's death. The fact Rothstein came through with clean legal linen all through his career proves either that he was a much maligned citizen, or

129

else he was stretching a point when he told lawyers
that they "were too full of tricks" for him.

When asked what steps he had taken to find where
he had bought the Liberty Bonds that he had testified
were the collateral put up for the loan, Rothstein
said:

"I racked my brains and looked over every paper
in my office."

"It is perfectly obvious," Chadbourne said, "that
the witness has not only been evasive but untruthful."

It's only fair to include Rothstein's view of the
lawyers. He said at one of the later hearings:

"I've been here twenty times or more, and the
questions I've been asked have been one per cent
relevant. The other ninety-nine per cent have been
asked by lawyers looking for publicity."

Not only lawyers, however, were accusing Rothstein of not being strictly on the up-an-up at this
period. On November 5, only a few days before
Chadbourne made the charges that Rothstein was
lying, Colonel Samuel James, noted sportsman and
handicapper, described what he termed the "double
cross" that was given him by Rothstein, who had
been his intimate friend.

Colonel James was testifying in proceedings before
Referee Terence Farley, which grew out of contempt
charges brought in connection with a suit instituted
against the Colonel by Miss Mildred Adams, for
whom Fallon and McGee were lawyers.

The Colonel testified that someone, who described
himself as a clerk in the office of Rothstein, had called
him on the telephone and had told him that a war-

rant charging bigamy had been issued against him, and that Rothstein would be glad to attend to his bail.

"A day or two afterwards," Colonel James testified, "Rothstein himself came to my house and said, 'Can't we settle this thing?'"

Questioned by his lawyer, Samuel S. Berger, Colonel James said that a few days later he received anonymously through the mails a copy of an alleged marriage certificate. Berger said:

"Now, after you received this marriage certificate, did you again see Mr. Rothstein?"

"I don't think so," was the reply. "I don't think I saw Rothstein after that. You know, Mr. Rothstein and I have not been on such friendly terms owing to this. I made a request through friends of mine for Arnold not to go bond for her, or for Fallon or McGee. He said he would not, but I am led to believe that he guaranteed those bonds."

At the time of Rothstein's death no decision had been rendered in a suit brought against him in the Supreme Court by George C. Sprague, receiver in bankruptcy for Fuller and McGee, to recover the $366,768, which it was charged had been paid by them to Rothstein for gambling losses.

Rothstein's last of several appearances in Court in connection with this case was on June 22, 1928, when he repeated denials previously made that checks for the amounts mentioned represented gambling debts. He said he had cashed them for Fuller and McGee purely as a matter of friendship.

On this last appearance as a witness, the "Big

Shot" testified that he made only one bet on a horse race with Fuller, and that was when Fuller won $25,000 from him on a Kentucky Derby.

He denied the testimony of a previous witness, and what still are the assertions of his intimates, that he would "bet on anything."

"I never bet on football games," he said, "and I seldom bet on prize fights."

These forms of wooing the Goddess Chance, by the way, are not regarded by those who make a living by gambling, as the safest forms of investment in their chosen field. But Rothstein really took bets on everything because his system was betting that the other chap would guess wrong; and, as has been pointed out, he was in a position always to take advantage of odds in all sports because so many bets came to him.

Rothstein, in the witness chair, continued to explain. He said he never went to Sunday baseball games, and that he risked money only on championship series. (He used to be described in newspaper articles as "the man who backs the Giants against all-comers.")

"I haven't any interest in the American League," he said.

In answer to questions as to who had won the World's Championship in baseball from 1919, the year of the fixed series, through 1921, he said that he didn't know. But he had heard that the White Sox had gotten into difficulties one of those years.

Rothstein was asked especially about two of Fuller's checks, one for $10,000, and one for $19,000. He said:

"They were very small checks. Fuller on many occasions had given me checks for $100,000. My confidential man, Tom Fuller, would go to Delmonico's and get Fuller's 'tabs' showing the losses of the day before, and in paying them I gave hundreds and hundreds of checks to the bookmakers and clubhouse commissioners. They were always Fuller's checks."

"What is your business?"

"Frankly, I ran gambling houses. Fuller was a large player."

"Did you ever act as a bookmaker?"

"No, but in 1914-15 I was a betting commissioner. I believe in our dealings Fuller quit more than even. He was a very desirable patron of my club and I went out of the way to oblige him. I always used Fuller's checks in paying his bets, and sometimes he sent me thirty a day."

"Did you ever pay any of your own racing losses with Fuller's checks?"

"I wouldn't pay my own debts with another man's checks."

"I had partners in the gambling house," Rothstein said in answer to other questions. "If we won we divided the money and if we lost we made up the bankroll."

"That wouldn't happen often."

"You'd be surprised how often."

Joseph F. Levins, betting commissioner, testifying for Rothstein, said Fuller's losses were always paid

133

by his own checks endorsed by Rothstein. "They always had to be endorsed by Rothstein or the bookmakers wouldn't take them," he said.

There certainly is nothing very romantic about ,THAT appearance of Rothstein.

One never could tell from the account of this hearing that it was the last appearance in any court on this earth of Arnold Rothstein in the role of a misunderstood and grievously wronged gentleman—a gentleman who liked to take a sporting chance now and then; a gentleman who was willing to do a good turn for a friend at any time; but a gentleman who drew the line at any of the various forms of sculduggery, of which, by some strange trick of a malignant fate, he always was being accused.

No, there was nothing in the fullest account of that proceeding that might have been written to show any of the long chain of dramatic incidents that had led up to it. It was the last flash in the pan of the famous bucketshop scandals which agitated the courts and the body politic of New York for several years, and which grew out of a painful parting by many trustful individuals from their hard earned savings.

Rothstein's really big day as a witness in the Fuller and McGee mess was on June 25, 1923, before Harold P. Coffin, Referee in Bankruptcy.

The proceedings opened with Fuller being granted time to confer with new lawyers he had chosen. Fuller then was in Ludlow Street jail on a contempt charge.

Former Sheriff Thomas F. Foley, a power in Tammany Hall, who had appeared as the agent through whom Charles A. Stoneham, owner of the New York Giants, had financed Fuller & Co. to the extent of $147,500, with their lawyer, former Supreme Court Justice Edward E. McCall, also a figure in Tammany, had been called, but they were told to return another time.

Then Rothstein took the witness stand. He said he was forty-one, but he looked ten years younger. He was smiling constantly that day, revealing his store teeth. He was most tastefully attired, as usual, in an unfinished blue serge suit, a white silk shirt and black bow tie, with modest white figures, and wore tan socks and tan shoes. No one, as usual, ever would have taken him to be the biggest gambler in New York—the biggest power in the underworld.

Two hours of blistering cross-examination by Coffin, and by Chadbourne and Kohlman, the lawyers, left him blissfully serene. Chadbourne appealed to the referee frequently that Rothstein "assumed a bland, child-like attitude of not being able to understand the plainest words in the English tongue." That did not make Rothstein any less bland, however. Invariably, his reply to difficult questions was:

"I don't know what you mean; I'll be glad to tell you all I know about it."

At the outset, in response to questions, he said that his business was insurance, and that he had known Fuller and McGee eight or ten years. He had brought with him a number of memory refreshers in the form of documents, and said he was going to tell everything he knew.

And he began at once by telling everything he

135

knew—which already was known by the public at large.

Q. Did you borrow money from Fuller & Co.?
A. Certainly. I have the checks right here.

Among the checks was one for $34,000, which he said represented a loan for which he had pledged twenty-nine Anglo-French bonds, in September, 1920.

Q. Why did you go to Fuller & Co. instead of a bank? A. Money was tight at that time and it was hard to get a loan. Furthermore, I saved two per cent. by going to a broker.

For a few minutes his testimony flowed smoothly.

On June 1, 1920, he bought four hundred shares of Chandler Motors for which he gave a check for $39,660, and June 3 he sold three hundred shares and received a check for $30,616, and on June 22, a hundred shares.

In September he said he borrowed amounts ranging from $2,000 to $27,000, for which he pledged Liberty Bonds valued at $25,000. He guaranteed the $2,000 for a friend named J. J. Hynson, and when the friend failed to pay it he did.

Between January and July, 1921, he testified, he borrowed about $80,000, specifying in detail the various transactions. But he couldn't remember distinctly one loan of $30,000. He didn't know whether or not he put up $30,000 in Government bonds as security.

Q. (By Kohlman): I would remember all about it if I borrowed $30,000. A. Probably you are not in the habit of borrowing large amounts.

Q. Are you sure you gave him Liberty Bonds?
A. Some kind of collateral. I used different kinds, but I always gave security.

Q. (By Referee Coffin): Where did you get the Liberty Bonds? A. I bought them.

Q. I assume you did. I am not intimating that you stole them. A. Thank you.

Q. (By Kohlman): If this account does not show the delivery of collateral, are you prepared to say it is not a correct account? A. I will swear that I left security. I never borrowed five dollars without giving security. I never broke my word in my life, and I wouldn't tell you a lie. I am under oath.

The name of Jay O'Brien, well known in gambling and sporting circles came up. There was one loan for $20,000 which he made good for O'Brien. A deal was made of the fact at the time that Account No. 600 could not be explained satisfactorily. Rothstein's name appeared in it, and so did O'Brien's. It was obvious that the investigators were hopeful of getting some extremely helpful admissions from Rothstein in connection with this account. But they did not.

They got nothing helpful from him. Here is another sample of questions and answers:

Q. (By Kohlman): It appears that sixty Liberty Bonds were delivered out of the account; we don't know to whom. We also find in the same account checks for $7,700, and $52,776.08. The blotter of Fuller & Co. merely stated the receipt of the checks. There is no entry on the blotter as to whom they were received from. I ask if they represent pay-

137

ments to you by Fuller & Co.? A. I don't remember. It doesn't mean a thing to me.

Q. Don't you recall receiving sixty Liberty Bonds? A. I do not.

Q. If you had received them, wouldn't you remember it? A. I think I would.

Q. Is your answer, then, that you didn't receive them? A. I didn't say that. I said I didn't remember receiving them.

Rothstein promised to look in his records and see if the fifty-five bonds came to him. He was very agreeable about it, and continued to be agreeable, even when he was told that an eminent jurist had said "I don't know," is a fraudulent answer.

"I'm not trying to hide anything," he said, equably.

Q. (By Kohlman): You can't expect the Court to accept at face value "I don't remember" as an answer to questions concerning a transaction of $60,000, can you? A. That is the only answer I can make.

Q. The charge has been made that Fuller took considerable sums from E. M. Fuller & Co., and lost them at the race track, and that you were the agent with whom they were placed? A. I refuse to answer, on the ground that it might tend to incriminate or degrade me.

Q. Did he lose large amounts of money with or through you? A. I refuse to answer.

(All refusals to answer were based on the witnesses so-called "constitutional privilege." That is, no witness may be forced to testify against himself.)

Q. Did he lose large sums of money with you at

Belmont Park? A. I refuse to answer. I always heard he was a very good player and a big winner.

Q. And you are informing the distinguished newspaper men present that Fuller often won large sums of money? A. I always heard he was a successful player.

To questions about the $35,000 Fuller and McGee bail bonds, Rothstein readily admitted that he had "helped."

"I would do the same thing for any unfortunate friend," he said.

So far as Charles A. Stoneham was concerned, he said he did not know the owner of the Giants well, and that he had no part in, and knew nothing about, the loan of money by Stoneham to Fuller through Foley. He asserted he had nothing to do with paying the legal expenses of Fuller and McGee.

When he was asked if he was connected in any way with the baseball scandal, he said emphatically that he was not, and added that the question was unfair.

He said, in answer to further questions that he knew Louise Groody (Mrs. McGee, of whom it was said at the time that she was in Paris having a pleasant time on her husband's money, but who, it developed later, was paying her own expenses from her earnings as a theatrical star.) He said he had heard of Florence Ely (Mrs. Fuller) but did not know her.

It was Chadbourne who asked the questions about baseball. He also asked if Rothstein ever had employed the firm of Fallon and McGee as attorneys. Rothstein's "No" aroused the lawyer's wrath, and he turned to Referee Coffin, and said:

139

"This witness is giving deliberately false answers. I ask that you direct him to answer. He has stated he never employed Fallon and McGee."

To Rothstein, he added:

"Do you wish to change that testimony?"

Rothstein said pleasantly:

"Yes, I refuse to answer on the ground that it might tend to incriminate or degrade me."

Whereupon, Chadbourne said to the Referee:

"It is quite apparent that perjury has no terrors for the witness. I ask that he be cited for contempt."

Referee took this motion under advisement, but he smiled as he did it, and the belief of those present that he had no serious intention of committing Rothstein for contempt was borne out afterwards.

Rothstein said his businesses were insurance and "dabbling in real estate," and he said he was interested in a finance company and a mortgage company. Chadbourne said:

"How about the business on which you claim your constitutional privilege?"

Rothstein, one of the wits of the round table at Jack's Restaurant, said:

"You don't call that a business, do you?"

And that ended a session which gives the best and most authentic example of Rothstein's attitude under verbal attack.

CHAPTER EIGHT

THE JAIL ROBBER

B Y far the most brilliant and romantic personality which figured in the reign of Rothstein in New York was that of William J. Fallon. Fallon was not of the underworld but he was the idol of it.

He had the good looks of a matinée hero, the poise of a dancer, the brain of a student and a most profound knowledge of the criminal law. Where other lawyers might hesitate for a word, or go to a book for a precedent, Bill Fallon was never for an instant at a loss. Not only prosecuting attorneys, but judges also grew to fear the deadly thrust of Fallon's knowledge, backed by his remarkable oratorical gifts and his uncanny ability instantly to locate the weakness in an enemy's armor.

There is no need of mincing matters. Judges and prosecutors during the successful years of Bill Fallon's career were more than ordinary legal foes. They firmly believed that he was the most effective barrier in the country to the orderly enforcement of the law. They were his enemies.

Fallon's progress from one courtroom to another was a sight worth seeing. He had an entourage in which more often than not was conspicuous the tall and handsome figure of "Dapper" Don Collins, otherwise "Ratsy" Tourbillon, and which always included past or present clients among whom was an indicted detective or two.

I saw the late Maurice, the dancer, and Jack Dempsey when he was heavyweight champion, dividing the honors at a crowded dance one night. Each luminary had its great tail of followers. In the courts and in the night life of Broadway Bill Fallon had no rival luminaries. He sat alone during his brief day in the sun as the most admired individual in the gay life of the town.

There was something pathetic, however, about this feverish semblance of success. The very adulation, which Fallon loved so much, was final proof that he had built his reputation upon sand. Many great law firms of New York would have liked to employ Fallon to do their trial work, but the word had gone out that the District Attorney's office, the United States Attorney's office, the Appellate Division of the Supreme Court and the Bar Association, all were delving industriously into Fallon's activities. The nature of his successes rejoiced the underworld, but were a matter of grave concern elsewhere.

The racketeers and other denizens of the underworld who grouped themselves around Fallon and patted him on the back and cheered over his victories didn't mean anything to him, or wouldn't mean anything to anyone else, so far as real achievement is concerned.

Bill was something like an actor. He loved to go into a court room and be the star, which he always was. The only difficulty was that if one looked beneath the glamor created by the personal magnetism of the man, and by his rare eloquence, his amazing gift of cross examination and his audacious sallies at judges and prosecutors, one could not help but feel that here was a man dressed in knightly armor equipped for mighty deeds riding in tournaments for the favor of a scarecrow.

Fallon was born in Westchester County, and his well-to-do family still live in Mamaroneck. He went to college at Fordham where he distinguished himself in logic and at debating. He also played tennis a great deal, and this may have given him the graceful poise which was one of his appealing attributes.

In college Fallon behaved himself neither any better nor any worse than his fellow students. On only one occasion did he come into notable conflict with the faculty and that was one hectic day when he amused the undergraduates by making stump speeches against the college authorities. Those who heard the speeches bear witness that they were remarkably amusing and witty. Nothing came of this mild outburst except a short session behind closed doors with the Dean.

After graduating at Fordham, Fallon went back to Westchester County and soon became an assistant on the staff of former District Attorney, Frederick E. Weeks. There, his amazing abilities as a trial lawyer quickly brought him a reputation which spread outside his native bailiwick. Even the fact that the great war was taking most of the space in the newspapers couldn't crowd the achievements of young Fallon from their pages. He had one

143

of those personalities which would take more than the world war to smother. One of his unusual feats was the conviction of a score of Blackhanders in one batch for a murder.

Various reasons have been given for Fallon's going to New York and setting up practice for himself about 1918. On two or three occasions, Bill himself told me substantially this:

"I had convicted a man of murder, and he was all set to be electrocuted when we got evidence, quite by accident, that he was innocent. We had time to save him, but it was a narrow squeak, and it made me feel sick. I decided right then that I wasn't cut out to be a prosecutor of my fellow human beings. I decided I wanted to help them and not hurt them.

"My experience was that District Attorneys go just as far wrong in their attempts to secure convictions and make good records as defendants' lawyers may go in trying to protect their clients. Personally, I feel much happier over the thought that I may have prevented a guilty man from being punished than I would over the thought that I had been instrumental in securing the conviction of an innocent man. I wouldn't be a prosecutor again for all the money in the world."

I am sorry that I kept no record of that and similar conversations I had with Fallon. I asked him on several occasions if he wouldn't take the time to go into the details of cases—incidents of which had interested me, because I saw wonderful material in him for one of those "human interest" articles. I never jotted down the odds and ends, because I always was hopeful that some day, he would sit still long enough to tell the whole story. But our ways parted before the end, and Bill Fallon died without having had time to tell anyone even as much as he told me, so far as I know.

Bill's first case in New York didn't attract much notice at the time but it was significant in the light of later developments. It was the first brick in the reputation that he was going to rear by the boldness of his methods, by his marvellous mental agility and his knowledge of every loophole in the law. It was the start toward the time when, in the heyday of his success, accused bond thieves, bucketeers, badger game workers and racketeers of all sorts, with the knowledge of Fallon's ability and his known backing by Arnold Rothstein, were going to adopt the slogan:

"Get Fallon and get out."

This first case was that of "Dandy Phil" Kastel and his wife Daisy who were charged with having worked the badger game against a wealthy manufacturer of New Jersey named Heller. The Kastels and Heller told diametrically opposite stories in the various legal proceedings which followed and nothing came of it except unwelcome newspaper publicity for Heller.

"Dandy Phil" was one of the lucrative clients of Fallon until in 1921 the bucketshop of Dillon & Company, which was merely a false front for "Dandy Phil," failed with losses to clients of about $500,000. A pretty good line on the care taken by the stock buying and speculating public in selecting brokerage houses with which to do business, is splendidly illustrated by this instance. After three trials "Dandy Phil" finally was sentenced to a long term in Atlanta for his bucketing activities. He was a friend of "Nicky" Arnstein, "Big Nick" Cohn, and the other high class Broadway and Fifth Avenue racketeers.

Fallon's next case and one which got him a great reputation was that of Mrs. Betty Inch. Mrs. Inch was a charming and attractive woman, a former actress, who was charged by Eugene P. Herrman, President of the Herrman Motor Truck Company, with having tried to extort money from him by telling his wife that he had other women in his home when Mrs. Herrman was away. According to the evidence at this trial, Herrman and his wife and three children were dining one evening when the telephone rang. A woman's voice asked for Mrs. Herrman, and said: "I am Mae Hayes. Last March, while you were in Atlantic City your husband and a friend met me and a friend and took us to your apartment where we spent the night."

Mrs. Herrman had called her husband as soon as she caught the drift of the conversation and he had listened to it with her. Next afternoon Herrman said that he heard the same voice say over his telephone at his office, "Well, old man, how did you like the message your wife received last night?"

"Who are you and what do you want?" Mr. Herrman asked.

"I am Mae Hayes, and I have to undergo an operation."

The voice then went on to say, it was testified, that money was needed for expenses for the oper-

146

ation. The owner of the voice continued that she was not Mae Hayes but a friend. Herrman made an appointment with the owner of the voice at the Hotel Woodruff next day, having taken the precaution to plant detectives at the hotel. There he met Mrs. Inch who told him she would have to ask her friend how much money was necessary. Mrs. Inch ostensibly went to a telephone and when she returned said that her friend would leave the amount to Herrman's generosity: otherwise, Mae Hayes would meet his wife the next day.

Herrman testified that Mrs. Inch told him that if he paid her, Mae Hayes wouldn't bother him any more. So he gave her $215, in marked bills, while the detectives who were behind a screen used their ears and eyes. Then they came out and arrested Mrs. Inch.

Bill Fallon always insisted in his talks with me that this Inch trial cost him personally about $2,500. I never believed it, and told him so, but he said that it was true. He said he had gotten into the case expecting to get a good fee out of it, and then after he got into it he became interested in winning it for the prestige he saw it would bring and spent his own money, mostly in efforts to find Mae Hayes (who the prosecution claimed in the first trial was a mythical person) and in paying her expenses to come to New York from Cincinnati. There were two trials, both resulting in disagreements, not an unusual outcome for a case of Fallon's and one which in many instances was regarded by Broadway as a victory for him.

In the first trial the newspapers had made a great fuss about Mrs. Inch's display of ankles, particularly when she was on the witness stand. In the second trial a bright newspaper reporter deduced that he could get a better story for his paper by having Mrs. Inch's ankles concealed than he could by having them show. That is the real solution to the mystery of how a rail came to be built about the witness chair for the second trial. At the time, the papers said that nobody connected with the court or with the prosecutor's office or with the defense knew who was responsible for the ankle-shrouding device. As a matter of fact, no one knew the answer better than the newspapermen themselves. Mrs. Inch called this railing a spite fence. In his summation, Fallon said:

"Look at that monstrosity, that outrage on justice. Just because of that we have refused to let Mrs. Inch take the stand, to sit there behind the barricade. It seems that they have tried to make this a comic opera case."

Mae Hayes's appearance in court was expected to be the most sensational moment of the affair. However, it wasn't so pulse-stirring after all. She looked at Herrman and said she knew him, and Herrman looked at her and said he had never seen her before. She wasn't allowed by Assistant District Attorney Alfred J. Talley to say very much.

She testified that she lived at the Parkside Hotel with Peggy White in April, 1918 and met Herrman that month. Fallon asked Mae Hayes a good many questions about alleged meetings with Herrman and

148

about telephone calls. Objections by Talley prevented her from answering but she nodded her head affirmatively until Talley got the judge to order her to stop.

According to her testimony she had telephoned to Herrman about three weeks before and he had had the charges reversed at her request. Her testimony continued:

"I said, 'Is this you, Gene? This is Mae.' He said, 'I don't know any such person.' I said, 'You know me; I'm married now.' I told him my husband and I were happy, but felt worried about Betty and thought something should be done. He told me to get into communication with the District Attorney.

"I said, 'Must I come to New York and testify?' And he said, 'Do as you like.' He asked me if I had ever slept in his apartment, and I said, 'Why, no, Gene; I have one of my own.' He said, 'Well, there is a warrant out for you,' and I said, 'Why, that's so silly. I have done nothing to be arrested for.'"

Talley didn't ask Mae Hayes any questions. He contented himself with getting into the record the fact that Herrman said he didn't know Mae Hayes, who by the way, had been married and was now really Mrs. Irving Benjamin.

In 1925 it might be mentioned Supreme Court Justice Wasservogel dismissed a suit for $10,000 for false arrest which Mrs. Inch had brought against Herrman. This trial had just been getting under way when the Justice was told that the indictment

149

against her on the charge of extortion was still in force. However, the two disagreements had resulted in her practical freedom, and Bill Fallon's growing reputation was greatly enhanced at that time.

The next case of any importance that came up was the "Kid" Regan trial, which already has been mentioned in some detail. This was another instance where Fallon was credited with a victory although what he really got was two disagreements.

Tourbillon, who had become a client of Bill's, was one of the claque recruited from Broadway which daily followed Fallon's triumphal progress in the courts. It used to make me smile to see the detectives around the Criminal Courts Building watch "Dapper Don" with hunger in their eyes. "Dapper Don" strolled elegantly around in the wake of his legal protector, serenely indifferent to detectives, judges, assistant district attorneys, and the rest. He knew he was safe with Bill.

It was during one of the Regan trials that the District Attorney's office suddenly became very much upset one day. Assistants bustled here and there, the speed of their passage making the corridors rather breezy. One of them told me that some sort of legal action had been taken to prevent anyone from removing papers in a safe uptown. The safe was supposed to contain money, as I recall it, which belonged to a client of Fallon, who was accused of having acquired the money in some illegal way.

Fallon, during the noon recess of the Regan trial, had been told of the action of the District Attorney

150

with regard to the safe, and had taxied uptown and buffaloed whomever it was necessary to buffalo, into letting him get what he wanted from the safe, and then he had returned to continue with his defense of the "Kid."

The District Attorney's office was beside itself. Fallon was a thorn in its flesh anyhow. One of the assistants said:

"No one else but Fallon ever would have done anything like that."

They were going to do all sorts of things to Fallon, as a result, but all Fallon did was grin about it.

"What can they do?" he asked.

Somehow, observation of Fallon and Fallon's methods in Courts didn't increase one's respect for the Courts. If Fallon were wrong, as Judges and Prosecutors were saying all the time, why didn't they do something about it? They complained enough.

Fallon maintained up to the time of his death that he didn't use any more tricks for the defense than were used by the offense. And he went to his grave with a clean slate, so far as indictments and convictions for any sort of offense were concerned. As a matter of fact, I don't think there even were any formal charges pending against him at the end. The last thing the Appellate Division did was give him a clean bill of health.

Friends of mine who knew I was writing this book have jokingly advised me to buy a bullet proof vest. Other friends have told me I probably will have to be prepared to take one witness chair after another and refuse to answer questions on the grounds that they will "tend to incriminate or degrade me."

This thought came to me in connection with this question of the courts. I was a bystander in one case in which I saw a defendant pay $2,800 to a lawyer. The understanding with the lawyer was that an assistant district attorney got $150, that two detectives got $750, that a third detective, who was the go-between in this bribery affair, got $100, that another lawyer, who had a hand in it, got $250, and that other less important persons got a few dollars.

I didn't see any other money except the original amount paid to any one. I do know that the detectives in the case became friendly with the defendant, who was discharged for lack of evidence. To cap the climax to this story, I should like to add that the original evidence of the detectives was framed anyhow. But they knew that the defendant might just as well have been guilty as not, so that probably satisfied their consciences.

I certainly would answer any questions about this affair by saying:

"I refuse to answer on the usual grounds."

My conscience in that affair is clear. That particular defendant was up against a bad situation. It happened that the defendant had a bad record, and the detectives were out to make a case. The defendant paid for a bad record by paying to get out of a situation in which he never could have been trapped except for his unsavory past.

I've seen enough policemen take enough money in my time not to be at all unsettled by the idea that they take it. Why, parking privileges in the business section of New York are rented out by individual policemen. It's a business. You pay them so much a week, and then squabble with them if some one steals a tire from your car—but you don't get back the tire, and you keep on paying for the parking.

And how many drinks I've had with policemen in speakeasies I wouldn't like to have to count. The only rule I used to have when I frequented speakeasies was that I would never take a detective or a policeman into one. You could never tell when he might forget that he was supposed to be a paying guest, and start in to become a collecting guest.

This doesn't mean, at all, that all policemen are grafters and drunkards. The facts are just the opposite. The majority of them are splendid citizens, doing a splendid work. Their average is high. But they do have their backsliders among them.

My opinion is that the New York Police Department is the best with which I ever have come in contact. I think it'll be better since Grover A. Whalen has been made Police Commissioner. I think he has the admiration and support of every one who is at all familiar with him and his abilities. He should make a great Commissioner. And since I'm damning some persons with extremely faint praise I certainly should have the privilege, once in a while, of telling what I think of a friend for whom I hold the very highest regard.

While on this subject of the police, I wish one occasional idiosyncracy would be abolished, and that's the occasional idiosyncracy of using night sticks, and beating up prisoners who don't need to be beaten up.

Now that I've ingratiated myself with the District Attorney's office, the police force, various members of the underworld, and divers persons known to Broadway, I will resume with Bill Fallon. He's big enough, and romantic enough to have a whole book to himself, let alone a section of one book.

Just as the newspaper boys reached for crowns when they were describing Tourbillon, so they snatched at rockets and meteors in describing Fallon. And both the rocket and the meteor are applicable to the career of that interesting individual. He certainly went up fast, and came down faster. And he certainly flashed across the criminal and night life sky of New York, and faded out.

There are those of his old friends who contend that he should have been content to pursue the even tenor of his ways and stay in his native Westchester, basking in the warmth of the home fires, and in the companionship of his charming wife and their two children. Those persons assume that Fallon indubitably would have risen to a high place on the bench in the orderly course of events.

But Bill Fallon was not the type that sits around the old fireside at night, or waters the lawn, or busies himself with sprays for the rose bugs. He was a chap who had to be in the biggest city there was, showing the rest of them how to do things.

All Bill had to do was win one or two of his first cases, get his reputation established, then keep away from the underworld, and associate with those worth while in business and in his own profession, and he would have been really top of the heap in no time. He would have had the really juicy plums that come to the great trial lawyer—a lawyer like Max D. Steuer—who is a master of his art (I almost said craft) and wins his cases, but doesn't come to be identified with professional racketeers.

At the time of the Regan trial, business was just beginning to look up for Fallon, and his extremely able partner, Eugene F. McGee, whose acquaintance in Broadway circles was wide. Money had begun to pour into their offices. Retainers, and then more retainers were left by eager clients. Which ever one of them happened to drop into the office stuffed the retainers into his pocket and went out and looked around the town with his friends. Neither one of them was of what may be called a saving disposition.

I remember a friend of mine met Gene McGee one morning, and Gene said:

"How're you fixed this morning?"

"I'm fixed all right," was the reply. "Why?"

"Oh," Gene said, "I thought you might need some money. I got down to the office first this morning and went through the mail."

Bill and Gene took the money that came into their offices just like that—like manna from Heaven. Bill told me once they kept no accounts, just put the money in their pockets and walked out.

Another friend was in their offices one day when Fuller walked in and asked for some money. Bill said he would try "uptown," which meant Rothstein. Some one said that perhaps uptown had been tried too often. However, Bill telephoned, and a few minutes later an envelope containing five $1,000 bills was delivered.

Bill left the envelope on his desk, and Gene slid one out, winking behind Bill's and Fuller's backs. Bill handed the four grands to Fuller without counting them, and Fuller went out. In a moment he returned telling Bill there were only $4,000.

"There had to be five," Bill said. "I didn't even bother to count 'em."

"May be you dropped one of them down the elevator shaft," said McGee. "Why don't you take a look?"

I know one of this crowd who tottered into a restaurant one night with a strange beauty in tow. He had $28,000 in negotiable bonds in a wad. He lost them all over the floor a couple of times, and the proprietor, after having them gathered up, pleaded in vain to have them put in his safe.

"I can look after 'em," said this one.

Next day he came in and asked the proprietor if he had left the bonds with him. The proprietor reminded him of what had happened. He grinned and wagged his head.

"I guess I was tight," he admitted. "But she was a good-looking doll, wasn't she?" he added brightly.

The trail of easy money is a hard trail for normal persons to comprehend.

It was while he was following this trail—actually while he was in Washington trying a case for Nicky Arnstein—that Bill Fallon met Gertrude Vanderbilt, former stage star, and so far as I ever have heard, she was the best influence in his life from then until his death. She brought a loyalty to Bill that no one of his other Broadway associates on the feminine side provided.

Naturally, a friendship could not be other than hectic when Bill was living that sort of existence.

Available records indicate that the first public connection of Gertrude Vanderbilt's name with that of Fallon came in the hearings that grew out of the failure of Dillon & Co., brokers, whose backer was "Dandy Phil" Kastel. Fallon was lawyer for Kastel.

There was a $3,000 check, dated June 21, 1921, drawn to William J. Fallon, and deposited three days later to the account of Gertrude. Both of them declined to testify about this and another check for $1,000, similarly drawn, endorsed and deposited.

A man I know in Boston came to New York on business which necessitated seeing Fallon at about this time. When he called Fallon's office he was told that Fallon would see him in a café. He went to the café, and found Bill and Gertrude Vanderbilt. Bill transacted the business right there, which made such a deep impression on this friend, so far as New York legal methods were concerned, that it became one of his favorite anecdotes.

I recall a story at this moment that one of Fallon's law associates told about him, which is illustrative of Fallon's ways outside a courtroom. This man told Fallon that he had to see about getting a chorus girl client through the customs. The chorus girl had taken a bit of time from her work, and had spent it abroad. She was bringing back with her about a million dollars in jewelry, and she needed legal advice—and was in a position to pay for it.

Well, Bill went along with his partner and met the chorus girl, and promptly attended to her case himself. His partner asked Bill to wait until the next day before he became too attentive; the partner could see a possible fee of $10,000 taking unto itself wings and flitting forever from his ken.

And that's exactly what happened to the fee, whatever it might have been. Next day Fallon said soothingly to his partner:

"You wouldn't want to take any money from that sweet little girl, would you?"

Bill Fallon certainly never took any money from any sweet little girls. As a matter of fact, although he made and spent hundreds of thousands of dollars, he never got money enough in his life to repay him for the ability that was his.

And if in these pages the idea is created that Bill Fallon was popular with women, and many of the greatest beauties of the day were among them, the fact that he was popular with men in all walks of life shouldn't be overlooked. And he was the idol of the Underworld, where "Get Fallon and go free," was the popular slogan.

They were a great team, Fallon and McGee: Fallon, tall, suave, easy, eloquent; McGee, dark, bull-shouldered, and bull-necked, with a slight hesitation in his speech which marred his court presence, but which detracted nothing from his remarkable knowledge of all there was to be known by any one human being of the crooks and crannies of the criminal law,

158

as well as of the crooks and crannies of the criminal
himself.

McGee was a football player of parts in his Fordham days, and he had the same sort of mentality that
he had body. It was built for crashing the line. But
it also could gracefully skirt an end, on occasion,
which was more than his physical entity ever could
have done.

Fallon found his pie baked, and cooling for
him. The war had increased the wealth of the country to a vast degree. Every one had money and
wanted to invest it. There were so many Liberty
Bonds floating around, that houses handling them
had grown careless. They were sending bales of
Liberty Bonds from one brokerage office to another
by mere lads, about whose antecedents, and about
whose habits they had only knowledge of the most
perfunctory sort. The stock market was on the up-
grade. Men and women who knew nothing of bonds,
owned them; men and women who knew nothing of
stocks were buying them. It looked pretty good to
the racketeers, and it was good.

Brokerage houses, artfully designed to look like
real brokerage houses, but which in reality were
bucketshops, were opened, and did a flourishing
trade. I myself worked for about a month for one
of these houses. My job was writing stock letters to
customers. I didn't know anything about the stock
market, except such information as any newspaper
man might have acquired most casually, but I could
stick enough words together to make a sentence, and
enough sentences together to make a paragraph, and

so on to the end of a letter advising customers to buy stocks. I wrote seven or eight letters the first day I was on the job. That is, I dictated that many. I never counted, during the month I sat around the bucketshop, how many letters I dictated, or how many stenographers I used doing the dictations. There were other chaps doing the same thing.

All these letters were signed by good pen men who could imitate the signature of the man in whose name the house was run. I grew suspicious of the place, when I found, quite by accident, that a letter I had dictated to a widow to hang on to her Liberty Bonds, and not sell them to buy stocks, never had been sent to her. I asked a friend of mine, a newspaper man in Wall Street, about my house, and he said it didn't have a very good reputation. He wouldn't say any more than that. But I knew the house had bank officials on its list of speculators—even one president of a big life insurance company was sucked in. I had an opportunity to get out of there, and I took it on the run. I saw, by the way, that the widow got her letter.

The chaps that wrote those stock letters didn't know any more about the stock market—less perhaps—than the most ignorant lay reader of this page. They got to think they knew about the market because they wrote so many letters about it. To hear them talk you would wonder why J. P. Morgan didn't send for them right away in order to be sure always to have the latest information a couple of weeks before it leaked out on the ticker.

This stock brokerage firm, which was one of the

bucketshops that went under when the crash came, was begun with a mail order list and a bankroll of $10,000. The men behind it spent the first few days of their venture writing and sending letters. After that they had to hire boys to empty money from envelopes into wastebaskets. It was as easy as that.

After a while they graduated from an office into a building full of offices. And they hired experts from authentic and reliable houses to prepare the statistics from which the letter writers took their sketchy but important sounding inside information.

Those racketeers who decided it was a good plan to open brokerages, opened them; those who didn't think that much time was necessary went to work in another way. They got together, and fixed up a simple scheme to take bonds from messenger boys. And they had gotten away with $5,000,000 in bonds when the howl went up to the skies.

A killing or two was incidental to this raid upon the bonds, but these killings never were tied up with any one suspected of having taken part in the general looting.

Nicky Arnstein, husband of Fannie Brice, and formerly mostly distinguished for his reputation as a transatlantic card specialist, immediately was named by the federal authorities, and by the District Attorney's office as the "Master Mind" behind the robberies. As a matter of fact, these authorities made no secret when I talked with them, of the fact that they believed Rothstein was the "Master Mind." They hadn't anything more than suspicions to go on, so far as the law was concerned, however. It was no surprise to any one who knew the inside conditions of that time when, following Rothstein's murder, statements were made that $4,000,000 of the bonds might be found among his effects. Neither were the suspicions that Rothstein was one of the king pins in the "International Dope Ring," or "Syndicate" any surprise. The authorities for years had considered that back of every nefarious enterprise in New York, and of many such underworld goings-on from Maine to California, were the machinations of Arnold Rothstein. They whispered his name behind closed doors, and tried to figure out ways and means to get him with the goods. But he always seemed to be able to figure out better ways and means for them not to get either him or the goods.

If the truth be told, I have a certain sense of shame in writing this about Rothstein after he is dead and planted far underground in his nice, solid bronze casket. Rothstein is so much easier for every one to say things about, now that his place in the game is vacant. I would have liked this job much better while he was alive.

I would have admired more the various authorities, federal and state—if they had "gotten" Rothstein while he was alive.

Rothstein was a great man in his way. I know he was a most reprehensible character, and yet I must confess to a sneaking admiration for him. A lot of tough characters were in awe of Rothstein, and many smart genus homos were outsmarted by him.

I'd hate to have a cheap grafter in the family. If

I were going to have one at all, I think I'd like a ru
Arnold Rothstein. After all, as I emphasized before,
even Rothstein had his human qualities. For instance, he not infrequently sent checks for thousands
of dollars to his honorable father, A. E. Rothstein,
to be devoted to charity. This was a secret about
Rothstein that many persons knew. Somehow or
other, his private charities became widely known.

Rothstein also was very kind about lending his
automobile to the clergy, particularly the clergy engaged in ministering to the aggravated spiritual
needs of those in the various jails. This made it
pleasant when Rothstein wanted a little favor done
by one of the clergymen in connection with a
prisoner.

No one in New York could get meals, and cig-
arettes, and other dainties of all sorts to prisoners
with the celerity of Arnold Rothstein.

When Nicky Arnstein, sought in vain for a long
time by the police and the Department of Justice and
other agencies, finally made his grandstand parade
down Fifth Avenue with Bill Fallon in that shining
Cadillac described in the first pages, and went to the
Tombs momentarily because of a slight misunder-
standing over the amount of the bail that should
have been ready, he never complained of mistreat-
ment.

I've forgotten who told me that he spent $5,000
right away, and had champagne, and plenty of con-
genial company. Probably it was an exaggeration.
I may have libeled the Tombs entirely. I don't
know. But those with funds aren't so likely to see

163

the rougher side of our penal and correctional institutions. There is something about money that greases the way.

There I go, reminded again of a personal experience—in night court this time. There is a cage outside of the door to the courtroom in which are detained prisoners awaiting appearance before the magistrate. On the evening of my memory an indignant gentleman, who said he lived in Kansas and was stopping at the Biltmore, was walking up and down wondering audibly about the ways of New York police. He said he had been arrested in the afternoon for a traffic violation in driving his automobile and had not been allowed to telephone his wife, whom he visualized as having hysterics at the hotel. I told him he probably had had a drink or two too many. And he admitted maybe he had.

"But," he said, "I thought it was against the law to shoot craps. And look at them rolling the dice right here at the door of the courtroom."

I didn't have to look. They were right in front of my eyes then—the crapshooters. And just at that moment, one shooter who apparently had all the money in the game, was picked up by a big policeman and borne outside the cage. A howl went up from the other players, who saw any chance of recovering any of that money go a-glimmering. But the chap in the policeman's arms waved the tired and soiled bills, and yelled:

"Ay-yah! Ay-yah! I'll get half of it anyway."

I hoped the chap was not too optimistic.

It has been printed in newspapers that this Arnstein matter really was the "beginning of the end" for Fallon; that through Arnstein, and Arnstein's friends he met the gay revellers of the Boulevard, and went like a moth dancing to his destruction.

This is, to put it mildly, an exaggeration. Fallon needed no Arnstein to introduce him to friends willing to help while away the liquid hours in Broadway and in the various roadhouses which vary the monotony of an average big time Broadway night, by providing an excuse for a quick dash into the alleged country, and a quick dash back again. Fallon needed no introducer. They introduced themselves to him.

At the time of the return of Arnstein to town, Fallon was very fond of a dancer in the "Follies." She had a Stutz roadster, which Fallon said he gave her.

I didn't hold anything like that against Bill Fallon. I would have been passing around Stutz roadsters myself if I had been able to get the Stutz roadsters to pass.

Bill had another tender little romance at this time, which always impressed me with its dramatic possibilities. I had met the lady in the case before he did. She was from out-of-town, and was stopping at one of the most exclusive hotels. Her name was known nationally. She had come to New York, as did many another person in those days, to consult the great William J. Fallon, on a rather delicate legal matter.

I was introduced to her by a woman who was a friend of both Bill's and mine. After the introduction, she had a rather hectic petting party with an extremely well and favorably known boulevardier.

165

Then, she met Bill, and instead of talking business, they told each other how fond of each other they were. Meanwhile, Bill was supposed to be most romantically attached in another direction.

What intrigued me about this affair was that first the lady would tell me how much she loved Bill, and then Bill would tell me how much he loved the lady, and then each would slip over a little of outside romance, if it may be termed that for lack of a better word, on the other. They both acted separately and individually as if I didn't see what they did with the other persons.

Bill would say to me:

"She is the most wonderful woman I have ever met. I never was really fond of any one before."

The lady would say to me:

"I could die for Bill."

Bill would say:

"Do you think she really cares for me?"

And with memories of what I had seen her doing when Bill wasn't around, I would say, "Sure, Bill."

And the lady would ask me: "Do you think Bill really loves me?" and I would say, "Sure," thinking what a faithful wench she had turned out to be.

I never did figure who was being kidded in this merry-go-round. But, if any one thinks that Nicky Arnstein had anything to do with Bill Fallon's Broadway nights—beyond wishing he would curtail them when he had Nicky's liberty and pursuit of happiness in his legal hands—he's crazy.

Nicky always took a drink. Maybe he might occasionally have had more than enough for purely beverage purposes. But I never saw Nicky when he wasn't in full control of every faculty, and when he wasn't charming and pleasant, and forbearing. He has a nice personality, has Nicky. One could see why Fannie Brice was fond of him.

Nicky Arnstein had more balance, more sanity than Bill Fallon, more of a normal emotional reaction to life. If Bill Fallon's intellect had been equipped with an emotional balance wheel, he would have gone far, wide and handsome.

One shouldn't blame Bill Fallon for what he did with his life. One shouldn't blame any one for Bill Fallon's failure to achieve real greatness. One should blame the Nature that formed him of unequal parts. He was a boy, with the body of a man, and a mind fired by something akin to genius.

Bill Fallon had reached the beginning of the high noon of his career with the spectacular surrender of Arnstein. He was going to keep Nicky out of jail for long months, in which he employed every legal device, every brilliant artifice, every adroit maneuver in his magician's bag of tricks.

Nicky surrendered on May 16, 1920, and he didn't go on trial in Washington, D. C., until the following December. During that period Fallon was extremely busy in directing the ramifications of Nicky's case in the Federal courts but he found time for a deal of other legal work, which brought a golden flood into the offices of Fallon and McGee.

In April of that year, it might have been mentioned, Fallon successfully defended "Curly Joe" Bennett, who had been indicted on a charge of white slavery. This trial was held before Judge Mulqueen in Special Sessions. Assistant District Attorney Jim Smith, who was prosecuting the case, said that "several well known tenderloin gamblers were involved," and that he had been threatened with death over the telephone and offered $3,500 "to go west."

On August 18, 1920, Fallon was attorney for John J. McGraw, of the New York Giants, in litigation which grew out of a fight on August 8 in the Lambs Club. This fracas in the leading theatrical club of New York caused a stir at the time. McGraw and an actor named William H. Boyd had a disagreement which ended in an exchange of blows, variously described. Later on the same evening John C. Slavin, a friend of McGraw's, was taken to a hospital suffering from injuries mysteriously received. McGraw was put on trial for the possession of alcoholic liquor, his excuse for getting in the fight having been that he had been drinking at the club with friends.

This was an easy case for Fallon. He merely put McGraw on the stand and McGraw simply denied that he either bought or owned the liquor. He merely drank some liquor that was handy, and didn't know to whom it belonged. There was no law against that, so Fallon and McGraw strolled out of court.

In October 1920, Fallon was attorney for Abe Attell who had been named in connection with the world series baseball scandal. Before Fallon had come into the case Abe had done a good bit of talking. Among other statements attributed to him was one that Rothstein had made $60,000 on the series.

After Fallon appeared upon the scene Abe Attell not only had nothing to say but vanished from public gaze for a time. Fallon's answer to the authorities who wished to have a chat with Attell was in effect:

"If Abe Attell is charged with anything he will come to court and prove his innocence."

In December of this year Fallon was in Washington, where he defended Nicky Arnstein in his first trial, and where he continued his high living much to the distress of Nicky. It was part of Fallon's procedure, however, to take every situation, no matter how serious, with apparent jauntiness and ease. It was a most successful procedure up to the time of his own trial and acquittal on a charge of bribing a juror. This trial in Washington of Nicky which Fallon defended resulted in a disagreement. It was a subsequent trial which ended in conviction, and sentences to Leavenworth, for Nicky Arnstein and "Big Nick" Cohn. Fallon was busy in New York during this second trial.

The case of Edward J. Donegan, which came up in 1922 was one of the rough spots in Fallon's amazing campaign in the courts, as defendant of men accused of badger games, white slavery, coin matching, bond stealing, bucket shopping and every variety of racketeering on the books.

Donegan, like other characters who bloomed in the easy money days of the dominance of Rothstein, is a subject for a volume himself. Donegan was referred to in newspaper articles at the time of his trial and conviction as a former dock worker, who became a contractor on ship's repairs. He was sentenced to

169

serve ten years in Atlanta, and pay a fine of $65,000. Besides that, the Government announced it was going to collect $1,653,797 in overdue income taxes from him.

The truth is that Donegan was a dealer in kindling wood in Brooklyn when Prohibition brought him his opportunity. At the time of his arrest in the Hotel McAlpin in New York, the Government charged that his income was $30,000 a day! Donegan got permits from the Prohibition Director's office and had them forged. He did an enormous business in withdrawals.

He lived as one might imagine a "King of the Bootleggers" would live. When he went to close business deals, he rode in one bright limousine of the latest and most expensive model, and his retinue of gun bearers rode in two other limousines, no less gorgeous.

Donegan would not descend from his automobile until his bodyguard, ready for emergency, had deployed on either side of him. There was reason for those precautions. It was not all show. On one of these occasions, he counted out six hundred $1,000 bills and handed them to the men with whom he was trading. Donegan promised one agent, who he didn't know was on his trail, $100 for each barrel of whisky that could be gotten out of bond as a result of the agent's connivance.

He was a big shot in the bootlegging business, this Donegan. He had money, and he didn't want to go to jail, so he got Bill Fallon to defend him and, so it was understood, gave Fallon $125,000 as a fee.

170

Now, I never talked with Donegan, but Donegan has been quoted as saying that if he lived long enough he would get square with Fallon for what he considered a dirty deal Fallon gave him in not giving sufficient attention to his trial. One set of stories had it that Fallon, who promptly spent $25,-000 of the fee for a present for one of his feminine friends, had gotten too interested in the bright lights to pay much attention to the law.

It was said that when Fallon disappeared from his usual haunts at the time the indictments against him for jury bribing and conspiracy were returned, he offered to give himself up on condition that he wouldn't be sent to Atlanta where the vengeful Donegan was jailed.

I always believed Fallon when he said that he did the best he could for Donegan. One might just as well have said that Fallon won cases because he spent his nights at high living, as say that he lost cases for that reason. The Fallon method in his halycon days was not to sit up all night with fusty law tomes for company. The companions with whom he spent his hours of relaxation were not fusty, and they were bound in silks, satins, chiffons and velvets, and not calfskin.

Bill, however, had spent numerous hours with the law books in the past. That was obvious to every one. He was a perambulatory law library. Some one said he could pick up a telephone directory and read precedents from it. Certainly, it was no unusual device of his to pretend to be reading something that,

171

as a matter of fact, he was spinning from the wheel of memory.

This idol of the underworld couldn't defeat every case that was prepared by the experts of the sovereign state of New York and by the organized forces of the government of the United States. He couldn't turn loose every crook.

I don't believe that Fallon ever offered to surrender himself on any terms that indicated guilt. Fallon always said he didn't, and I trailed with Fallon on that score.

After Fallon's indictment, and when most persons believed he surely would be convicted, stories got into some newspapers to the effect that he would invent any excuse in court in the later days in order to get out and get a drink of alcohol—to brace his frayed nerves.

Bill always would do that very thing, when he was feeling low. As he grew older, and didn't mend his ways, the periods when he felt low grew more frequent.

But, at the time I knew him extremely well, he was not the sort of drinker that took a pick-me-up in the morning. None of that "hair off the dog that bit you" for him. He would drink a cup of black coffee and get himself to court. Later in the day, he needed a stimulant. In court is where Bill Fallon lived a hundred lives compressed into one. There is where every nerve in his body, and every cell in his brain was concentrated on the greatest contest in the world, the greatest sport in life to him—the outwitting of the prosecution.

172

Bill frankly regarded the law as a game, which is the same way I always have regarded it. I didn't get all heated up in the Regan case when Bill got something across to the jury by some dodge that couldn't go into the record. I had seen enough of prosecutors and judges on the other side to know that it wasn't at all unusual for them to combine energies to get a conviction by every means available. A defendant certainly isn't held innocent by a judge until he is found guilty. A judge knows a whole library of data that never can get to a jury because of the rules of the "game."

Under the rules of the criminal law, as it is practised, I can't see, even in cold retrospect, that Bill Fallon ever did anything in the actual courtroom that wasn't all right. That isn't because I have respect for Bill's methods; it's because I haven't any respect at all for the criminal law. I think it's a howling, screaming joke. And Bill Fallon proved it to my satisfaction.

If, instead of weeping and complaining over what Bill Fallon did, persons who stand for law and order, which are the standards I advocate, would do better to set about getting a new code of laws, a new criminal procedure.

Bill showed how far you could go with the rules as they stand. Why not change them?

How silly it is, for instance, to believe for an instant that because a judge rules out questions which are asked in the courtroom, that jurors will not consider those very questions in arriving at a verdict.

If I were innocent I certainly would beg for a

173

trial by a judge; if I were guilty I wouldn't want anything else but a jury. But that doesn't mean necessarily that the jury system is bad. It means that all the material facts don't get to the jury. The rules of evidence are an impenetrable wall between the jury and the truth.

The present situation is—and how well the crooks know it—that the right lawyer is nine-tenths the battle in getting loose. Crooks are prepared for trials; innocent men aren't. Crooks know the best lawyers; innocent persons don't. Why, I recall that two clients of Bill's finally were turned out without a trial by a judge because, though their cases had been on the calendar seventy-odd times, they never had been called to trial.

Let a chap like Bill Fallon hypnotize only one juror, and he will get a disagreement, which is all a guilty client needs. A lawyer gets business on disagreements from a clientele that understands.

Then, there is the indistinguishable drool which so many lawyers affect in criminal court. They object for incomprehensibly tautological reasons. When I was a young reporter and was hearing my first cases in court I thought I was even more stupid than city editors and copy-readers had led me to believe.

Then I heard Martin W. Littleton try a case. Ah ha, I thought (not having heard Littleton's name mentioned in court, and never having seen him before) this chap is too open and clear to be a lawyer. Even I can understand everything he is talking about.

"Who is that dumbbell?" I asked.

174

A look of withering scorn greeted me. And I was told plenty about Martin W. Littleton. Then rapidly I made the discovery that great lawyers and great jurists are as easy to understand as an expert tutor trying to poke a mess of nit wits through college to a degree.

It's a glorious delight to listen to a lawyer like Max D. Steuer try a case—better than reading any book, or watching any play. One of my great pleasures was listening to arguments in equity cases in the room of Lindley M. Garrison, when that eminent jurist was a Vice-Chancellor in New Jersey. I liked to hear the lawyers on both sides of a big case in equity argue their points, and then hear Garrison dictate a memorandum, summing up the situation. More often than not, the Vice-Chancellor would point out to the lawyers that neither of them was hitting at the point that interested him. And they would be instructed to file briefs. It is all so clear and fair in equity. It is all so messed up and sordid and tricky in the law.

Fallon was so easy to understand in the courtroom that he might have been your next door neighbor, whom you'd known all your life, leaning over the back fence chatting with you. In that murder case in the Bronx, mentioned in the earlier pages, he even had his medical expert trained to call a liver a liver, and a stomach a stomach. When the other experts were on the stand talking in medical terms, Bill seemed to become a part of the bewildered jury. He and they looked at each other in mutual sympathy and ignorance.

175

Lucid as they make them, was Bill Fallon; an actor, a poseur, a man willing to take advantage of every situation in any way that would get by, a darned smart criminal lawyer, whom all his detractors would have retained in an instant if suddenly they had been arrested for crimes of which they were guilty.

This period of the bond robberies, and the bucket-shops failures and resultant trials marked the peak of Fallon's career. He went down into a well of discredit, soared higher than ever for that brief moment in his own defense, and then sank back into a brief interlude of half-hearted endeavor which ended in death. Anything that came after the trial had to be anti-climactic.

He had worked like a master for Fuller and McGee, and had gotten three disagreements for them, when Rendigs was indicted of perjury for saying when he was qualifying as a juror in the Durell-Gregory trial, that he wasn't acquainted with Fallon.

At this time Fallon was not, never had been and never could be a model of fashion. His suits were just suits; his hats were just hats; his shoes were just shoes, and they weren't always shined, either.

It has been said of him that he was stingy—that he rode in subways, met ladies in restaurants to save taxi fares, shaved himself, and even trimmed his own hair with the help of a three-sided mirror. Well, he may have done all of those things, but it wasn't because he was stingy. It was because it suited him at the time to do them.

He never took Peggy Hopkins Joyce, for one, on

a subway—I'd like to see the man who would dare!
And I was with him on many occasions in taxicabs
and automobiles, but I never saw him in a subway.

If he were stingy, then giving automobiles and
costly gewgaws to members of the opposite sex, and
tossing around thousands of dollars a night, and
dying with nothing but debts after having earned an
enormous income for five years, is stinginess.

A one thousand dollar bill meant no more to Bill
Fallon than a dime does to another man. He had no
sense of money at all. He liked to hand a waiter
a thousand dollar bill to pay a dinner check, as he did
now and then, but in the set with which he was
travelling thousand dollar bills seemed to grow by
spontaneous generation. They were no luxury—
nothing but "grands."

Maybe Bill was showing off when he handed a
waiter a thousand dollar bill. My idea was that
when a chap has thousand dollar bills to spend, and
has a check to pay, and has nothing smaller than thousand dollar bills on him, and probably is going to
spend several of them that evening, a thousand dollar
bill is a logical object to hand to a waiter.

Thousand dollar bills aren't so much when you begin tossing them about by the scores and the hundreds. W. F. McGee once said to Rothstein:

"Can you cash a check, Arnold?"

"Certainly," said Rothstein.

McGee handed Rothstein a check. Rothstein
glanced at it, and taking out a roll, peeled off thirty
yellow slips of paper, each a promise by the United
States Government to pay the bearer one thousand

dollars in gold coin. Thirty grand—$30,000—are figures that some persons merely dream about all their lives. And yet those are the persons, many of them, who each contributed his mite to that river of "grands" which flows unceasingly in the underworld, the land of easy money, and easy virtue, where the only improvement on the wide prospect might be the elimination of Sing Sing and Dannemora, and Leavenworth, and Atlanta, and the Tombs.

Those who bet on horse races, or play craps or card games with strangers, or buy stocks from any but reputable brokers, or who try to get something for nothing in an amateur way, are the ever bubbling springs from which flows this broad and pleasant stream of "grands," which makes diamonds sprout on fair wrists, and horses run in Saratoga and Havana, and finances Broadway plays, keeps hundreds of fussy little girls from the sordid necessity of having to use little old last year's automobiles, and sweeps much charming and frothy femininity to Europe and its broadening climate.

No, it wasn't showing off that impelled Fallon to hand the waiter a grand. I've seen him sign a check for more than that, and think nothing of it. Grands don't amount to much. It takes a hundred of them to buy a girl a decent necklace.

CHAPTER NINE

FALLON'S LAST STAND

THE turns and twists of the bucketshop scandals were numerous and intriguing. Fallon defended Fuller and McGee in three trials and in various other hearings in bankruptcy, and investigations that grew out of that mess.

Fallon and McGee were charged with contempt of court, and with destroying the records of Fuller & Co. Arnold Rothstein was dragged to court on numerous occasions. They hoped to get a lot from Rothstein, but what they got was nothing.

The contempt charges against Fallon and McGee failed to hold water. Some one mysteriously returned most of the missing records of Fuller & Co., in a way that indicated clearly that neither Fallon nor his partner, who always had insisted their offices had been robbed, had had anything to do with them.

On July 11, 1923, the indictments charging conspiracy and bribery against Fallon and Rendigs were handed down. Rendigs who also was a juror in the third Fuller & Co. trial, also had been a juror in the Durell-Gregory & Co., Inc. trials in October and November, 1922. The third Fuller trial also had resulted in a disagreement, four jurors, including Rendigs, holding out for an acquittal. Howard S. Beidleman, a juror, had complained that he had been

179

offered $1,000 to acquit Fuller. Beidleman voted for conviction.

In the Durell-Gregory trial, twenty-three defendants were in court. Seven of an original thirty had pleaded guilty before trial. The indictment contained eleven counts and charged using the mails in a scheme to defraud. The jury was out four hours and returned its verdict of acquittal of all the defendants, including six who had offered no defense at all.

First, Rendigs was tried for committing perjury in his examination as a juror in Fuller case, for on that occasion, as I have stated, he denied knowing Fallon. After his conviction of perjury, sentence was deferred. He finally made a confession that Fallon had given and he had accepted $2,500.

Fallon forfeited bail of $5,000 and disappeared. Later he always said in court and out that the reason he went away was to wait until he could find out what the final bail would be so that he could raise it and be at liberty to prepare his defense. He said in court that he had been in communication with the United States Attorney's office through his friend former District Attorney Frederick E. Weeks, of White Plains.

The New York American, however, and detectives, made a spectacular descent on Fallon's hiding place in a furnished walk-up apartment at No. 586 Academy Street, in upper Manhattan. They blew off plenty of flashlight powder, and my old friend "Jack" Moroso, who can't be beaten at that sort of stuff, popped thousands of skyrocketing words out of a helpless typewriter in honor of the event.

Gertrude Vanderbilt always said that she was not traced to that apartment because she did not go to it. She admitted, however, that she had visited friends in that far-off neighborhood, and that once she had seen thereabouts a man she knew was a detective.

Although she didn't know where in the United States, or elsewhere, Bill was hiding, she went into a restaurant which was handy and drank coffee until she saw the detective gaze in another direction. Then she went away from that neighborhood fast, and perhaps faster. She was sure the detectives had not learned anything from her.

It was unfortunate that Miss Vanderbilt hadn't known that Bill was concealed in Academy Street, because if she had known it she might have been able to select some other locality in which to do her calling. As it was, the agents, having seen her up that way, made a house to house canvass, and discovered Bill. When they found an apartment that had been rented within the past few days they took a peep at the tenant. One glance at Bill sufficed, although he had raised a little red, and rather scraggly moustache by way of disguise.

The detectives first disguised themselves as vacuum cleaner men and rang the door bell. After catching sight of Fallon they watched the house for twenty-four hours, certain that he could not escape. Then, reinforced by newspaper reporters and Assistant United States Attorney Millard, and plenty of revolvers and ammunition, and photographers and

181

flashlight powder, they moved in full panoply of the pomp and power, not to say majesty, of the law, upon Bill, and found him washing out his only shirt in the bathtub.

The man who tossed around the grands had been cooking his own meals, and rinsing out his own duds.

Gertrude Vanderbilt said she always would stick to Bill, and so far as I know she did. I know she still is the fightingest champion he has in New York City.

The story of Rendigs, which he told later when Fallon was finally placed on trial, was as follows:

He said he became acquainted with Fallon on October 6, 1922, the second day of the Durell-Gregory trial. Rendigs was a juror in this trial. He said on that day the telephone rang at his home and a voice said, "This is Fallon." Then Rendigs continued:

"He asked, 'Is this a private wire?' I said, 'Yes.' He said, 'Will you meet me at 8 o'clock to-night at Woodmansten Inn? I can do something for you financially.'

"I said I would be there. I went there. At 8:30 I saw Fallon come in the front door while I was in the foyer. He went up a stairway and beckoned to me to follow. He got almost to the top of the stairway and turned and shook my hand. There was a $1,000 bill in his palm. He said, 'The Gregory boys are fine fellows and I want you to do what you can for them. I'm going to get a lot of money out of this. Whatever I get I'll divide with you. I'll be

182

in touch with you from time to time.' Then Fallon went down to join his party and I went home.

"I kept the bill in my pocket until October 20 to disguise it. That day I went to the Manufacturer's Trust Company and got the paying teller to change it into two $500 bills. I deposited one of the bills with the receiving teller and carried the other until October 23, when I deposited it.

"Two weeks later Fallon telephoned me at home and said, 'You're going to be disappointed. I'm not going to get as much money as I expected, but I'll have some anyway.' I said I hoped that it would be soon, as I had a note for $1,800 to meet at my bank on November 8.

"About a week later he phoned me at home and said he'd have something for me in a day or so. I said all right. I didn't hear from him after that. On November 4 I phoned him at his office and told him the note would be due the following week. I said, 'There are about thirty defendants in this case. How can one act in a case like that?' He said there'd be a vote on each defendant and to acquit the Gregorys and do anything I liked with the others. (Fallon was attorney for Albert Dewitt LeBruns, one of the defendants.)

"On November 6 Fallon phoned me to meet him in the Knickerbocker Grill at 152 West Forty-second Street. I went there and the bookkeeper gave me an envelope with my name on it. I had dinner there. I opened the envelope and found $1,000 in it. Joe Pani, owner of the place, came to my table. I asked

183

for his check in exchange for the cash, so I could mail it to the bank. Pani gave me a check for the thousand dollars and I mailed the check to the bank.

"On November 12 Fallon phoned me to come to the Woodmansten Inn at 1:30. I went there. As a result of a message left there for me, I went to an address which was W. Frank McGee's apartment. Fallon met me at the door. McGee, Harry Tellfair and Fuller and some others were there. I was in a panic because of the crowd and went into a bedroom and called Fallon in. I asked what the purpose was in getting me there with that crowd present. He said they were good fellows and he wanted me to know them better. He said, 'Did you get that envelope at the Knickerbocker Grill that day?' I said, 'Yes.' Then I left."

Rendigs explained that when the ballots were taken on the guilt or innocence of the Gregorys the first vote was either seven to five or eight to four against him. Rendigs, of course, held out for acquittal which the others likewise voted after eight or ten ballots.

A brief sample of Fallon's method of cross-examination might not be amiss here. When, at his own trial, he got Rendigs on the witness stand the questions and answers went as follows:

Q. Did Fallon tell you to commit perjury? A. No.

Q. Did Fallon suggest it to you? A. No.

Q. During the Fuller trial did you talk to anybody about the case in which you were a juror? A.

184

Yes, you phoned me. You said you wanted to see me again. I said I didn't want to see you.

Fallon here employed a favorite device of his by repeating a response of the witness in his own words. In this instance the court interrupted to say sharply, "You can't misquote a witness." And it was only a minute later that the court said to Fallon when he was interrupting an answer, "You keep quiet and give the witness a chance."

Such admonitions from a judge had been commonplaces all through Fallon's career in the courts. Fallon's cross-examination continued as follows:

Q. Did you in your conferences with Millard and Wintner (an Assistant District Attorney) say you were at your wit's end in October 1923? A. No.

Q. Were you then at your wit's ends? A. Yes, I was.

Q. Yet you kept $1,000 in your pocket for almost two weeks? A. Yes.

Q. Was your phone number in the book? A. No.

Q. Up to October 6 you were a total stranger to me? A. Yes.

Q. Yet you say I phoned you, not knowing you at all, at your home, and said I was William J. Fallon and would help you out financially? A. Yes.

Q. Did I say what the money would be for? A. No.

Q. Did you guess? A. Yes.

Q. Were you willing to take money for that purpose? A. Yes.

Rendigs mentioned that on one occasion he had

borrowed money from Arnold Rothstein. An unidentified juror said, to the amusement of the courtroom, "I'd like to see a thousand dollar bill myself."

Joseph Pani, who had been proprietor of the Knickerbocker Grill and the Woodmansten Inn, was a rather embarrassed witness for the government. He testified that on November 6, 1922, Ernest Eidlitz, former confidential man for Fallon, who also became a government witness for the trial, gave him a check for $1,000 made out by Mrs. Agnes R. Fallon, Fallon's wife.

Pani was as confused a witness as one might hope to see in a long journey. Fallon's questioning of Pani was as follows:

Q. Didn't you deny the entire matter for months until you were arrested during the progress of the Rendigs trial? A. I never was arrested.

Q. Didn't you sell liquor to four detectives, two men and two women? A. No.

Q. Weren't you brought to Colonel Hayward's (the United States Attorney's) office during the Rendigs trial and threatened? A. No.

Q. Did Rendigs give you $1,000 in cash and ask you for a check? A. No. My office might have.

Q. Didn't Rendigs in your grillroom give you $1,000 for a check? A. I don't know.

Q. In your conferences with Millard and Eidlitz, didn't Eidlitz say over and over again that Rendigs came to your place and you gave him a check for cash? A. Something like that.

Q. In the middle of the Rendigs perjury trial

186

weren't two men and two women detectives sent by Hayward to buy liquor from you? A. It might be. I don't know. Maybe some of my men did. I don't know anything about it.

Q. Do you remember talking to Colonel Hayward? A. No.

Q. Were you ever charged with selling liquor during the Rendigs trial? A. No.

In questions that followed Pani said he had pleaded guilty in the Federal court to selling liquor, which contradicted all the testimony that he originally gave in that connection. He also admitted that the Knickerbocker Grill had been padlocked under an order closing it for six months, but that he had been permitted to open it after four months. Pani insisted that he couldn't remember that Colonel Hayward had threatened to close Woodmansten Inn, and he denied that he had ever told Fallon that Colonel Hayward had tried to "force me to say things."

Under Fallon's dexterous questioning Pani again denied having sold liquor at his grill, and then confessed that he had been arrested there by prohibition agents and had pleaded guilty.

Pani first said that Rendigs had visited him at noon on the day under discussion. Then he said it was either at four, five or six p. m. He didn't know just which. He said he didn't remember cashing a check of Agnes R. Fallon or giving Rendigs any check for cash.

Fallon explained that what he had been trying to do was to show that the Federal authorities were compelling Pani to testify against him by means of the liquor arrest.

This was a remarkable trial from all points of view. Here was the most sensational criminal lawyer of his day, still handsome, still audacious, fighting for his freedom, his reputation, and his career—everything in life that counts. Against him were arrayed, as he frequently said, the Government of the United States and *The New York American*, which newspaper had been carrying on a fight against bucketshops, and Rendigs, and Ernest Eidlitz, who had been Fallon's right hand man.

It looked like a foregone conclusion that the master prestidigitator of criminal law was beaten at last. He had bobbed buoyantly over contempt charges and accusations of destroying evidence, and things like that. But this was different.

A man, who had confessed to accepting a bribe from him, now was testifying under oath that he had accepted that bribe. And Eidlitz, confessed "fixer" for Fallon, was bolstering up Rendig's testimony. The powers in the state and federal courts had been gunning for Fallon for a long time. Now they all thought they had him. As a matter of fact, only a choice few of the old crowd believed any differently. And their hope was faint.

Knowing Bill Fallon, it is not strange that among the three stoutest friends he had were three women of unusual attainments and attractiveness. One was Peggy Hopkins Joyce, then Countess Morner, a second was Gertrude Vanderbilt, and the third was Miss Freda Rosenberg, who for long had been Fallon's private secretary, and at the time of this trial was secretary to Arnold Rothstein. Miss Rosenberg was a very brilliant young woman, I always had thought, and a most loyal one.

Bill and Peggy Joyce had been close friends for some time. She was called as a Government witness, and was treated with the distinction deserved by a lady of her international reputation—a reputation of having only to look natural to get a proposal of marriage from a millionaire or a member of the nobility.

The Countess was attired entirely in white for her début as a witness in this case, except for a large blue "P" embroidered on her hat. A corsage of red roses furnished relief to the general pallor.

Assistant United States Attorney Millard, who was prosecuting, addressed Miss Joyce as "Countess." She said that Fallon, Eidlitz and Miss Clara Phillips had been at her home, then at West End Avenue and Seventy-fourth Street, on the evening of October 6, 1922.

They motored to the Woodmansten Inn, and sat at a table opposite the orchestra. She didn't see Rendigs, but she did remember that Fallon had left the table, and that she finally had grown impatient and sent for him. She thought he was gone from the table about twenty or twenty-five minutes.

When Fallon arose to cross-examine Miss Joyce no one thought for a moment that it was going to be a hostile encounter. And no one was disappointed.

"You remember there were other occasions upon

189

which you and I were at the Woodmansten Inn, do you not?" Fallon asked at once.

"Yes."

Fallon then asked if she could not give the dates of one or more of those occasions. Miss Joyce drew the features that have been the admiration of two continents into an expression of concentration, and finally said that she couldn't fix the time of any of the visits to the inn, and, in fact, couldn't remember whether or not the time that Fallon remained away from her table was on the night of the dinner party or not. She said that Fallon was her attorney, and that it was part of his task to call at her home or to take her out to dine to consult with her on legal matters.

"You can't say I was away as long as twenty minutes, can you?" asked Fallon, smiling as if the idea was so absurd that it hardly was worth mentioning.

"It seemed that long," Miss Joyce replied, smiling sweetly back at Fallon.

"Well, mightn't that have been because you were hungry?"

No one heard what Miss Joyce said to that because the throng in the courtroom, in which was being staged the most successful and popular drama of the day, laughed so loudly. Judge McClintic thwacked his gavel on the bench and told the spectators he would have them put out if they didn't behave.

Miss Joyce agreed readily with Fallon when he put questions to the effect that he hadn't received a message while at the table, and that he had not mentioned Rendigs' name.

Miss Joyce's testimony certainly was not damaging to Fallon. As she left the courtroom she was handed a summons in a suit for annulment of her marriage to Count Gosta Morner, who was husband No. 4 on her list.

Miss Clara Phillips testified immediately after Miss Joyce, and corroborated her in every particular.

It was on another day that Miss Rosenberg made her appearance as a witness—a day on which Fallon himself, Joseph Shalleck, the lawyer, and Miss Rosenberg all testified that Miss Rosenberg cashed the famous $1,000 check so that Fallon might pay Shalleck $500 he owed. And nothing that Millard could do shook that testimony in the slightest.

Miss Rosenberg said she "practically ran the office" when she worked for Fallon and, cross-examined by Millard, later said, "of course she liked Fallon," and "would do anything in reason for him. But I wouldn't lie for him," she added with a touch of the pretty spirit which is said to go with Titian hair.

She told in detail of getting the check certified and of cashing it and giving the $1,000 to Fallon, and of Fallon handing $500 to Shalleck, and saying:

"Here's the $500 you've been yelling about."

Fallon was a sensational and convincing witness for himself. He told of a meeting with Eidlitz in which he asserted Eidlitz had given him the information which caused him to make a bulwark of his defense before the jury the claim that his indictment was the result of a conspiracy by William Randolph Hearst

191

and *The New York American* to get rid of him. Fallon said in part on the stand:

"He (Eidlitz) told me that when he first went to Watson (an editor of *The New York American*) he was incensed because I had discharged him, and he was afraid he was going to be arrested, that he knew of the animosity of the Hearst people against me. So he said he told Victor Watson that I had certain birth certificates that showed the birth of certain children to a certain prominent moving picture actress, and he also said I had evidence, or knew the fact, that Hearst had sent a certain well known woman, who had been supposed to be a countess, to Florida to obtain evidence against Mrs. Hearst.

"He said he also told Watson that I had the name of a man, the car and the number of the car and all of the details of a trip of Hearst and this other party to Mexico. And he said that he had told Watson that I intended to use that information for the purpose of blackmailing Hearst.

"And he said that a few days after that he, Watson, said he had communicated with Hearst and Watson said, 'We must destroy Fallon at any cost.'"

This issue of a conspiracy of great influences against him was the same sort of defense that Fallon had interposed in the trial of "Kid" Regan. In that case he insisted that *The World* was engaged in a scheme to persecute the poor, misunderstood "Kid."

Certainly, *The World* was interested in that case. I was handling the situation for *The World* at that time, and there was nothing done that wasn't perfectly fair and square. All we did was turn over to the District Attorney the facts and a witness. *The World* considered it was performing a public service. To hear Fallon talk before the jury, however, you would think *The World* was hounding poor men for the sheer pleasure of it.

The American always asserted it was active in the bucketshop scandals in order to do a public service. I have worked for *The New York American,* as well as for *The World,* and *The New York Times* also, for that matter, and I never observed any actions by any of those newspapers that made me doubt they would perform a public service, if it looked as if the general results were worth it.

The New York American simply had made public the drive that was on to try to get at the "Man Higher Up," who, it generally was agreed, but behind closed doors at the time, was Arnold Rothstein. Fallon was regarded as the ablest and most dangerous lieutenant of Rothstein. And they thought they had him.

This was a grim battle that Fallon was waging. Hostile accounts written before the trial had painted Fallon as a broken man. He was supposed to be only a shadow of his former gay and brilliant self. He was depicted as down and out. *The New York American,* for instance, told daily that Fallon's sun had set. Physically, mentally, financially and sartorially he was supposed to be a wreck and a ruin.

To increase belief that Fallon was through, R. J. Shanahan, of Syracuse, was announced as Fallon's lawyer. Ah! So Bill didn't have the nerve to try his own case. Ah, hah! And Shanahan did begin

193

to try the case. But the day that Bill Fallon sprang gracefully from his chair, and raised those clear, bugle notes of the voice that had rung over many a charge to victory against overwhelming odds, the judge sat up with revived interest, Prosecutor Millard did not look quite so confident, and a new thrill ran through the old Federal Building.

And, as doubt changed to certainty, and it became apparent that Bill Fallon, not a whit changed from the sparkling blade he always had been, was going to lead his own fight, the rumor of voices ran out of the Federal Building and penetrated the Roaring Forties:

"Bill Fallon is defending himself."

And those same Roaring Forties sat up and took notice, because it was there that Arnold Rothstein sat on his throne, and it was there that Fallon still was regarded with awe for the witchery of his ways with a law case.

Perhaps the old time sparkle in Bill's eye, the old time lilt in his musical voice, the old charm and assurance of manner, the flash of wit and quick riposte of repartee, and the magnetism of the man, were due in no small measure to the loyalty of Gertrude Vanderbilt. It was learned later that she had sold her home for $25,000. Gertie Vanderbilt never in public said she lent that $25,000 to Bill Fallon, but she did say, when she applied in vain for letters of administration after his death, that Bill was in her debt, and the records showed when she sold her house.

And Peggy Hopkins Joyce stuck to him, and Miss Rosenberg stuck to him, and any number of most estimable citizens, including former District Attorney Weeks, of Westchester County, testified to their faith in Fallon's integrity. Fallon wasn't so deserted as it had appeared. And he certainly wasn't deserted by his own powers as an advocate. He never shone so brightly as he did in this, one of the most amazing trials that ever occurred in any courtroom anywhere. And, strangely enough, he never shone again.

With Bill dominating the situation in his old way, his friends from uptown packed into that courtroom. They laughed when Bill made a sally, and watched with shining, adoring eyes as he fenced with the judge, or out-maneuvered the prosecutor. It was the old Bill, sure enough.

All the special Fallon tricks were brought out, and dusted off, and tried again. Bill would stick at it until the last possible instant to get across with something that wasn't allowed, and then, when he saw it was hopeless, he would bow gracefully and apologize to the court. But the jury had heard what he said, whether it went on the record or not. And that always seemed to me to be an important part of a Fallon campaign.

Judge McClintic, who presided, a jurist of the old school, came from West Virginia. Once, when Fallon had revealed that he had advised Pani that as long as he didn't serve alcoholic beverages, he couldn't be prosecuted because his guests drank them, the judge looked most surprised.

"You didn't tell him that as a matter of law, did you?" he asked.

"Well," Fallon parried, "that's pretty good law around here."

It may be imagined how this pleased the Fallon enthusiasts.

"It isn't good law in my district," the judge said.

"I wouldn't want to live in your district then," said Fallon in perfect good humor.

And how his supporters enjoyed that! They also were delighted when the judge said, referring to Pani, "This witness gets confused: you can see the kind of witness he is," and Fallon said, swift as light:

"If you have characterized him as the kind of witness he is, I have no need to go any further."

The jurors liked that too. Jurors were very much inclined to like Fallon, which wasn't so surprising, since he focussed every one of his unusual store of faculties upon bewitching them.

He was questioning a hostile witness when the judge said:

"This man now is your witness."

"I disown him," Fallon said.

At the close of this case, Former District Attorney Weeks, Mayor of White Plains at that time, had just testified to Fallon's excellent character. As he was about to leave the witness chair, Fallon suddenly turned, and trumpeted in his thrilling voice:

"Do you believe William J. Fallon would bribe a juror?"

Of course, a question like that is improper. That was the sort of tactics Fallon's enemies decried. Judge McClintic's gavel was racketing on the bench as soon as he could get it into motion, and before

196

Weeks had a chance to say a word, even if he had wished.

But Fallon had not expected an answer. The question wouldn't be on the dead record for the jurymen's consideration, but he knew that resonant voice of his still would be echoing in their living memories as they sat in their room with his fate in their hands. And he knew also that they would be pretty sure what the answer of that upstanding gentleman, Mayor Weeks, of White Plains, would have been if a hard-hearted judge, and a stupid law, hadn't prevented him from answering a question that any one of them would have liked to have asked a friend under similar circumstances.

The powerful effect of these off-the-record remarks during a trial was illustrated again in this very case. Once, the judge said to Fallon: "You have your back against the wall." Then he ordered the remark struck from the record. After the verdict one of the jurymen said:

"When Judge McClintic pulled that line about Fallon's back being to the wall, I didn't feel the same about the case. I had had the idea that some one was trying to get Fallon for something that wasn't appearing in the case at all, and now I was more puzzled than ever. I know that a man is supposed to be innocent until he is proved guilty. He hadn't been proved guilty by a long shot when the judge made that remark.

"I know that Judge McClintic withdrew his words, and said he was sorry for them, but they couldn't help but stir sympathy for Fallon."

The jurors who talked to friends said, however, that it wasn't a sympathetic verdict, that they merely hadn't believed the evidence against Fallon. One juror said it sounded "concocted" to him. That is, he would rather believe that the United States Attorney's office and *The New York American* had conspired to ruin Fallon for something he didn't do, than believe that Fallon would give a bribe. Or, of course, the jurors could have figured that Eidlitz and Rendigs were lying on their own account.

Comptroller Charles L. Craig, as a rebuttal witness for the Government, was the innocent cause of a typical passage between Fallon and the court. Fallon insisted on asking questions about the contract for the new courthouse then building, and about the Fuller Construction Company which had the contract, and Judge McClintic kept stopping him.

"I told you that was out of the case," the judge said finally. "I want you to understand you can't do these things. You can't run this court."

Fallon then asked a question about the resignation from the Comptroller's office of Walter J. O'Neill, who had been a witness for the defense. Judge McClintic thought he was misquoting a statement of Craig's.

"You are twisting the facts which no honest man would do," the judge said.

Fallon's cheeks blanched with rage, and he shouted:

"I except to the court's comment, and demand the withdrawal of a juror." (The withdrawal of a juror means a mistrial.)

"You can object and shut up," was the court's rejoinder.

"I object to that remark," Fallon said.

"You can object, but I tell you I am running this courtroom," said the judge, tapping the bench vigorously with his gavel.

Fallon took another exception.

"You can except; that is easy to do," observed the court.

"Of course, it's easy to do, and in view of your attitude, I ask that a juror be withdrawn," Fallon reiterated.

"You can't make a joke out of this case," the judge exclaimed.

"There are lots of things about this case that are a joke, but it's no joke to me," Fallon said. "In view of your remarks about me making a joke of this case I again demand the withdrawal of a juror."

Fallon referred to the fact that Craig had been convicted of contempt of court, so Millard said to Craig:

"You are still the Comptroller?"

"Yes," said Craig.

"Well, he won't be long," said Fallon.

Fallon's summation marked the high water mark of his stormy career at the bar. A speech such as Fallon made must be heard to be appreciated. The gestures of an orator, and the cadences of his voice, the play of expression on his features, the magnetism of his personality, and the constantly increasing bond of sympathy which he weaves between himself and his auditors are of more importance than his words.

199

Those same words spoken in the same room but empty of human beings would ring desolate on the empty air, and be lost in the hollow mockery of echoes. A glorious singing voice in a bare auditorium is baffled and overwhelmed by its harsh reception on the sound-reflecting walls.

Bodies of an audience absorb sound, and stop echo; minds in attune to the mood of the moment find and create sympathetic reactions each in the other. The cold word becomes a glowing symbol, which one finds pleasure in displaying, and the other equal pleasure in enjoying. A mesmeric harmony is created in which the orator and his hearers feel the orator's transcendent powers.

This speech of Fallon's before those twelve fateful citizens on the jury, and the thronged courtroom, and other gatherings in the corridors, ears alert to catch the trickle of eloquence that filtered to them through the partly opened doors, was such an oration. Persons who later read this speech in the papers and who did not stop to think that printed words do not sing, hastily revised their opinions that they had been listening to genius inspired in the courtroom. They decided on second thoughts that Fallon had done mighty well, but that Millard had done pretty well too—maybe better. His speech certainly read as well as Fallon's.

Away from the illusion, and more than that, disillusioned by the piecemeal reporting of the speech in the newspapers, which couldn't be helped, many of those who heard that last war song of Fallon's didn't believe their memories. However, a few of them did.

"I am not," Fallon declared, "with my back to the wall as the court has said. I am right in the front line. I have faced every accuser, and when I shall have finished I believe that you will find there is absolutely no truth or foundation for the charges brought against me.

"If you think I have been impetuous during this trial, let me say that it is not easy for a man who has stood here and defended others to stand here and defend himself. But I have done so. I could look every one of my accusers in the eye and tell them they were not telling the truth. Who of you could stand up and face your accusers without being impetuous and overbearing? If you heard men lie, and knew they were lying, wouldn't your animosity be aroused?"

Fallon was leaning over the jury rail when he said in a quiet, serious voice:

"You twelve men stand as the bulwark, under our system of jurisprudence, between me and an unjust conviction. I don't care about prisons. Reputation is what every one holds dear."

He repeated the basis of his defense which was that employes of William Randolph Hearst had entered into a conspiracy to ruin him. He said that he had the birth certificates of "the illegitimate children of a certain motion picture actress" right there in his pocket.

"You can guess why Watson wanted to see me," he continued. "You know it wasn't, as Watson said,

201

to see if I would involve others in this case. You know they wanted what I had; what Eidlitz saw I had; what Watson lied about.

"They knew what I had and that I got it to protect my clients. I got information no one else ever could get.

"I ask you to pay special attention, gentlemen, to the character of the witnesses who have testified against me here. If you had a brother or father on trial, with his everything at stake, would you believe the testimony against him of the witnesses who have testified against me here? We find strong reasons why they were all testifying against Fallon.

"Who would take the word of McGee, confessed bucketeer and robber of millions of poor people? Who would believe Rendigs, the juror, that miserable creature who faces ten years under a conviction for perjury? He is now in the Tombs. I believe he first said himself that he would not further disgrace himself by testifying against me, but a few weeks in a cell have had their effect. He saw ten more years in prison ahead of him.

"Doesn't the fact that Eidlitz, my former employe, was discharged for forging checks refute his testimony against me?

"I say to you now, and I say it is the truth, that *The American* deliberately started out to destroy Fallon, and if I were like Watson I would prove it to you in one second.

"You don't think he invited me to his apartment that day to suggest that I confess and give him information about some others, do you? You don't think I would say anything against any one? I now say to you publicly that I don't know anything about anybody, any big politician, or any big gambler that ever would put them in jail."

His last words were: "All that the whole world means to me I now leave in your hands."

Judge McClintic made it clear in his charge that the part *The New York American* played in the trial was "to help the proper officers of the law to enforce the law." Millard said the Government's case was proved.

The jury was out for four hours, retiring at 5 o'clock and sending word that it was in accord at 9 o'clock in the evening. The Federal Building was jammed with Fallon sympathizers among them Katherine and Charlotte Poillon, the famous sisters, whom Fallon had represented in court on occasion. They had been at every session.

When the verdict of acquittal was announced a few minutes before 11 o'clock, Judge McClintic having been summoned from a theatre to receive it, silence prevailed. The judge had made it clear that he would tolerate no demonstration, and he was a sorely harassed judge. The moment he withdrew to his chambers, however, a tremendous cheer arose. There could be no question as to the popularity of the verdict with the spectators in the courtroom, and the overflow in the corridors of the building.

Fallon had smiled and stepped forward to shake hands with the members of the jury as soon as he heard their decision. Now he was picked up and carried by enthusiastic admirers, who were shouting their throats raw.

A sort of snake dance march was made around the corridor on the trial floor, and then a rush was made for the street. Hats were waving and handkerchiefs were fluttering. An uninformed passerby might have thought a national hero was being welcomed home from the wars. It was the biggest ovation in memory any one ever had gotten in a New York courtroom.

Bill Fallon, flushed and happy, and having a great ado to prevent himself from being torn apart, finally was rescued by friends in the street below. They called a passing automobile and stuffed the hero into it. And away it went for Forty-second Street and Broadway, and a victory libation.

I'm going to digress for a moment here. One of the bravest men I ever knew was one of the worst murderers whose gun ever spat death-laden lead. He was the chap who went to his death in the chair at Sing Sing under the name of Gordon Fawcett Hamby.

I saw Hamby, with fresh color in his cheeks, and absolutely without any appearance either of bravado, or fear, or anything else but the normal attitude of one about to sit down for a hand at bridge, or a dish of tea, snap away a cigarette stub, smile a farewell to Warden Lewis E. Lawes, after thanking him for past kindnesses, and go cheerfully and unrepentantly to whatever bourne it may be that murderers go.

The late Nellie Bly, international newspaper woman, made quite an ado at that execution. She liked Hamby because he was a handsome young, blond lad, who never swore, and never told off-color stories, and washed behind his ears every morning, and talked in a soft voice and looked appealingly out of sweet blue eyes. She had wanted to save his life, and had worked hard to the effect. My recollection is that Hamby admitted all of nine murders.

My newspaper friends like to tell the story of how I kissed the executioner on the forehead after it was all over, and said:

"A very workmanlike job, my man."

Well, that's the way I felt at the moment, after having listened to a deal of hysteria over this callous murderer, and after having to suffer Nelly Bly's deep agony at the death scene.

Anyhow, some editors of *The World,* to whom I telegraphed my story of the execution adversely criticised me because I had made Hamby a hero to the public. Well, a reporter's job is to tell the truth as he sees it: if a murderer dies as Hamby died, what are you going to do about it—as long as newspapers go in for descriptions of scenes like that?

It is the same way with the characters in this story —Fallon, Rothstein, and the rest. I didn't admire Fallon for keeping "Dapper Don" Collins out of jail, but I admired the way he did it.

Put this matter of reporting persons and events in still another way by another analogy. I covered a series of revival meetings once which were conducted by the Rev. E. A. Torrey in Montgomery, Alabama. When I visited revivalist headquarters I first was asked:

"Are you a Christian?"

205

"I am a newspaper reporter," was my answer.

The Rev. Mr. Torrey prayed every day of that revival, matinée and night performances, for my soul. I went right ahead writing the accounts of the proceedings as they happened. When it was all over, Dr. Torrey said to me:

"You know, you have taught me something about reporting. Your accounts have been more valuable to our cause than the most violently partisan accounts anywhere ever have been. You haven't exaggerated, and you haven't detracted. You have told what you saw. At first, we did not like that attitude very well. Now, I see it is the only way to report events."

I never have changed my view that revivals are a form of organized mob hysteria—which I believe is the opinion of most persons who are unprejudiced about them—and I never could be accused of having been an ardent admirer of Dr. Torrey. But at the business of revivaling he knew his onions. And, also, I may add, I always have considered what he said the greatest compliment my theory of writing about persons and events for newspapers ever received.

I never cared a hoot—or even two hoots—whether the newspaper for which I was working was supporting editorially the program or the individual which I was writing about. I tried to write what I saw.

Those persons who didn't cheer at the sheer brilliance of Bill Fallon's defense of himself in that bribery trial, are the sort of persons who do not make any distinction between intellectual achievement and moral issues. The brilliancy of some distorted intellects may have worked against the public welfare, but, by Godfrey, they were brilliant just the same. And, if all lawbreakers were stupid, and all police and prosecuting officers were geniuses, life wouldn't be anywhere near as thrilling as it is. I couldn't imagine anything more stupid than a perfect world.·

A reader might be pardoned for thinking Eugene F. McGee, Fallon's partner, was nowhere around during this trial. But he was right at Fallon's elbow all during the sessions, right up to the end. And Gene McGee was a man for any trial lawyer to have at his elbow.

They used to call Bill the steam, and Gene the safety valve. Gene McGee, who later was disbarred for some dereliction of duty in connection with an obscure client in Brooklyn, was generally credited on Broadway with being the best preparer of criminal cases in New York. What he doesn't know about criminal law, and the criminal world, isn't supposed to exist. Right to-day, it's my bet that McGee is one of the soundest advisers in his field. He generally was given credit for bringing Fallon to New York, in the first place. It's certain that they made a marvellous team. I always liked to believe Gene when he said his disbarment wouldn't have occurred if "they hadn't been after me." It pleases me to see the criminal codes kicked around because the more they're kicked the sooner I believe they may be changed. And there was no one who could kick more to my satisfaction than McGee—with Fallon.

Fallon didn't live long and didn't do much after that. He was acquitted August 8, 1924. On May

12, 1925, Emory R. Buckner, who had succeeded William Hayward as United States Attorney, filed formal notice that there was insufficient evidence to proceed further against Fallon on the indictment charging conspiracy to obstruct justice, which was the second charge in the Rendigs matter, and with conspiracy to conceal assets, which was in connection with the Fuller & Co. case. This cleared the books of all criminal charges against Fallon, as well as Eugene F. McGee, his partner.

On March 26, 1926, the Appellate Division of the Supreme Court dismissed proceedings brought by the Bar Association to discipline Fallon. "Until a few years ago a leading lawyer" is the way some reporter described him in *The World* of March 27.

The Bar Association had objected to his conduct in the Fuller cases and in the instance of a suit for $1,000,000 by Carolyn M. Connors against Isaac H. Dickenson for alleged breach of an oral contract. This case had been thrown out of court. Fallon acted as his own attorney before the Appellate Division, where his knowledge of the law won just as many victories in proportion, by the way, as his eloquence did in the lower courts. To that body Fallon said:

"No attorney ought to be harassed or annoyed by the bringing of such proceedings as this, based on no substantial violation of any of the canons of ethics of any of the various bar associations."

This might be as good a spot as any to emphasize an oversight by persons who freely have commented on a Fallon they didn't know. It's not out of the ordinary to hear every once in a while nowadays some person, who should know better, refer to Fallon as something in the nature of a trickster, and nothing better, who had a great, antique throne-like chair in palatial offices in the Knickerbocker Building (from which he was later evicted for non-payment of rent) and who sat in it imagining himself a Napoleon, gazing down upon a subservient world. A chap told me about that chair only the other day, taking it for granted I'd never heard of it, and describing Fallon as a little fellow who perched himself in it rather grotesquely. And that chap, further described the monogram that Fallon had had worked in the back of the chair, "W. J. F.," along Napoleonic lines.

He wouldn't believe me at first when I described the real William J. Fallon to him; the reality was so different from his mental image. Fallon did sit in that chair, as described, and, no doubt, he got a deal of solace for his vanity out of it, too. But he never looked ridiculous in it. William J. Fallon had height, breadth, poise and personality—a big, handsome, graceful body, topped by well shaped head covered with a profusion of tawny hair. He filled the chair when he sat in it, and he probably looked more like an emperor in it—poor old Bill—than many a real emperor would have looked.

And William J. Fallon was not only a lawyer to try cases before juries. He was one of the finest pleaders before the high courts in the history of jurisprudence. The reason the judges were afraid of him was because they knew he knew the law.

What they didn't know was when he was telling facts or fancy.

Take the instance of Alfred J. Talley, as assistant district attorney, and as judge. Talley fought Fallon as assistant district attorney as they all did, and when he was judge he certainly had no friendly feelings for Bill Fallon.

Fallon was once trying a case before Talley as judge—the case of William Stern, a jewelry salesman, who admitted killing a man in self-defense. Stern was convicted of manslaughter in the first degree and sentenced by Judge Talley to from ten to twenty years in prison.

Fallon asked Judge Talley to charge the jury that the State must prove the falsity of Stern's story that he acted in self-defense. He told the Appellate Division on appeal that Judge Talley had refused his request, but had charged that the defendant must show that he had a reasonable ground for fearing a desire to take his life or property.

The members of the Appellate Division are not jurors. They are judges. The law is what they are interested in. The Appellate Division agreed with Fallon on this occasion, as it had on others, and ordered a new trial. Supreme Court Justice Dowling wrote that opinion, and said in it:

"It is the duty of the defendant to go forward with such proof, in order that the issue may be presented, and in this sense only must it be shown he had reasonable grounds to believe that he was in great peril and that the killing was necessary for his escape—or that he was actually resisting an attempt to commit

210

a felony upon him. But in either event, whether the evidence tending to show justification appears from the case of the people, or from the case of the defendant, the burden still remains upon the people to show the guilt of the accused beyond a reasonable doubt."

Justice Dowling's opinion was that the jury which convicted Stern might have received an impression from Judge Talley's charge, "that the burden of proof did not always rest on the prosecution, but when a prima facie case of murder had been made the burden of proof shifted to the defendant who sought to excuse or justify."

Now you know where you stand when you kill some one and have self-defense as an excuse.

Judge Talley presided at the trial of Rendigs on the charge of perjury and, after the acquittal of Fallon, he directed that the record of the testimony in the Rendigs trial be sent to the Bar Association "for such action as it sees fit" against Fallon. He released Rendigs with a suspended sentence and said to him:

"I have not the slightest doubt that everything stated by you in your confession as to your previous dealings with the attorney in question (Fallon) was true.

"I have seen no man in this court who has satisfied me so completely of his regret for the commission of a criminal act as you have. You not only confessed your guilt, but you have endeavored to aid the legally constituted authorities in the prosecution of another person charged with crime in connection with yourself.

"The United States Attorney has sent to me in writing a request in which he states you rendered him every service that it was possible for you to render, and he has asked consideration at the hands of this court in return for the services which you did render."

Right after his trial Fallon was photographed with his wife and their daughters. He announced that he was going to leave criminal law alone, and devote himself to a civil practice. His name was mentioned in connection with few cases.

On August 16, 1926, a woman entered Fallon's apartment in the Hotel Belleclaire, where he was enteraining a man and two women friends, and slashed at one of the women friends with a dog whip. When Fallon tried to protect his guests the woman threw acid in his face. A newspaper mystery was made of this unfortunate episode. The woman who threw the acid was one of those who were very fond of Bill. She took that method of showing that she thought her affections were being trifled with, and that she didn't like it.

On April 29, 1927, William J. Fallon died, ostensibly of a liver complication, but really of a broken heart and disillusionment.

Bill Fallon's funeral was attended by men and women from every walk in life. There were race track touts and Supreme Court Justices, gamblers, racketeers, leaders of the bar, public officials, ladies and others not so lady like. Bill Fallon's brains were

212

respected by his peers. He was admired by the underworld. He had taken a wrong path, and every one, who had a heart, was sorry.

After his death Gertrude Vanderbilt applied for appointment as administratrix of his estate. She said through her lawyer that she knew he had died without any cash but that he had told her of some $15,000 which was owed to him in fees, and which he had not collected. Her lawyer said that Bill had died owing Miss Vanderbilt $25,000. Her friends said it was nearer $40,000. Miss Vanderbilt would say nothing about it. After Fallon's death she went into the business of serving legal papers. There is something pathetic about the end of the easy money trail.

Mrs. Fallon, who said the estate wouldn't amount to $500, was appointed. Miss Vanderbilt took the matter philosophically. She had stuck to Bill from start to finish. She had sold her house and gone on his bond when all his "grands" had been tossed away.

If a man ever hopes to have a friend he might not be very badly off if he had one like her.

Mrs. Fallon, about whom naturally, very little has been said, was quietly wed to Dennis P. Nash, a lawyer, and World War veteran, at a decent interval after Fallon's death. Contrary to many reports, Fallon and Mrs. Fallon had been living separate lives for several years. She had come forward during the trial to give him that aid, which every real human being always will give another in distress.

As a parallel to the devotion which Fallon was able to inspire, it is interesting to note that Louise Groody and Florence Ely, married to two of his most impor-

tant clients, were just as loyal to their husbands—
William F. McGee and E. M. Fuller. In fact, the
frequency with which their ladies were permitted to
visit their husbands while the latter were held by
the courts on Governor's Island threatened, at one
time, to cause a scandal.

Both the actresses, however, strenuously denied
stories that they had helped spend the millions lost
in the failure of Fuller & Co., at gay parties in Broadway, and trips abroad, and expensive motor cars.

"I married Mr. McGee five months before the
failure and he wasn't in a position to give me any
money at all," Miss Groody said. "I married him
for himself. I haven't profited. In fact, I'm a credi-
tor of the firm.

"I've taken care of myself ever since the failure.
I didn't live luxuriously in Paris. Mother and I had
two rooms and a bath in a modest hotel and I was
taking singing lessons I paid for before I went abroad.
Every summer I've been going abroad. My cabin
coming home cost $640, not $1,800.

"I ought to be able to afford to go abroad. I made
more than $100,000 in 'Good Morning, Dearie.' It
ran eighty weeks, and I received $1,250 a week. It
was part of my savings that I loaned Mr. McGee—
nearly $50,000—when the firm got into trouble."

"We had just a two-room and kitchenette apartment," Miss Ely said. "I didn't even have a maid.
I did all of my own work."

"If someone you loved was in trouble you'd do

214

anything you could to hasten the end of his trouble, wouldn't you?" said Miss Groody. "They aren't so bad as they've been made to appear," she added. "We know."

CHAPTER TEN

QUEEN OF EASY MONEY

THAT iridescent butterfly, Peggy Hopkins Joyce, was known as Marguerite Upton in what may be termed the caterpillar stage of her evolution. Samuel Upton, her father, who died in April, 1928, was a barber, who ran his own shop in Farmville, Va., about one hundred and fifty miles west of Norfolk.

If the blonde and beautiful Peggy ever had a chrysalis experience it was when she was sent to a girls' school at Chevy Chase by her grandmother, with whom she had spent her adolescent years, and by whom she was both adored and spoiled.

If there is any question about Peggy having been a spoiled child, the error is hers. In one of her many bursts of confidence, she has admitted it herself. If there is any doubt about Peggy having been adored by her grandmother, it must be engendered in the mind of some one unfamiliar with the natural ability of Peggy to arouse the spirit of adoration in any bosom—except of those persons whom she has designated as "jealous females."

To me by far the most intriguing romance in the astounding Peggy's imposing list of romances was the first one of which any trace can be found. From this lover Peggy received no pearl necklaces, diamond

216

rings, or country homes. In fact, she didn't even get a kiss from this amazing lad. And she never forgot that, either.

This first affair of the heart began when Peggy was eleven, and the boy was thirteen. She was wont to follow after him in silent and loyal adoration. She was a helpless love slave.

Even when he was eighteen and she was sixteen she still thought the sun revolved around him for its orbit, and that the moon shed no lustre over the Mediterannean of her reveries unless he smiled.

This lad, however, rather took Peggy for granted. He was absorbed with the task of shaving off the first down which struggled hopefully through the tender skin of his upper lip; trying to keep an eccentric voice entirely in its lower register, and otherwise was busied with the chores of being a man.

He was so self-centered—this unfortunate lad—that when he went to the village railroad station to see Peggy off to school he failed to observe the tender emotion that caused Peggy's bosom to flutter, her red lips to tremble, and her big blue eyes to glow softly.

Peggy has confessed since that she was dying to have her Romeo kiss her. But she was too bashful to tell him. What that young lad missed is what many another youngster has missed in his earlier blunderings around in this peculiar vale of tears.

It is not the purpose of this chapter to go into similar details in connection with Peggy's subsequent affairs with members of the opposite and weaker sex. I feel more sympathy (and by sympathy is meant fellow feeling) with that village lad than with any of the other big, brave men who have come and gone in Peggy's life. He stands for the Blue Bird with Peggy. He is the pot of gold beneath the rainbow, the unattainable romantic goal for which we all may yearn and strive but never attain. That kiss, ungiven and unreceived, at that country railroad station, is one of the sweetest and most wonderful kisses no doubt, that ever was conceived.

Peggy rather preferred dancing to studying while she was at the school. She was quick to learn from her newly made friends that nothing was to be gained by letting nature take its course in the matter of beauty. And she became a willing assistant to what had been in her case a most bountiful nature.

If Peggy neglected her books, she didn't neglect herself. No one ever had to tell her to wash her hands, or brush her hair or her teeth, or to hold herself straight, or to be careful of her complexion, or that the heels on her shoes were run down.

Peggy was born with the outward attributes necessary to the creation of an international beauty, and she had the inner urge to make the best of every opportunity.

I have known many world famous beauties in my years in New York. I have lunched with them, dined with them and interviewed them. I remember one beautiful creature, in particular, with whom it was most embarrassing to be caught for an instant on the sidewalk. A throng collected around that girl with magical speed—small boys, large men, and all sizes of women. I took her to the Ritz-Carlton many

218

times for lunch, and she always drank one small bottle of milk and that was all—except on one memorable occasion she went on a debauch of gormandizing, and ate half a grapefruit too. That girl was Claire Windsor. I wrote an article shortly afterwards, which ostensibly was to make Miss Windsor a trifle better known to the public. But the real reason was that I always felt it was too bad that the average girl, and the average woman, didn't take somewhere near the pride in keeping themselves fit that is taken by their professional sisters.

The great beauties of the world aren't stuffing with confections, and aren't swallowing unwholesome quantities of food of any sort. They may drink alcohol now and then, but none of the fair ones who have kept their beauty through the years have done anything that any dietitian, or any physician wouldn't heartily have approved.

That was the way with Peggy Joyce in those early years. She didn't let well enough alone. She made it her business to keep herself right up to snuff all the time.

Everett A. Archer, a young millionaire, of Denver, was a guest at one of the many school dances. All the girls were rather aflutter over him, and Peggy never was one to sneak out and hide herself behind one of the palm trees in the conservatory when a millionaire was around—not unless the millionaire were with her.

A dance or two, a kiss or two, and the first any one knew about it Peggy and the young man from Denver had eloped, and were married.

But matrimony didn't mean much to Peggy then, or ever. That is, in the abstract, Peggy had many delightful ideas about the hymeneal state, but in the concrete, it was a case of too much concrete. In this instance, the romance ended on the honeymoon. Peggy returned to Washington.

In that city, in that day, the young ladies had a quaint custom, and may have it yet, of foregathering at the Saturday afternoon performances of vaudeville at Keith's Theatre. Many present day matrons recall the supremely lovely, golden-haired, blue-eyed Peggy, if for no other reason that at those Saturday matinées she sat alone in a box, which all the other girls knew had cost three dollars. Ah yes, Peggy Joyce always had a way with her. The idea was that Peggy was doing just what most of the other pretty girls would have liked to do, if they had the nerve and the three dollars.

Perhaps, after all, Peggy Joyce's success in annexing husbands and admirers isn't any more of a mystery than that she has been perfectly natural—hasn't let any artificial inhibitions stand in the way of doing what she would like to do.

Always a graceful dancer, Peggy overlooked no dances, and soon she found herself dancing with young Sherwood Hopkins, son of a wealthy and prominent lawyer. All the girls had their best smiles oiled up for use on Sherwood. He was another good catch. Peggy caught him—or let herself be caught by him—in short order.

Peggy and her husband found almost immediately that they were not suited to each other, and Peggy left him, or he left her. Anyhow, she came to New York, which is one of the great natural parks of the Big Game world, where there is no closed season, and where the butterflies hover daintily over the fields abloom with diamonds and emeralds and shining automobiles, and silks and satins, and rare perfumes, which grow richly in a soil made fertile by easy money, and in an atmosphere rendered intoxicating by public adulation.

That's the natural stamping ground of the "grands"—the thousand dollar bills, which are just a name to many hard-working earnest citizens of these United States—which are handy bits of yellow paper to toss at waiters in the Big Game country.

Of course, right now, and for the past few years, as has been pointed out, the pickings are unusually rich. The bootleg multi-millionaires, who are more numerous than the oil millionaires ever were, and get their money more easily, if less legitimately, are responsible for that—those bootleg plutocrats who are the greatest menace to the country to-day, the fruit thus far of Prohibition, brought about by people who know nothing at all of the issues involved, poor blind people, who say a thankful prayer to God because the saloon at the corner is closed, and do not see the rushing millions which are flowing into outlaw hands.

That's another story, however, the story of the bootleg multi-millionaires. I'll never buy myself a bullet-proof vest, and write that story. I don't blame the bootleggers for taking advantage of the situation, any more than I blame otherwise estimable citizens for drinking the alcohol. I do think, however, that

221

a law should be passed providing for Government supervision of the bootleggers. As it is, there are bad bootleggers, and good bootleggers, and there is no method by which the public can tell the difference.

Peggy Joyce didn't have anything to do with bootlegging, let me hasten to remark. Far from it. But she knew bootleggers, as every one in New York does, and many of the grands that she has seen thrown around were the result of law violations. The same could be said of any most respectable citizen who has watched the grands circulate. Peggy has helped keep more grands in circulation than most ladies.

"Somehow," as Peggy said, "the news of my separation from Sherwood reached the newspapers and Florenz Ziegfeld sent for me, and I went to work in the 'Follies.'"

Peggy was a big hit in the "Follies"—one of the toasts of Broadway, in fact. That was in 1918. In the following spring, she opened in "A Sleepless Night," which was deemed not a bad title for a dramatic vehicle for Peggy. It had to do with beds and bedrooms.

When Peggy was in Chicago a little later with this opus she met J. Stanley Joyce, a lumber man, who Peggy said later had an income of $5,000 a day, and who was reported to have forty millions of dollars. Joyce fell in love with the beautiful star of "A Sleepless Night." Peggy always had figured that matrimony should be an ideal state. If one were seeking the ideal, one shouldn't be baffled by the fact that forty millions would go in the same package. So when Joyce asked her the important question Peggy whispered:

"Yes."

Naturally, she couldn't become Mrs. Joyce until she had ceased to be Mrs. Somebody Else. So she promptly brought a suit for divorce from Hopkins, and went to Miami to cool her ardor in the surf until the decree should be granted.

Joyce went to Miami too, and he stayed there during the seven months of Peggy's wait, letting subordinates manage his big business affairs, and throwing around the grands in a style that impressed even Peggy, who had become accustomed to the idea that there was something about her that made money itch to be dancing at her smile.

Peggy was enjoying a spin on a bicycle when news that the decree had been handed down was received. Joyce didn't wait for her to pedal back. He dug out one of his imported motor cars—or it may have been one of Peggy's—and burned up the road in the direction she had gone.

When he caught up with her he stopped with a great shrieking of brakes, and a great skidding of tires, jumped out, grabbed Peggy from her bicycle, jumped back in the car, and headed for a Justice of the Peace—the nearest one. They were made one in less time than it takes to tell it, so Joyce—and Peggy—were happy.

Their bliss didn't last long. Peggy went back to the stage, and went to Europe. And then Joyce brought suit for divorce in Chicago in the Spring of 1921.

Peggy had said that she was going to fight this suit which was brought on the grounds of cruelty and unfaithfulness, but she didn't. She and her lawyers were in court, but they interposed no defense.

Joyce got the divorce and Peggy got about $1,000,000 in jewelry and furs, which he had given her, and $80,000 in cash. The trial was enlivened by the testimony of Hannah Nordstrom, Peggy's maid, and Mrs. Julia Sawdon, her secretary.

"We made one trip to Venice," Mrs. Sawdon asserted on the stand, "with Mr. Letellier [Henri Letellier, the French multi-millionaire publisher.] On the train there and back Mr. Letellier and Mrs. Joyce occupied the same compartment day and night.

"At Venice we stopped at the Europe Hotel. Mr. Letellier and Mrs. Joyce occupied the same room after the first night. We were there seven days. He paid the transportation, and hotel expenses."

Of Peggy in London, Mrs. Sawdon testified:

"The first night we met Edgar James in the grill. A night or two later I opened my door and saw Mrs. Joyce come out in her night clothes. She said, 'All is well.'

"Then I heard Mr. James tell her good-night and saw him leave.

"When we got back to Paris, Mr. James was there. They were together a good deal. When he left she sent him the following radio:

"'I miss you; very lonely. Return. (signed) Peggy.'"

"Did she see much of Mr. Letellier after her return from Paris?" was asked.

224

"No," was the reply, "she had met Prince Noureddin Vlora, of Albania, and was with him most of the time."

At this point, thought of a dinner in the suite of Prince Vlora and Helen Kelly Gould when they were in New York immediately after their marriage, flashes to mind.

One of the wildest rides I ever had as a newspaper man, and one of the most exciting, was taking the then Princess Vlora's sister, Eugenia Kelly, from the Ritz to the Pennsylvania station, so that she and Al Davis could be married in Elkton, Md.— secret nuptials, except for me.

A cordon of other newspaper men were guarding the Ritz that day, but I got Eugenia into a taxi without them having seen either of us until just as she stepped in. There was a great roaring of gas stimulated motors, and a jangle of meshing gears, and howls of rage, as our taxi jumped ahead.

Eugenia took all that as a matter of course. What she said to me was:

"If I get married in Maryland will it be easy for me to get a divorce if I ever should want one?"

I was telling the taxi driver to break his neck, or wreck the car, but lose the pursuit anyway, but I found time to reassure her, and give her a cigarette. She was perfectly calm after that. In fact, I never saw Eugenia, and I saw her in most trying situations, when she wasn't as calm and cool, and as pleasantly detached, as any great lady of fiction.

This is going far afield, maybe, from the story of Peggy Joyce, but it's all a part of the period with which we're dealing. The affair of Al Davis and Eugenia Kelly led to action against the cabarets and tango parlors of that day, and caused great thunderings by preachers. Mrs. Henry Moskowitz led a campaign to tidy up the Broadway dancing places, and Police Commissioner Arthur Woods announced they must look to their knitting.

That well might bring a smile, in retrospect. Dancing of that sort now is taken as a matter of course. Drinking now is done behind closed doors, and there is more of it.

Al Davis also knew Arnold Rothstein and, in fact, on the occasion once of his spectacular arrest at Murray's old place in West Forty-second Street on a charge that he and Jay O'Brien had been running a wonderfully circumspect roulette wheel, Rothstein had furnished the bail. Jay O'Brien and Davis said they were innocent of the charge, and no one proved anything different.

I always liked Al Davis, and I never had any reason to change my mind about him. He was always square in his dealings with me. And it was through his kind offices that I later met the Princess and her Prince in the Biltmore at dinner.

Before I go on, I would like to finish the story of Al's and Eugenia's marriage. Eugenia and I shook off the chase by crashing through north and south traffic on Broadway just as it began to move. I had a police card which made that possible, although not legal.

When we got to Elkton, we interviewed several

ministers, one after another, and none of them would perform the ceremony. Eugenia said:

"Why is it, as soon as they see us, they look supercilious, and say they can't do it?"

"It isn't looking at us, it's smelling us, I guess," I said, "that makes them look supercilious. They're sniffing those Orange Blossoms which we had at the hotel."

As a matter of fact, we each had had two cocktails to celebrate the occasion.

I asked a taxi driver to take us to a minister who would be agreeable to Orange Blossom aromas, and a newly signed divorce decree, which Al, whose first wife had just divorced him, had. And the driver did.

Unknown to any of us, that minister was a Mormon. And, after nearly breaking all of our necks to keep the story of the wedding from other newspapers, I had the pleasure of reading in them next morning, that Al and Eugenia had been married by a Mormon.

"Well," I said to them next day, "That's fine. It's only Al's second marriage, and only your first, Eugenia. Now, you can go ahead and get married under a different brand every time."

It was this same Prince Vlora, who was Eugenia's brother-in-law for a short time, who was referred to by Mrs. Sawdon at this divorce trial of Peggy's. Mrs. Sawdon said further:

"She (Peggy) told me that the Prince was in love with her and she was going back to America to get a divorce and would return to France and marry him."

227

This Prince was a tall, dark, handsome chap. But it was Helen Kelly Gould Thomas he married at that time—not Peggy Joyce.

Hannah, the maid, said that Peggy had scratched Joyce's face several times. She also testified about a visit she made with Peggy to Hot Springs.

"She met Barton French there," Hannah testified. "Mrs. Joyce spent lots of time in his home. When Joyce called her long-distance, they made a connection from our home to Mr. French's home so that he could talk to her. She and Mr. French got up a code so that he could talk to her."

Hannah also told of an affair she asserted Peggy had with Evans Spaulding.

"Mrs. Joyce would come home early at night, and Mr. Spaulding would come in a little later. He had a key to the door downstairs and we left the upstairs door unlatched for him. He would go into her bedroom. In the morning he would call me to lock the door after he had gone out.

"Mrs. Joyce told me that Mr. Spaulding had lots of money but was not as good looking as some of the other men she knew."

Peggy at that time was toting her $1,000,000 in jewels around with her. Of her marriage, Peggy said:

"One night before the curtain went up when we were playing in Chicago, Francine Larrimore came to me and said there was a man in front crazy to meet me. It was Joyce. When I met him he told me he would do anything for me.

"After we were married he didn't want me to go

out or meet any one. He wanted me to be always alone with him. Wealth, beauty, youth, luxury, extravagant tastes—all these he wanted to have for himself. It was cruel. I had everything I could wish except happiness.

"His jealous rages became worse. He hired a companion for me who really was a spy. She knew everything I did. It is preposterous for him to charge that I did anything wrong.

"Our life in Paris was a frightful experience. Every day there were quarrels. One day I met Henri Letellier, of *Le Journal*. He asked to be presented to me, and entertained for me. My husband was infuriated; he accused me of indiscretion and we had a scene.

"I danced with Maurice once at Deauville, and when I returned to our table my husband struck me, knocking a tiara I was wearing so that the edge cut a gash in my nose. I cried all night.

"He bought me a Russian sable coat for $40,000, and twenty wrist watches, one of sapphires and diamonds that cost $35,000. A diamond tiara cost $50,000. Two twin mesh bags that you can't tell apart cost $5,000 apiece.

"Men are all right—quite jolly to take one about, but marry one of them again? Damn! No. That is, not right away."

Joyce said she had cost him $1,380,000, as nearly as he could figure.

Jack Dempsey was reported to have been seen with Peggy when he was abroad while heavyweight champion. Asked on his arrival here if there was any truth in a rumor that he was planning to become a Mr. Peggy, he said:

"Peggy is a nice little girl, but she talks too much."

Jack Dempsey certainly was one of the lithest and most graceful humans I ever met. He also is a charming, and boyish character, and with excellent manners. Jack had a hard spot to hold as world's champion, and so did Maurice Mouvet, the great dancer now dead—hard spots because women of all walks in life chased them persistently. Of Jack Dempsey, Peggy said once:

"He's a peach with a white soul."

I decided long ago that there's no mystery about women. Don't look for something for nothing from a woman, any more than you do from a man, and you won't have any trouble. You can't buy the friendship or the love of a woman with money, any more than you can buy the love or friendship of a man with money. You've got to pay something of yourself to get part of some one's else self, be it male, or female, in return.

Of course, there are bad eggs in both sexes, but there are good spots even in the worst eggs. And now that sermon's over.

In the "Vanities of 1923" Peggy Joyce and Fannie Brice, "Nicky" Arnstein's wife, and the mother of his children, played together.

Bill Fallon, of course, long had known Fannie Brice, who unquestionably is a great comedienne. He had met Peggy Joyce for the first time, so far as I know, May 17, 1922 when she returned from Europe on the Mauretania. She brought with her the jewel case, famous on both continents. She told customs officials it contained gewgaws valued at $1,700,000.

How many grands Bill spent on Peggy, I suppose no one knows. She said once that he and she were lawyer and client, that he was busy in court, and in his office day times, and that the only chance they had to talk business was at night.

This business took them to many of the night clubs in New York, and to many of the inns conveniently situated about it. Bill Fallon was extremely lavish with his client.

I never was around when Bill and Peggy were having one of their conferences, but friends we had in common told me that Bill seldom had seemed as interested in a client. I was told that he spent $25,000 on some present or other at one clip.

It didn't make much impression on me, because I had seen Bill myself roll out of a taxicab and spend three or four thousand dollars for a doodad for a lady.

Peggy Joyce also had at least a speaking acquaintance with Arnold Rothstein, as indeed, had every one who was a figure in Broadway life, and Peggy Joyce, in her own field has been as much a "Big Shot" as Rothstein was in his.

Certainly, Peggy never got housemaid's knee, or needle pricked fingers making her jewelry collection. She worked in shows, and was the recipient of charming gifts.

There was the famous Black, Starr and Frost Blue Diamond, which Peggy accumulated. This is one and five thirty-seconds inches one way and one and nine thirty-seconds inches the other, and weighs 127 carats. It was mined in South Africa, and brought to New York in 1912. Peggy dropped into Black, Starr and Frost's one day, and picked it up for three hundred of those grands.

This stone is the one that you may see referred to as a "$450,000," or an "$800,000 diamond." Cheer up. It is only a $300,000 diamond.

Why, as Peggy said herself, Joyce tossed a $75,-000 diamond over to her at lunch before they were married. It's pleasant to live in a land where diamonds drop without even having to shake the trees.

A book of very pleasant reading, and of many pages could be woven about Peggy, which is true of all the main characters of this volume. Peggy would have been a great character in any historical era, and it is just as well to recognize her merits while she still is alive and beautiful, as to wait until she is dead and gone. I submit that any one who attempts to compile a general history of this period, and doesn't give due attention to Peggy Joyce, has lost a deal of the color.

Peggy is a symbol, a living proof of the eternal verity that one beautiful woman is more powerful than an army corps of men. There are empires of that past she might have run—if she'd had the time, which she probably wouldn't.

For present purposes this sketch of Peggy is deemed sufficient. But it must include the trial of Stephen G. Clow, publisher of that noxious periodical *Broadway Brevities*, and three of his advertising solicitors. That was early in January, 1925.

I have heard it said of Peggy Joyce that she is a doll-faced female without brains. My conception of Peggy always was that she had more than the average of mental acuteness. If any one has balance it is this same Peggy Joyce, toast and beauty of two continents, and as noted in Paris and London, as in New York.

Miss Joyce was a most important witness in the trial of Clow, and largely instrumental in sending that individual to Atlanta, convicted of having misused the United States mails with intent to defraud.

Bill Fallon was lawyer for the defense, but was absent from court on the day that Peggy was a witness. His place was taken by Edward Reynolds. This saved Bill any embarrassment that might have arisen in questioning Miss Joyce in a matter about which she felt very sincerely aggrieved, although I do not know whether or not that was the reason for his absence.

The interesting fact is that the beautiful Peggy Joyce was clever enough to do what no one else, so far as the records show, ever was able to do, and that was to secure from a representative of *Brevities* a receipt for money paid for "advertising."

I always wondered at the time why more emphasis was not placed on the acumen of Peggy Joyce, and also why more credit was not given her for her talent for persuading the hitherto unheard-of from supposedly smart men. The receipt read:

"Received of Miss Peggy Joyce the sum of $200, same to be used for advertising. Miss Joyce is hereby guaranteed that articles are not to be used derogatory to her without her written permission. Broadway Brevities, Inc., by D. J. Thomas."

Peggy said on the stand that Clow himself called at her dressing-room for the advertisement, but that Thomas, supposed to be Clow's secretary, signed the receipt and gave it to her. A. B. Brown, one of the defendants, tried to get it back, she asserted, but she wouldn't part with it. She continued to hang on to it even when Thomas came to her and reported that he had lost his job because he had given it to her.

Oh, that Peggy Joyce! When one knows how many men and women had paid money to *Broadway Brevities,* and to other similarly managed publications to keep themselves from being slandered. And it was left for Peggy, of all of them, to get a receipt, and to keep the receipt under pressure, and to have it ready for evidence when the time came.

Peggy simply acted natural again and naturally got what she wanted. Plenty of persons—probably every one who paid money to *Broadway Brevities*— would have liked receipts. Peggy would like a receipt; she asked for a receipt; she got a receipt. Certainly, them that don't ask, don't git.

On the stand Miss Joyce said that after she paid the $200 *Brevities* ceased printing articles which annoyed her, and referred to her as "famous, charming, sweet Peggy."

Several of the paragraphs which Miss Joyce didn't like were read into the record. One mentioned that she was as generous as the Scotchman one meets in humorous stories. When that was read, Peggy shot to her feet in court, and exclaimed:

"I consider that the greatest insult I have ever had. And they put that in, too, after I had given them $200 not to do such things."

Tex Rickard was a witness on the same day. He said uncomplimentary articles about him ceased to appear after he had given two checks for $125. After that, he said, he was "Rickard the Great," a man "who enriches charity," "an asset to the game," and "the friend of clean sport."

Broadway Brevities did quite a business. A. B. Brown, on the stand, admitted under cross-examination by Assistant United States Attorney Mattuck, that he had collected for advertising the following amounts from the following persons:

Otto H. Kahn, $250; James B. Seaman, President of the Seaman Paper Company, $1,250; Julius Fleischmann, $500; Arthur S. Friend, President of Distinctive Pictures Corporation, $250; Arch Selwyn, $200; Paul Bonwit, of Bonwit-Teller Company, $350; Tex Rickard, $250; Frank J. Godsol, President of Goldwyn Pictures Corporation, $200; Colonel Jacob Ruppert, $250; Rosina Galli, $150; Percival Hill, President of the American Tobacco Company, $100; W. Averell Harriman, $500, and Jesse Lasky, $500.

I had one talk with *Broadway Brevities* shortly after I left the newspaper business and went with Goldwyn Pictures, now incorporated in Metro-Goldwyn-Mayer. Some one at *Brevities* wanted an advertisement from an actress. I started to swear at the person, but suddenly thought I was in a new enterprise and had nothing to do with that particular end of it, so I told Howard Dietz the director of the department I was in, what I had done, and he said:

"Swear some more at him."

As a matter of fact, no one had to give *Brevities* a nickel. It was admitted on the stand that none of the men whose names were mentioned above had done anything which *Brevities* could print that would hurt them. Nothing *Brevities* said could hurt any one anyhow.

I'll never forget when one of the most charming chaps I ever knew, who had been an aviator in the war, and who served a brief spell on *The Herald-Tribune*, went through *Brevities* office like a Texas Norther, and cleaned everyone and every object in it out of his way, because a paragraph had been printed about a lady who was writing also at that time for his newspaper.

And here's a chance for another sermon. Tell a blackmailer to go ahead and be damned, and he'll leave you and go to some one else. Most blackmailers couldn't get into print even a real scandal about you.

During my newspaper reporting days on *The World* I went away up in the Bronx on information that a pretty story of domestic infelicity had been brewed there, one that might make piquant reading over the morning coffee.

I found a perfectly frightful mess in a family, one that no newspaper could print under the laws of libel, or would print under the rules of common decency.

The mother in this tragic domestic group followed

236

me out on the porch. She had a bank book in her hand. She said:

"I only have fifteen hundred dollars on earth, and I want you to take it, and see that none of this is printed. I feel I can trust you."

I spent half an hour trying to make it clear to her that no publication anywhere in this country possibly could print that morbid tale, and when I finally left her I think she would have been less worried if I had taken her money. As long as there are persons like that poor woman in the world, it is no wonder that the business of blackmail persists.

This sermon carries a postscript, and a most important one. It is a rule I have followed ever since I was a cub reporter and saw the trouble that might come from it, never to set a line on paper that I had not just as soon hear read publicly into a court record. Perhaps this rule may be followed too closely, but it is an excellent one to keep in mind.

If you think you are in love with a charming creature, and you haven't known her and her family from childhood, tell her how much you love her out in the middle of the street when no one is around. And when you are thinking "itty bitsy ducky" pretties don't perpetuate them in ink, unless you wouldn't mind hearing them read some time perhaps by a coarse and unsympathetic lawyer before twelve of your peers and a judge—not to mention reading them again in your newspaper.

This may explain to some delightful friends of mine for the first time perhaps, why the average temperature of my letters, is around tepid. I forget once in a while when I'm writing to my mother, and sign myself "As ever."

"As ever" is a great phrase. "As ever" what?

At the time of the *Brevities* trial Peggy Hopkins had met, married and divorced Count Gosta Morner. She met him in Chicago, when she was in "Vanities" in May 1924, and married him on June 4 in Atlantic City. He had a title but not many grands. Peggy hardly allowed the echoes of her assertions that she had found true love at last to cease echoing before she hauled the bewildered Count into court on a charge of non-support. She asserted that she had been paying the bills, and they had totalled $10,000.

The Count said he had thought Peggy was a society bud, that Peggy had been a trifle rough with him, and that he was quite puzzled over the affair. It all had happened so fast, you know. Peggy said once, in answer to inquiries about one of her reported forthcoming marriages:

"I really can't marry everybody I meet, you know."

Peggy only admits three marriages. To recapitulate, the generally accepted list at the present writing is as follows:

First, Everett Archer; marriage annulled: Second, Sherburne Philbrick Hopkins, Jr.; divorced: Third: James Stanley Joyce; divorced: Fourth, Count Gosta Morner, divorced.

An annullment means legally that the marriage hasn't existed, so that's probably what Peggy means by saying she only has had three husbands.

Peggy's old father, down in Farmville, Va., never

could keep up with his butterfly daughter. He called her "Margie." "You say she's married four millionaires?" he said once to an interviewer (who was slightly misinformed himself apparently) "and none of them suited her? Darn my kittens!"

If Bill Fallon enjoyed poking a grand or two at a waiter while under the Joyce influence, he wasn't doing anything that other men with grands handy hadn't done before him. The lay public would be quite startled if it could see some of the persons who don't mind keeping the grands in circulation in New York, gently stimulated in so doing by the soothing proximity of a beautiful, real blonde.

And Peggy is stimulating, don't worry. Now, L. Jerome Floum, for instance, once told the manager of the Miami Beach shop of Peck & Peck, Inc., that Peggy would be in within a day or two to buy a couple of odds and ends. Peggy went in and bought, according to the court testimony by which a judgment later was granted against Floum: eight suits, forty-one pairs of stockings ($2 to $15 the pair), three raincoats, three coats (at $120, $135 and $160), and four handkerchiefs at $4.50 each. The total bill for the one little drop-in was $1,345.

Young John Locke, a broker, gave two Isotta-Fraschini automobiles to Peggy before his brokerage house became defunct.

Peggy has foreign cars, maids, homes, jewelry, stocks, bonds, checking accounts and savings accounts, which isn't so bad for a country barber's daughter.

If Peggy wasn't the Queen of Easy Money during the Rothstein era, I don't know who was.

When she and Rothstein met at the races they both knew they wouldn't have to walk home, no matter how the horses ran.

CHAPTER ELEVEN

DAPPER DON AND THE LADIES

"THERE's the biggest crook of 'em all," said a detective to me one day in the Criminal Courts building in New York, where I was interested in the trial of "Kid" Regan. "That's 'Dapper Don' Collins."

Following the detective's gesture my eyes rested on the tastefully attired figure of a chap whom I already had known as "Ratsy" Tourbillon, and had considered for some time to be the handsomest and most striking human spectacle on Broadway.

His tall figure, wide shoulders, easy carriage and clean cut features would command attention in any gathering. It was only when one got close to him that one might form the opinion that there was something lacking about him that one felt in ordinary humans.

I remember one day sitting in Fallon's law office in one chair while "Ratsy" sat in another chair. He rose to no conversational ventures then, or ever when I was around, except to chat amiably with Fallon's unusually bright and capable secretary about commonplaces. That day I tried to figure out what it was that was different from ordinary mortals about him. And the only word I could think of was "opaque."

241

Words, after all, are only keys which are intended to unlock congruous pictures in the mind. I hope this word "opaque" may give a fair picture, because I never have been able to conjure up a better one.

"Ratsy's" eyes, for instance are not shallow. Yet they reveal nothing of the thoughts that go on beneath the surface. When he smiled I always was conscious of the feeling that it was a mere motion of the muscles. He was covered with a glaze.

It is said that he shed a tear or two on one occasion not so long ago when he was telling the District Attorney that he was going to be a nice, quiet, law-abiding person in the future. I have regretted that I wasn't there to see it. "Ratsy" must have been able to dramatize situations else he couldn't have risen to the eminence in the racketeering game that unanimously is accorded him.

He was the "King of the Racketeers" in the time of Rothstein. As a blackmailer, badger game worker, and prier of cold cash out of men of affluence by threats made of prosecution under the Mann White Slave Act, he had no superiors, and no equals, so far as word of mouth information in Broadway and its environs, and official records are concerned. The police files describe him as follows:

"Robert Arthur Tourbillon," alias "Dapper Don" Collins, alias "Rat" Tourbeville, alias Thomas Watson, alias Stephen Dailey, alias Gus Larsen, alias Charles A. Cromwell, alias Arthur Tyler, alias Edgar George, alias George P. Martin, alias Arthur Hussey; Bootlegger, Thief and Confidence Man."

But no one ever would suspect from looking at

242

him that he had any record other than might have
been written on the football gridiron, or the polo
field, or secured balancing dishes of tea and plates of
cakes in Mayfair's drawing-rooms.

This paragon among crooks, whom Judge Swann
once dubbed a "real Raffles" from the bench, was a
pet client of William J. Fallon. That brilliant lawyer, and playboy of the night life of New York,
seemed to take a perverse delight in keeping "Ratsy"
out of jail.

When Fallon was up to his neck in the Arnstein
case, and in numerous other legal skirmishes which
he constantly was pushing in the various courts, high,
low and middle, he always found time to put out a
helping hand for "Ratsy."

I do not remember all of the charges for which
this most interesting specimen of racketeer was held
during Fallon's time. I don't think "Ratsy" could
remember them either. He remarked one time that
he would consider that day misspent that he wasn't
either charged with a crime, or arrested for one.

It was for "Ratsy" that Fallon made one of the
many courtroom campaigns that won him fame. This
was in the Federal Courts. "Ratsy" and some pals
—seven of them altogether, I believe—had been
arrested and indicted on a charge of using the mails
to defraud.

The way Fallon used to tell the story—and the
way it generally was current in informed circles—
was that five of the defendants were on the point of
pleading guilty in order to get a lighter sentence.
But "Ratsy" held out to get Fallon. Fallon

wouldn't defend "Ratsy" unless he could defend all of them. So that was arranged.

The trial came in December. The Federal Prosecutor was afraid that Fallon would make one of his famous summations with a strong pre-Christmas flavor—"the family is waiting at the fireplace with a row of empty stockings, while their Santa Claus is being kept here for a cruel law to send to jail unless you kind hearted jurors, who have wives and leetle cheeldreen of your own, step in and prove your Christianity, and your faith in the brotherhood of man, and the justice of the Constitution of the United States by sending this poor man home to his dear ones," and that sort of thing—so he kept putting in his evidence right up to Christmas Eve. That ordinarily would mean a recess over Christmas.

Fallon, however, was no ordinary lawyer. As soon as the Government rested—and rather satisfiedly too—Fallon made the usual motions for a dismissal because a case hadn't been proved. The judge refused. Then Fallon said he wouldn't call any witnesses. He would just sum up!

How-do-you-do! That was a new one for the book of that particular prosecutor. Fallon made one of his famous summations, and got all the empty stockings, and drooping Christmas trees, and lonesome mistletoes, and sweetfaced innocents into it that were possible. The way former United States Marshall McCarthy told the result, is as follows:

"After they were acquitted, the judge said to me: 'Tom, you might just as well throw away the keys to your jail. You won't need 'em much while that young man is practising law in these courts.' "

Fallon used to say that "all they had left" when he got into the case was $8,000. He said they told him they had spent $25,000 for legal advice to plead guilty.

Two or three books might be written about "Ratsy." One fair sized volume alone might be written about his affairs of the heart. What sort of eloquence "Ratsy" used—and may still be using, for that matter—on the fair ones, I don't know. Every one who knew anything at all about him, however, knew that when "Ratsy" really "fell" for a woman, and wasn't just tolling her along for his own ulterior purposes, she was red headed.

There was nothing to indicate at any time during the period that I was more or less in touch with the goings on of "Ratsy" that he had "one million dollars fall money" put aside for an emergency. But there was every indication that he always could get heavy bail—up to and including $50,000—and that he could pay lawyer's fees, and at least had credit for a remarkable wardrobe.

One of the few times a sentence followed an indictment in his case, was in 1919 when he was sent to Atlanta Penitentiary for two years, on charges which had their origin in his activities as leader of a group of White Slave blackmailers. Operatives of the Department of Justice said at that time that they believed "Ratsy" and his gang of about fifteen, had made about $250,000 in a two-year working period.

Both men and women were swindled in this organized campaign.

Except for the time when "Ratsy" took a historic fling at bootlegging, this probably was the most prosperous period of his life. No matter, however, how many thousands, or hundreds of thousands of dollars, passed through "Ratsy's" hands, they passed, and passed rapidly.

"Ratsy" probably was the most successful of all the blackmail experts in securing the coöperation of beautiful women. A man of wealth or social standing who flirts with a beautiful woman whom he doesn't know, or at least know something about, is running mighty serious risks. On the other hand, a woman of wealth or position who flirts with a handsome man, with whose character she is unfamiliar, may awaken to find that she would rather be in a kettle of hot water than in the particular blackmail situation she finds herself.

One wealthy woman's case may be told as illustration. A member of the "Blackmail Syndicate," as it was called, met her in a café in New York. He made love to her, and she believed his protestations. She took him with her to her home in Philadelphia.

After he had grown tired of the affair he took her to a hotel in New York. Two other members of the "Syndicate" forced their way into the room, knocked down and handcuffed the man, showed false credentials as Government agents, and said this was a Mann Act case and they would go through with it unless they were paid to keep still. The woman paid.

'But this wasn't done without careful preparation.

246

The woman's companion and his friends put up such an excellent fight, that real black eyes and split lips resulted. The woman's companion wrote a check for what was supposed to be his share of the hush money. But the pretended agents wouldn't take the check: they required cash. So one of them took the woman to her home, and the other one went out with her companion.

Public accounts at this time described the feminine allies of the blackmailers as most accomplished and charming adventuresses. My information from first hand sources was that the girls, in many instances, were attractive but not so sophisticated—"beautiful but dumb," in other words.

I was told by those who certainly should know what they were talking about that one of Tourbillon's methods was to get a girl infatuated with him; tell her to let a man to whom he introduced her by one means or another, make love to her; and then at the proper moment, make his dramatic appearance, either in the guise of a federal agent, or a detective, or an indignant husband. He didn't even thank the girl for her more or less hazy, but most effectual assistance.

The matter-of-fact way in which the unexpected can happen in the borderland between the upper and underworlds is really astonishing.

I knew a girl, very well known along Broadway, and very pretty. (Her chum, by the way, married a son of a noted millionaire, and still is married to him.) She told me that she knew most favorably a chap with a deal of money. One day a couple of friends in the Tourbillon coterie dropped into her flat, and for lack of something else to do, she idly tossed out a couple of dice, saying, "I'll shoot you for a quarter." The wealthy chap, and she and the two racketeers rolled the dice until they were shooting for high stakes. Then loaded dice were run in, and her wealthy friend was "taken" for several thousands of dollars.

That girl knew she had made a false move as soon as she had made the first toss of the dice. She would have given anything to have been able to save her friend a trimming. But she didn't dare offend the two racketeers. That would have been against the unwritten, but universally understood code of her and their world. And, besides, if she had done anything to prevent this easy money from flowing into their hands, she couldn't have lived in New York with any degree of comfort.

Her friend awoke about the time his money was gone. He felt he had been cheated, but he had to pay. He couldn't do anything else. The code of his world made it necessary for him to keep his mouth shut and take his medicine.

I was relating this to one of the most eminent lawyers in New York one day, and he told me, interestingly enough, of a similar incident that had happened in the flat of one of the best known actresses on the stage. Stage folk, like newspaper folk, are likely to have a wide range of friends, or at least of acquaintances. In this instance, some of the persons in her flat this night were racketeers.

Some one spun out a couple of dice on the rug in

248

front of the fireplace. A couple of hours later, a young man of Fifth Avenue, who was getting acquainted with Broadway, had written a check for $45,000.

When this check was presented at the young man's bank the next morning, the bank officials were curious, and asked the young man about the check over the telephone. He told them that he had lost the money shooting dice and to pay the check. When he told them with whom he had been playing, the bank officials said they doubted the game was an honest one, and he indignantly replied it must have been because it was played, merely as an after-the-theatre pastime in So-And-So's home.

The bank officials, still hesitant, notified their lawyers. Their lawyers, in turn, consulted over the telephone the lawyer who told me the story. This lawyer said:

"I told them to pay the check, of course."

Earlier in this book, you may recall, what a fuss was made about young Charlie Gates losing $40,000 in the old days in Rothstein's gambling house, which, to all intents and purposes, was a public place. At least, any one who went there knew that he was going to gamble, or else he wasn't going to be very welcome.

Here is a young man, under modern methods of "bootleg" gambling, who merely was out for a bit of excitement, a drink or two, and a laugh or two, with a celebrity of the stage. He had no idea of gambling. He probably wouldn't have gone to a gaming house if it had been suggested. But that crap game, under those conditions, beginning insidiously for a few cents, bit a $45,000 chunk from his bankroll before he knew it. And the cocktail—with a dash of absinthe—and the champagne in that particular flat, are very soothing. I have been there.

Charlie Gates got a little excitement out of his $40,000. This poor chap didn't get anything but a lesson. Playing games for any stakes at all with strangers is dangerous—and don't take it for granted because a friend has introduced the strangers that the friend is responsible for them, either.

Beautiful, charming and talented women—and girls who only have the incomparable charm of youth —are just as likely to attract wolves as lambs. And, a wolf always can find time to try to pry a few loin chops loose from a lamb.

This "Ratsy" Tourbillon outfit has been called all sorts of "Syndicates" and "Empires," and "Gangs." Wherever "Ratsy" was, men and women were complaining about getting robbed, gently and roughly, by force and by art.

It has been said of "Ratsy" that he was a coward. I would hate to call him that. I never heard any one that knew him say that he was anything but a person with a colossal nerve, who would prefer not to fight, but who could and would fight any time that it was necessary. But that is superfluous. No one without a barrel of courage could ever have done a hundredth of the acts that "Ratsy" has done.

Tourbillon has said that he was born in Canada, and in other countries. The police say he was born in Atlanta, Georgia. There is a story that his father was a wealthy planter of the South, and that it was from his mother that he learned to speak French so perfectly.

Tourbillon first appeared around New York in 1901. He had given up clerking in Atlanta, and had gone with a circus. In Newark, N. J., at nineteen, he was billed as "Tourbillon, Dare Devil of the Motor Bike." He rode his motor bicycle over a den of lions. He always asserted that he was the only person who ever had the nerve to do that particular feat. They called it the "circle of death." He would have made a good-looking meal for the lions if he had slipped.

During the winter Tourbillon shot craps a bit in Jersey towns, and drank a little beer in saloons in New York. He never drank much of anything anywhere—like Rothstein.

He began to make acquaintances in "Curly" Bennett's poolroom in Broadway, and in Danny Clancy's saloon in Seventh Avenue. There he met "Nicky" Arnstein, "Big Nick" Cohn, and others of the gambling fraternity. He also rubbed elbows with racketeers of all varieties.

Among those racketeers was one badger game expert who had seen Tourbillon doing his specialty with the lions. This luminary in his own field was interested in the young man, and said to him one night:

"Are those tame lions that you ride over?"

"Don't be foolish," was the answer. "They are

251

the real thing. If anything happened they would get me for a quick lunch. That's why I've got the biggest act going."

"How much do you get for it?" the badgerer asked.

"Seventy-five dollars a week," was the answer.

"Well, all I've got to say is a guy with your looks, and your front, and your nerve is losing a lot of time. Let's have a talk.

"All you've got to do," added this new-found advisor, "is get a swell looking dame or two, and wait around where the guys with the dough hang out. When one of 'em gets too thick with one of the dolls, all you've got to do is frame him, and take what he can afford."

There is no official record to show that Tourbillon acted on this advice at once, although there is plenty in the record to indicate that he never forgot it.

In 1911, Tourbillon was working as a walking advertisement for a Fifth Avenue tailor. "Ratsy" is the sort of chap who couldn't help being an advertisement for a tailor, whether he were paid for it or not. And even if the tailor wasn't very good, the chances are all in favor of "Ratsy" being a good advertisement. He is that kind.

"Ratsy" learned all that he hadn't already known about the value of a "front" while he was at this refined occupation. He learned how to carry a walking stick of just the right sort, with just the right sort of clothes, and also perfected his native grace in wielding real amber cigarette holders. He picked up tricks in the way of giving an indefinable air to a felt hat with a deft touch or two that must have been worth the hardships of the employment to him.

On the night of June 15, of this same year, "Ratsy" fell into the hands of the police for the first time in a way that he couldn't escape. He and two other men went to the Hotel Roy, in West Thirty-fifth Street, poked a gun at the clerk, and took $160 from him. In sentencing him for this robbery, Judge Swann said:

"He is as smooth a rascal as ever came before me. He is a real Raffles. I consider this man a very dangerous character, for he is such a smooth talker and such a fine dresser."

Tourbillon next was arrested in connection with looting of coin boxes in telephone pay stations on the Upper West Side of Manhattan Island. The "Upper West Side," for those who are not familiar with New York City, is, roughly speaking, territory north of Fifty-ninth Street, and west of Central Park to One Hundred and Tenth Street, and not much further north than that. This is a region in which are many most respectable dwellers, but it also includes areas in which a large number of speedy ladies, and extremely fast moving men, make their homes. That's where there are not a few of the "call flats," which have taken the place of the old fashioned bawdy houses. One telephones the presiding genius of a "call flat" that one would like to play a hand of bridge with a blonde, and the presiding genius "calls" a blonde—or a half-dozen of them, if necessary. Bridge is a popular afternoon pastime in New York.

I might mention that among the girls who go in for bridge, and for the Broadway company of Tourbillon and others, are many who are thought by their families to be hard-working females. It's easy to fake pay envelopes and occupations in a city like New York. Quite a few married women play bridge. One excellent bridge player I met was sending her son through college on her winnings.

Tourbillon never had to face the charge of stealing nickels from telephone coin boxes. As soon as the Federal authorities learned that he had been arrested with a number of other persons in that round-up, they asked for him. They had indictments all ready for him on charges of being the leader of the "White Slave Blackmail Syndicate," described above.

It should be pointed out somewhere, and this is as good a spot as any, that victims of these blackmailing schemes, and most of the so-called "rackets," never want their names published. That's why they are easy victims in the first place, and that is why they are hard to persuade to act as witnesses in the second place.

In this case, apparently, the victims played true to form and didn't make good their charges against "Ratsy." But the Government had another card up its sleeve in the case of Tourbillon. The wonder was it hadn't more.

Tourbillon already was under $7,500 bail on a charge of compelling a prominent banker to sign two $2,500 drafts by threatening to tell tales about him if he didn't. But the indictment that was used effectively against him was one charging use of

254

the mails to defraud in connection with the sale of fake peat lands in the South.

They didn't "have the goods on" Tourbillon in the Banker's case, if results mean anything; and apparently they couldn't get anywhere with the "White Slave Blackmail" charges, although the Federal people said that the victims they knew about included a judge of New York State, a Representative in Congress, and a wealthy resident of Washington. But the peat lands affair was so clear cut that Tourbillon pleaded guilty to an indictment and took two years in Atlanta. It seemed to satisfy both parties to the deal.

In the land frauds, Tourbillon worked a rather ingenious turn of an old game. He received letters from an accomplice who worked for a trust company that dealt in oil lands. The letters were couched most confidentially, and explained that certain lands were about to be purchased. The concluding paragraph was:

"Keep this strictly to yourself. Don't let a soul know about it, but the company is going to buy up this land soon, and you'd better get a piece of it yourself. . . ."

The letters looked rather effective on real trust company stationery.

Tourbillon wrote some letters himself, among them, one to his associate. In this he referred to purchasers of the land as "saps," and to money as "filth." He remarked that one sap had only been able to get together $2,500, and wasn't worth bother-

255

ing about, and that another "louse didn't know enough to bite."

You may see the great respect with which the racketeer regards the sucker.

After he got out of Atlanta, Tourbillon was arrested on a charge of robbery of a hotel in Middletown, N. Y. At last reports he still was under bail for this partly forgotten interlude.

Then came one of those tragi-comedies that occasionally crop up in the doings of the denizens of the underworld. Frederick C. Robb, an employe of the American Railway Express, disappeared from his car in 1920, with $5,150 in cash, a $435 watch, and other jewelry. While the police were looking for Robb, Tourbillon posing as a member of the Narcotic Squad of the Police Department found him in an apartment in West Sixty-fourth Street, and gently removed from him the money and the gew-gaws.

When the honest-to-goodness police found Robb a few days later he didn't have anything left except unpleasant memories of the energetic narcotic detective. The police always had said that one of the specialties of "Dapper Don," as they always called him, was robbing robbers. So, with a deal of hope they had Robb run through the portraits in the Rogues' Gallery. Sure enough, he picked out Tourbillon.

For this little odd job "Dapper Don" was convicted and sentenced to a year in prison.

But, he didn't go to prison right away, as he was out on $5,000 bail—a chronic state with him—pending appeal to a higher court.

This was his situation, when early on the morning of May 15, 1921, John H. Reid, a wealthy manufacturer, was mysteriously and thoroughly drilled full of bullet holes in the home of Mrs. Hazel Davis Warner, No. 1892 University Avenue, the Bronx. Mrs. Warner was a former close friend of Tourbillon.

Not long after the shooting, and while Reid was making a miraculous fight against death in hospital, Tourbillon called at the apartment of Helen Paterson, and said he hurt his hand in a door. A physician was called in and the wound was dressed.

And now to pause while that wound is being wrapped with bandages, and tell something about Helen Paterson, beautiful, passionate and wilful, whose romance with Tourbillon forms one of the most interesting chapters in underworld history of the past fifteen or twenty years. In fact, this affair got so hectic and all-pervading before it was over that it assumed the proportions of an international complication.

Helen was only nineteen years old then. She had come to Broadway from some undetermined village in the lonely West Virginia hills, bringing with her an air of freshness and innocence, and an apparently inexhaustible fund of vitality, just two years before when she was seventeen.

She was a beautiful girl—an unusually beautiful girl,—even in a city which attracts beauty as distilled sugar attracts butterflies. She didn't have to ask for a job in the Winter Garden. They asked her to take it as soon as they saw her red gold hair, her peaches and cream complexion, and her dreaming blue eyes.

Girls like Helen have the world at their feet, if they are wise. They are likely to become footballs for the feet of the world if they haven't that saving faculty.

Helen had a quaint Southern drawl, an ingenuous, trusting manner, and a positively delightful way of thinking that everything was too perfectly wonderful for anything. Unfortunately, in her case, her ingenuousness and simplicity were not pose. They were real. She had enough force of character to make her widowed mother take her to New York, but she did not have the strength of character to use the means that came to her hands to forge permanent success from them.

She immediately was a prize for whom the beaus of Broadway, old and young, and honest and not so honest in their intentions were striving. She could have had her pick from a large, and not so unchoice collection of admirers. She did pick Otto Young Heyworth, of Chicago.

This lad, new laid by college, was heir to a great fortune. His grandfather, the late Otto Young, had been associated with the late Levi Leiter, and was one of the largest holders of real estate in Chicago. The plot where the Blackstone Hotel now stands once belonged to that old gentleman.

Youthful Mr. and Mrs. Heyworth went to live with his grandmother in one of those hotel homes on Lake Shore Drive. Her new grandmother could not help but be fond of her. Helen was so young, and so lovely, and so appreciative of everything.

Society in Chicago is said to have given her a warm and unreserved welcome. She had everything that money could buy for her, and that praise and affection could give her, except freedom. She had tasted freedom during those months she was on the stage in New York. And now she felt like a bird in a cage.

It wasn't long before Helen went back to her home in West Virginia. It was known that she and her young husband hadn't been able to get along, and it was understood that a divorce was only a matter of time.

Helen couldn't tolerate the country, however. And she hadn't intended to. She was back in New York almost before Broadway had missed her. At first she lived with Mrs. Samuel K. Martin, an aunt of her husband. Mrs. Martin called her "my baby," and made much of her. But Helen wanted more freedom, and took a bachelor girl apartment in the East Thirties.

In this apartment she met another girl, and a friend of that girl, who was a racketeer. Through them she met Tourbillon. She didn't know anything about either of the men except that they both were unusually handsome, unusually well dressed, and that Tourbillon, in particular, was one of the most charming and persuasive individuals she ever had met.

After the physician had gone, Tourbillon remained in Helen's apartment until night, and then he went to Philadelphia.

Meanwhile, the police were trying to find "Dapper Don" again. Although Reid refused then, and refused ever afterwards to say who had shot him, indictments charging him with the shooting were returned against Tourbillon by a Bronx County Grand Jury. The police theory was that Tourbillon was fond of Mrs. Warner, and that jealousy caused him to fire the shots.

A deal of excitement—in the newspapers—existed at the time. Five days after the shooting William J. Fallon, as her counsel, surrendered Mrs. Warner to District Attorney Glennon, in the Bronx. Two days after that, Frank Boylan and Lila Wiley, presented themselves to the District Attorney. The three were held in $10,000 bail each.

Lila Wiley was a name generally glided over in the accounts of that shooting. But, Evelyn Wiley, as she as known in Broadway circles, was a very close friend of Tourbillon. In fact, he was always understood to have been more attached to her than to any one else up to the time of his romance with Helen.

Mrs. Warner, afterwards, in commenting on the affair, which rather had the town by the ears, and gave the police occasion for wondering if it was a sort of aftermath to the unsolved murder of Joseph Elwell, the bridge expert, and if it had anything to do with "blackmail" rings, and things like that, said:

"I did not see him (Tourbillon) there that morning, and I have not seen him since. Statements that I ran away with him are untrue. I have not even seen him. They are like the police statements of a blackmail ring—pure bunk. If Don Collins did shoot John Reid, jealousy is the only motive I could conceive."

The point that was not emphasized at the time was that the jealousy, if any, probably would have been over Evelyn Wiley, if those who pretend to know their Broadway really know it.

If Mrs. Warner did not go with Tourbillon, as obviously, she didn't, and if Helen didn't go with him either, some beautiful blonde did.

What Tourbillon was doing while the police were after him was pretty good proof that a chap, not too meticulous about violating laws, can have a good time and still have the police after him.

He went right to Philadelphia where he took the name of Charles A. Cromwell, and said that he was related to one of the leading bankers of Philadelphia, the fact that names were similar allowing him to be accepted as the banker's step-son.

The fact that the rather swanky Cromwell bought a United States submarine chaser and had it refitted sumptuously as a yacht, caused no surprise to any one. The police were looking for "Dapper Don" Collins. They weren't interested in the idle vagaries of a wealthy young yachtsman.

With a crew of six men and "Mrs. Cromwell," the new member of the "400" embarked upon what he referred to as a cruise in southern waters. It turned out to be one of the most dramatic and romantic episodes in the history of rum running. After it was over, Tourbillon had won a new title. It was "King of the Rum Runners."

In this craft, Tourbillon put in at the Bahamas,

261

and took on 850 cases of Scotch. You can call this 1,600 cases, or 2,000 cases. Those who made the trip tell different stories. Anyhow, there was quite a flock of Scotch.

With the lady of red gold hair, Tourbillon—and three of his crew from New York who toted revolvers, and three of his crew from Philadelphia who did the work—arrived back at Philadelphia on December 11, 1921. Tourbillon headed the Nomad straight for the Mathis Yacht Shipbuilding Plant at Camden.

"You can't dock here," said a watchman.

"Don't be an ass, me good fellow," said Tourbillon, in his best Cromwellian manner. "We're putting her on the marines railway for repairs in the morning."

"Oh," said the watchman.

Then the watchman saw a motor truck drive up to the dock.

"What's going on here, anyway?" asked the watchman.

"Why we've got to get the furniture off, haven't we?" said Tourbillon good-naturedly.

And the watchman went away again. Half the cargo of Scotch then was unloaded right there. The rest was dumped off in Chester, Pa. But a truck broke down, and the Scotch was traced. And Tourbillon, the unidentified golden blonde, and his crew were indicted. And that, by the way, was all the good that ever came of it, except a fine of $500, which Tourbillon paid long afterwards.

No brief account can do justice to this sea adventure of Tourbillon. He had a magnificent wardrobe with him that included an array of suits made by the best tailors in the world, haberdashery of the best, and a gold cigarette case that is supposed to have cost $1,000.

With a gesture that is typical, Tourbillon hid himself by returning to New York and living for a while in excellent style in a hotel near Fifth Avenue. He was quiet but exclusive. He figured that no one from Broadway, including detectives, ever poke their noses into a hotel of that sort. And he turned out to be correct.

In a leisurely manner, he moved along up to Canada by easy stages. There, he adopted the name of Arthur Hussey, became a Canadian citizen by his own permission, secured a passport, and sailed for London. He wandered here and there over Europe, leaving a broken heart here, a flattened pocketbook there, and more wisdom in most places. He made big killings at baccarat, and generally had a grand time.

Helen and her husband, meanwhile, had been divorced, and she had received a cash settlement of $85,000. With this money in hand she also sailed abroad. She and Tourbillon met in Berlin.

After a long courtship Helen, very much in love, promised to marry Tourbillon. Despite the fact that he already was shadowed by French detectives on suspicion that he was active in smuggling narcotics, Helen and he both insisted that she knew nothing of his criminal career.

Tragedy struck on New Year's Eve, 1923. They

had attended a party, and had had a gay time. Tourbillon gallantly saw her to her third floor apartment. She said she felt nervous, and asked him to get her a bromide. When he came back, she was gone. He ran to the open window, and saw her lying on the pavement.

She was taken to a hospital where it was found that her pelvis had been fractured, and that she had suffered internal injuries. Her forehead, also, was badly cut. She told Tourbillon—known as Hussey then, of course—that she had fainted and fallen from the window.

Events moved rapidly after that. No one could have been more tender and devoted than was Tourbillon. He was constantly at her bedside until she was out of danger. But the publicity was disastrous for him, and he knew it. He was wanted by the police in the United States, and he was being followed by the police in France.

He made a short trip to Germany, and on his return was arrested. Identified by two New York detectives who happened to be in Paris on another errand, he was thrown into La Santé prison on a technical charge of having narcotic drugs in his possession. That made him the "King of the Dope Smugglers" with those persons who loved to crown him with a new title ever so often.

Helen Paterson, now convalescent, but doomed to permanent lameness from her injuries, limped to his prison, bent upon marrying him there and then, despite the pleas of her friends, and the advice of every one who spoke to her. And here is a letter which Tourbillon wrote to her:

"As for your marrying me, sweetheart, think it over seriously first and you may change your mind. I personally think you would be very foolish. You can do so much better. I am ruined from every angle, and have a prison sentence before me. When I come out I will be of little use to anybody, and what use would I be to you or any one after prison? When I would come out I would be broken in health and a burden on society, and I know you don't want that.

"You are still young and have the world before you, with many opportunities if you keep your head up. You will be a million times better off by not marrying me and by forgetting such a miserable creature ever existed. So think it over and understand. I haven't forsaken and will never forsake you; I love you more than my liberty or anything else, and my consideration of you, and your welfare is the reason I am writing this way.

"Please be careful, dear heart. Don't catch cold, darling. Do you know, I didn't recognize you yesterday until you called me, and then I was so surprised I was almost speechless. I would have given the world to have picked you up in my arms and hugged and kissed you. You looked so thin and pitiful—I had all I could do to stop the tears.

"Don't let anything worry you, darling. All my love to you."

Tourbillon was brought back—he insisted in making the trip in a $4,600 suite for which he paid—and was sent to Welfare Island to serve his sentence for robbing Robb. While on the island making balloons he said:

"The name of that little lady (Helen) never should have been mentioned in the same breath as mine. I am what I am, a convict. She thought I was what I pretended to be, a gentleman."

When Tourbillon finished that eight months' sentence, he called the attention to detectives who came to take him to the Bronx where the indictment for the shooting of Reid was still hanging, that under the extradition law of France he could not be tried in this country on any other charges. This turned out to be true. He was given "a reasonable time" to return to France.

But Tourbillon didn't go. After thirty days he was arrested on the indictments that grew out of his rum adventures, but the smuggling charge was dropped, and he only was fined $500 on a "possession" charge. Later he was charged with beating a hotel, but was acquitted.

He was arrested in April, 1928, charged with having taken $700 from two men while he posed as a Government agent. The two men couldn't identify Tourbillon in court the next day. Magistrate Corrigan asked one of the complainants:

"Has any one spoken to you since last night?"

The complainant said "No," and that was all.

Items in the newspapers from time to time, say "Dapper Don" is wanted here for a gold brick game, and there for some other racket. Judge Swann once said from the bench that he thought Tourbillon was a "dope fiend."

The fact that the Paris police suspected him of, and arrested him for dope smuggling, was interesting anyhow. That trail of dope, which the Federal authorities have followed to Rothstein, is an interesting one.

CHAPTER TWELVE

FOR THE WIFE AND KIDDIES

Nicky Arnstein, the most charming crook with whom I've ever drunk a highball, is a sentimentalist. He says that what he admired most about Fannie Brice as a wife was her ability as a seamstress—he loved to see the dear head bowed over the sewing basket, and the shining needle flying in and out, as she fashioned underwear for him, and cute wearables for the children.

What ruined their romance, Nicky adds, was the fact that his wife had to work nights, which caused a certain regrettable irregularity in his hours, if he cared to see her awake, and her insistence on singing her famous song "My Man," which sets forth that her man isn't any good, and is a faithless, wife-beating brute, but that she loves him anyhow.

Fannie Brice, in her suit for divorce, which was granted in Chicago, September 14, 1927, merely told the judge that she had found Nicky and an unidentified female of the species together in a Chicago hotel.

Before she left for Chicago to testify, however, she told friends that Nicky had grown cool towards her as soon as she had her nose altered from Roman to Grecian, which was accomplished by Dr. Harry Schierson in Atlantic City, August 15, 1923.

She said Nicky complained that the new nose made

her too beautiful, and that it gave him an inferiority complex. He couldn't stand so much feminine pulchritude, so he went out looking for something down nearer to his deserts—and found plenty, she averred.

After getting the divorce Fannie said she was going to file an alienation suit against a wealthy New York society woman, but nothing came of that.

I couldn't violate any confidence with Nicky Arnstein, even if I were given to such practise. He never told me anything except that he was a domestic, home-loving, much misunderstood creature, who always had been blamed for crimes some one else had committed, and with which he had had nothing at all to do.

"I have been the innocent by-stander," Nicky said. "I will admit that I have gambled. I have a gambler's heart. It is a great thrill to me to play a game. I get a kick out of it. One of the biggest kicks I ever got was when I saw Arnold Rothstein lose $500,000 once on the turn of a card without a sign of emotion.

"I admire sportsmanship, and sporting men. Perhaps, it is because of that fever in my blood that I gave up contracting and building, which is the field I entered first, and in which I was making a success. I wanted the lights, the action, the suspense that comes from adventure.

"But I love a home, a fireside," he added earnestly. "I think of my wife waiting for me, with the children, and my heart warms. A wife and children, and the future to look forward to together!"

269

And many a night, and many a day, the little woman and the little children would be sitting there waiting, I used to think. Many a man has sat around a café drinking all night dramatizing the fireside, while his real better half is home warming a flatiron, or making practice swings with a rolling-pin against her idealist's return.

While Nicky was speaking of those sterling domestic virtues I thought of the perhaps $2,000 a week that Fannie was lugging home every pay night (maybe it wasn't quite so much then, but I understand it's $4,000 a week now). I said once:

"Well, if she was a housewife she'd be a liability instead of an asset, Nicky."

He said earnestly:

"I would only love her and cherish her more. I can earn money. I would like nothing better than to have a real home and no more of the stage."

There was more along this vein, which I always felt maybe Nicky believed himself for the moment: he was so much in earnest.

Nicky Arnstein's real name is Jules Arndstein. For years on Broadway he was known as Nick Arnold. He has used many other names, including Nicholas Arnold, Wallace Ames, John Adams and J. Willard Adair.

He tells his friends and acquaintances that his family is good. And that is true. He said to me once:

"My father was a Jew, and was born in Berlin, of excellent parents. His father was decorated several .

270

times for gallantry in the Franco-Prussian war of 1870.

"My mother was of Dutch ancestry, came to this country when she was very young and was reared in the Episcopal faith, and my father and all of us children were communicants of St. Joseph's Episcopal Church, right here in New York.

"No boy could have been brought up with more love and care than was I, and I always have loved the beautiful things in life—beautiful pictures, good books, and birds and flowers. My fondness for gambling, however, led me to live a life rather apart from my family. It is one of the penalties I have payed for my fondness for the cards, the dice and the horses."

Nicky acted hurt if he were asked about his activities as a racketeer of parts. He always was perfect in his role as a gentleman of high instincts who has been grievously wronged, but for whom every little wrinkle will be ironed out in the life to come. If I had not known Nicky's record I am sure I would have believed his stories. Rogues' Gallery photographs do not lie, however, and an innocent man could not possibly associate with crooks so closely as has Nicky without having had some ideas in common with them. That is entirely outside of police assertions regarding him. Those assertions by detectives always were vitriolic and sweeping.

But, what annoyed the detectives rather titillated my fancy. They were a bit upset because Nicky could get away with what they said was so much, and serve so little time for it, and that most comfortably.

If Nicky had been a bungler who spent most of his time in jail, rather than basking in the warm glow of familiar spirits, excellent wines, delectable viands and not unprepossessing femininity, he would not have been a character for this book.

Nicky's schooling was rather sketchy—as was the case, it will be recalled, with Rothstein and "Ratsy" Tourbillon—but he was born with a remarkable gift for making himself attractive, especially to the fair sex.

An interesting point in connection with his love affair with Fannie Brice is that he not only won her affections to the extent of making her glad to marry him, but he also enmeshed her heart to the point where she was happy to become the mother of two beautiful children. And when an actress goes in for motherhood it means money out of the family stocking in more ways than one.

Of course, it might be said there were no ancestral castles in Fannie's background: her first public appearance was in 1907 selling newspapers at Bergen Street and Vanderbilt Avenue in Brooklyn. But Fannie has something that is of more account practically than castles; she has genius as an actress, and she has plenty of common sense. Any estimate of Nicky Arnstein must include the fact of Fannie Brice's real devotion for him.

Also, there is something in Nicky's plaint that Fannie would make any sacrifice for her career on the stage. Artists have been that way since the beginning. He didn't want her to sing "My Man," because of the certainty that the public would associate

272

him with the hero, or rather the villain, of the ditty. But she sang it because she could see that it meant greater success than she had then attained.

Nicky first came into the hands of the police in July, 1912. Detectives Barney Flood and Joseph Riley were in London on another chase at that time. They had caught their birds—two racketeers—but the birds had produced $100,000 bail and thus escaped being brought back to the United States to trial.

While Flood and Riley were consoling each other for this not unusual mishap, they received a cabled message from Charles S. Whitman, then District Attorney in New York, to bring Nicholas Arnstein back with them. He was wanted for putting over a variation of the "sick engineer" racket on William E. Shinks, of Springfield, Mass. The amount was $15,000.

Detectives Flood and Riley decided that the best way to get trace of their new quarry was to find the best looking and smartest woman with underworld connections, and follow her. On the register of a hotel they found the name of Anne McCormick. This Anne McCormick, in question, was known as one of the most dashing and versatile, as well as one of the most beautiful, of Continental sports. They knew she was acquainted with Arnstein.

A good story is lost by not going into details of how they worked so that their cab was ahead of Anne's at the beginning of the chase and how they hoodwinked her throughout. However, it is enough for present purposes to know that by trailing the lady

273

they got Nicky, who was just mellowing under the influence of a magnum of vintage champagne.

The really excellent detective work I can omit, but I can't omit the behavior of Nicky under these distressing circumstances.

Nicky is a tall, slim, graceful chap with dark hair, and blue eyes, set a trifle close together. He always wears a tiny, tidily waxed and twisted moustache. His clothes, ever the result of care by a modish tailor, are worn with an air. When the detectives interrupted him, Nicky did not bat an eye. They just had time to observe that Nicky had turned blond, when he said in a lazy drawl:

"Raaly, this is a surprise. You quite have the advawntage of me, don't you know. I rally cawn't say that I evah saw you befoah. My name is James Wilfred Adair."

This didn't prevent the detectives from packing Nicky up and lugging him off with them. But, Nicky didn't drop the James Wilfred Adair name and pose, or his British accent, until after he had been arraigned in New York. He was still "aw"ing the ship news reporters when he landed on this side.

And that's another item that should be included in considering Nicky Arnstein. He has quick wit in an emergency, and he will play a hand through until he is beaten, and then play the hand some more.

Stories have been written in newspapers that poor Nicky has been made a goat by smarter men. Well, maybe; maybe. But Nicky has made quite a few goats on his own hook, in his time, and don't forget that.

Nicky's bail of $25,000 in this case was furnished by his father. After a deal of stalling and delay, Nicky finally was convicted of grand larceny by a jury of the Court of General Sessions and was sentenced by Judge Otto Rosalsky to serve two years and ten days.

He arrived at Sing Sing March 18, 1916, and was pardoned by Charles S. Whitman, then Governor, July 16, 1917, which meant that eight months and fourteen days had been chopped off what would have been his minimum sentence.

But that is not all. The records at Sing Sing are proof that he had one of the preferred "trusty's" jobs, and it was said that he was a star boarder. What influence brought this state of affairs about never was established. The wise chaps just grinned—exactly as they grinned later, when Nicky was in the Tombs, and the word was out that he was living on partridge and champagne, or their equivalents. Nicky, as has been mentioned, was a friend of Rothstein.

As Jules Arndstein, Nicky had married Carrie Greenthal, May 5, 1906. During his sojourn at Sing Sing, Fannie Brice was a constant visitor. Her mother, Mrs. Borach, had pleaded in vain with Fannie to give up Nicky. Fannie wouldn't. She loved him and believed in him. Not only that, but Fannie was said on excellent authority, to have pawned all of her jewelry during that time, and to have spent thousands of dollars on Nicky, while he was a prisoner. A friend of Fannie's said that the amount she realized on her jewels was $20,000.

Fannie herself had married Frank White, a hotel

and barber shop proprietor of Schenectady, N. Y., and Springfield, Mass. Or maybe it was a beauty parlor he had. It doesn't matter. That marriage occurred Feb. 4, 1910. It was three years after Fannie had finished selling papers in Brooklyn by making a big hit on an amateur night, and it was the same year that she graduated from burlesque and vaudeville into Ziegfeld's "Follies." She lived with White three days. Asked why she married him, Fannie said:

"To kill time."

She got a divorce from White in 1913.

On October 28, 1917 Mrs. Arndstein, in an affidavit accompanying a motion for alimony and counsel fees in a counter-suit for divorce against Nicky, said:

"The plaintiff (Nicky had brought suit first) is a notorious confidence man, having been convicted in the Court of General Sessions, and was released from Sing Sing Prison quite some months ago.

"That he was a man of ability, and while I lived with him and while he supported me we were able to live in the finest style. That I always was under the impression that he was a broker and promoter.

"That our friendly relationship continued even during his incarceration in prison and that the first intimation I had that he was released from prison was a telephone message from some person unknown to me that my husband desired to meet me at the Hotel Ponchartrain, on August 11, 1917.

"That when I reached said place I met a gentleman who approached me at the door and asked me

276

if I was Mrs. Arndstein, to which I replied, 'I was,' and asked him where my husband was, and this stranger told me that if I would go into the ladies' waiting room, that my husband would meet me there.

"After waiting about fifteen or twenty minutes or thereabouts, I became impatient and came down the elevator from the ladies' waiting room, and met my husband with another gentleman.

"That my husband started in to accuse me of having come to the hotel for immoral purposes. That I never entered any room in the hotel except the ladies' waiting room, and have never had any relationship with any man except my husband to whom I have been a faithful and loving wife since our marriage.

"The defendant wrote me a letter while I was in prison, which I annex hereto, in which letter I particularly call attention to the fact that he requested me to represent myself as his sister-in-law. I am now informed the defendant was receiving visits from Fannie Brice while he was in jail, and whom he represented as his lawful wife.

"That during defendant's term in prison I was thrown upon my own resources, and when my health permitted, I acted as a demonstrator of ladies' garments. That my average earnings during the year are about $9 a week.

"That I have a grown daughter who helps to keep up the little home by her own earnings and that my said daughter and myself reside at 200 West One Hundred and Ninth Street.

277

"That I am without means to pay my lawyer, Aaron A. Feinberg, for the defense of this action.

"That plaintiff (Nicky) rides around in an automobile and meets said Fannie Brice nightly after her performance at one of the New York theatres."

Nicky's letter to her showed that he was Convict No. 67,050, and in it he asked her to be a sister-in-law if she called on him. Mrs. Arndstein showed some poetry that Nicky had written her before he met Fannie Brice. Any book should have a poem or two, so here it is:

"I have lived and I have loved,
I have waked and I have slept,
I have sung and I have danced,
I have smiled and I have wept.
All those things were weariness;
And some of them were dreariness.
Of all these things, but two things
Were emptiness and pain,
And love it was the best of them."

Nicky must have been reading Keats—or "Mother Goose."

On July 31, 1918, Mrs. Arndstein sued Fannie Brice for $100,000 damages on the charge that she had stolen Nicky's love. A settlement by agreement was reached November 8, 1918.

The most amazing feature in this amazing situation is that Mrs. Arndstein accepted $700 for the release after her amazing husband took her on a Broadway party. Maybe he got a chance to whisper another poem in her ear.

Fannie Brice always said that she met Nicky in Baltimore in 1914. Their friends said they met in London in December, 1913, when Fannie was playing at the Palladium. There is no doubt that they met, anyway.

The final decree of divorce was granted Mrs. Arndstein on June 11, 1919 by Supreme Court Justice Leander Faber, in Long Island City.

Fannie Brice said that she and Nicky were married in Brooklyn. Wherever they were married, they were devoted to each other during the days I knew Nicky fairly well, and Fannie slightly.

The bond robberies, in which Nicky got his greatest notoriety, became known to the public in February, 1920, when three men were arrested. It was not acumen on the part of the detectives that caused this arrest. It was the desire of a man who had a criminal record to save his own hide. He tattled to benefit himself.

One of the prisoners was a young chap named Joe Gluck. He said that during the preceding two years more than two million dollars in stolen bonds had passed through his hands. He arranged with messenger boys to steal them, he said, and then turned them over to Arnold. He was taken to the Rogues Gallery where he said Arnstein was Arnold. At about the same time that the alarm was sent out for Nicky as the "master mind," an alarm was sent out also for "Big Nick" Cohn, a former pickpocket.

From February until May, Nicky remained in hiding, despite a country wide search, extraordinary publicity, and a reward of $5,000 for information leading to his arrest. He merely lived quietly in Pittsburgh—where there is plenty of smoke.

Gene McGee, Bill Fallon's law partner, cheerfully admitted in court that he had seen and talked with Nicky, but Nicky didn't come in and surrender, as was related earlier in this account, until the bond had been arranged with Arnold Rothstein. Fannie Brice made the arrangement.

Every effort was made then and later to trace the stolen Liberty Bonds. Upwards of $1,000,000 were recovered, but $4,000,000 have remained untraced up to the time of this writing. Many officials connected with the affair were disappointed because the bonds in question have not been found in Rothstein's effects.

Guided by Fallon, Nicky refused to answer most questions asked him on the ground that they would "tend to incriminate and degrade" him. He was jailed for contempt for not replying, and the indefatigable Fallon got him free.

It finally was decided that the best chance of getting a conviction in the case of Nicky, "Big Nick," William Easterday, David W. Sullivan and Norman Boles, was in the District of Columbia. The charge was conspiracy in bringing stolen bonds into that bailiwick.

The authorities had become convinced that the stolen bonds had been turned over to David W. Sullivan & Co., who pledged them as collateral on loans. The banks took the Sullivan company on faith as a reputable house, and did not investigate the collateral. Bankers are something like laboratory scientists; they are used to believing labels on packages. If they didn't they couldn't do business. If a scientist had to test every ingredient he used for an experiment to prove the guarantee that it was pure, he never would get anywhere; if a bank were to question every piece of paper that came through it, business would be much slower.

That is lucky for crooks. In this case they were getting along in great style, and were dreaming of many more millions, when the end came so suddenly.

Sullivan and Co. confessed that their business was a subterfuge. Gluck's confession had wrecked the whole crooked structure.

Nicky never has been happy over the conduct of his first trial in Washington by Fallon, and he thinks Fallon treated him rather shamefully by not defending him in the second trial. The first trial ended in a disagreement, and the second in conviction. Nicky still asserts that it was not fair because in the District of Columbia the "uncorroborated word of an accomplice" was accepted as evidence, and because Judge Gould, who had presided, died of heart failure near the end of the second trial.

Nicky and his co-defendants landed in Leavenworth, May 16, 1924. Nicky emerged December 21, 1925, with seventy-two days off for good behavior.

Fannie Brice was a constant visitor while Nicky was a prisoner, and she thought the fact that he shoveled coal and worked as an electrician did him good. She remarked that he would be handier around the house in the future.

After he had been free a few months Nicky blos-

281

somed out with an electric sign, which he himself had invented. He opened offices at 19 West Fifty-seventh Street, New York, and acted as his own sales manager in a country-wide selling plan. The device was supposed to be for advertising purposes, and to be ideal because it was cheap to operate, requiring no motor.

When this business died, Nicky's friends said that $75,000 passed away with it.

In December, 1927, the police closed the Newport Beach Boating Club, in Chicago, which was called "Nicky Arnstein's gift" to that city. It was a marvelous gambling house while it lasted. Attachés in tuxedos, with special pockets for revolvers, were in waiting to escort to their homes patrons who won enormous sums, so it was said. They probably didn't have much escorting to do. Closing the club didn't cost Nicky and his partners as much as it might have cost them if they hadn't gotten the rather dashing fittings on credit.

They were a strange married pair—Fannie Brice and Nicky Arnstein. When I was at their place in Huntington, L. I. on the day mentioned in an earlier chapter—and it's no $500,000 estate either, or anything like it, as has been reported—Nicky was most domestic and hospitable.

He took more pleasure in explaining the workings of his folding partition than he did in discussing any other subject except Fannie.

I thought then how ridiculous it is to imagine there is a sharp line dividing the upper world from the underworld, and also how true it is that the easy money isn't the money that pays the legitimate freight of life. I had no doubt then, and I have none now, that the beautiful homes of Fannie and her husband, were paid for by Fannie's genius and hard work on the stage.

After her divorce from Nicky, Fannie Brice was told that it was a big surprise; she had been known so long as "the steadfast wife."

"I have done the biggest thing for Nicky I ever did," she said. "I've given him his liberty and put him on his own responsibility. He'll have a chance now to keep out of the newspapers and do something."

CHAPTER THIRTEEN

BROADWAY FINALE

ARNOLD ROTHSTEIN ate his last dinner on earth on the fateful evening of Sunday, November 4, 1928 at the Colony Restaurant with Inez Norton, the blonde with whom he was enamored. Later she said of these hours:

"Arnold was very gay—his normal, natural self —and very much in love. He didn't seem to have anything on his mind. He certainly didn't fear anything.

"We spoke of many subjects, but mostly of love; and he said that he hoped soon to be free to marry me. He said everything would be mine—his property and the money—but I cared only for him.

"We went in a taxi to Lindy's where we separated. I went into the Rivoli Theatre with a girl friend to see a movie called 'The Wedding March.' And I never saw him again."

After he had left Inez Norton, Rothstein entered Lindy's Restaurant. About 10:30 o'clock, Beatrice Jackson, a telephone operator in the Park Central Hotel had a request from Room 349 to call Circle 3317, which is the telephone number of Lindy's. The occupant of Room 349 was registered as George Richards, but many witnesses later testified that Richards was George A. McManus.

284

When the telephone rang in Lindy's, Abe Scher, the cashier, lifted the receiver, and heard a voice he says he failed to recognize say:

"Tell A. R. I want to talk with him."

Scher called Rothstein to the telephone. A moment's conversation followed, and then Rothstein said:

"McManus wants to see me. I'm going to his room. I'll be back in half an hour."

Rothstein went out into Broadway and met Jimmy Meehan, in whose apartment on the northeast corner of Fifty-fourth Street and Seventh Avenue, the last great card game in which Rothstein ever took part, was played on September 8 and 9.

It was in this card game, which Rothstein entered late, that he borrowed $19,000 in cash from Nate Raymond, and lost $200,000 to Raymond, and more thousands to "Titanic" Thompson, whose real name is Alvin C. Thomas. Rothstein and "Titanic" cut the cards at $40,000 a cut after the stud was finished.

Meehan testified before the Grand Jury that it was between 10:30 and 11 o'clock that Rothstein handed him a loaded revolver outside Lindy's and said:

"Hold this for me. George McManus wants to see me, and I'm going up to his room. I'll be back in half an hour."

The Park Central Hotel in Seventh Avenue, between Fifty-fifth and Fifty-sixth Streets is about six blocks from Lindy's in Boardway at Fiftieth Street.

It was about 10:50 when Rothstein next was seen. He was crumpled against the wall in the entrance to the servants' quarters of the hotel on the Fifty-sixth Street side, about twenty feet inside the street door.

The first man to see him was Vincent J. Kelly, who ran the servants' elevator. Thomas Calhoun, a night watchman, appeared immediately.

Policeman William S. Davis, of the West Forty-seventh Street station got there a minute or two later, a telephone call having been sent to the station house. Davis answered the box call on his post.

Rothstein said, "I was shot; get me an ambulance."

Dr. Malcolm McGovern arrived in an ambulance and took Rothstein to the Polyclinic Hospital. Although he realized the serious nature of his injuries, Rothstein told no one, so far as the record is concerned, the identity of his assailant.

At the hospital, Rothstein lingered in a semicomatose condition until about 10:20 o'clock election day morning, when he died. He had bet about $1,600,000 on the election, and would have won $500,000 if he had lived. His death voided the bets.

An interesting witness before the Grand Jury was the maid, Mrs. Bridget Farry. She once had worked for Rothstein at his Hotel Fairfield. When she had been injured in his service Rothstein personally had paid her money. She knew him well and favorably.

Mrs. Farry said that she had been on duty all afternoon and until midnight on the third floor where 349 was situated, and that she had been in and out of 349 three or four times. She saw McManus with Ruth Keyes, a blonde of Chicago (who has testified

286

that McManus was getting up a party for a good time, and was serving drinks). Mrs. Farry asserted that always there was at least one other man beside McManus in the room.

Most important, however, for McManus, she testified that between 10:20 and 10:30 McManus left 349 and did not return again.

Another significant item was that she said she saw a man whom she could not identify, walk through an exit on the third floor, which led to the servants' quarters below. That was between 10:30 and 11:00.

It is not beyond the realms of possibility that the man she saw was Rothstein. Even though she knew him, it may be pointed out that the north and south corridors in the hotel are a city block in length, and that, as his face was turned from her, it was not strange that she failed to recognize him.

Anyway, if Rothstein was shot in 349, and until this is being written on January 1, 1929, no witness had been found who even had seen him near that room, he walked with a thirty-eight calibre bullet through his intestines the distance of two city blocks and down three flights of stairs, which are equivalent to six flights of ordinary stairs, to get to where he was found. As Dr. Norris, the Chief Medical Examiner, said, a man could walk quite a distance after being hit, as was Rothstein. But why should he take that unaccustomed course?

Bridget Farry heard no shots. No witness yet examined heard any shots. No witness saw Rothstein in Room 349. At this writing it is obvious that the District Attorney and the police are hoping to get a squealer, as they did in the Rosenthal case. If there is any one who is considered likely to squeal there may be another shooting before this book is published.

Enough theories are held as to how the shooting was done to fill a large volume. The official theory that the shooting was done in 349 is based on the fact that McManus had that room, that Rothstein was known to have been headed for it, that a hole had been poked through a screen in a window, and that the revolver with one discharged cartridge in it, was picked up by Abe Bender, a taxi driver, in the east surface car tracks in Seventh Avenue, just opposite.

Sergeant Henry F. Butts, the pistol expert of the Police Department, told the Grand Jury that this was the gun from which the fatal pellet emerged. It is an interesting fact, however, that the barrel of the gun was so twisted, by contact with the pavement presumably, that another bullet could not be fired from it to compare the rifling marks with those on the lethal bullet. The pistol barrel won't be straightened for the test until a trial is had, and it has been offered in evidence.

Authorities were clinging to the belief that Rothstein may have told some member of his family, or some intimate who shot him. But there was no indication that he did tell any one.

The nurses—Anna Kenson, Doris Shubert, Martha Goerdel, and Elizabeth Love—and the surgeons in charge, Drs. William A., and H. L. Kellogg, and Detectives Patrick Flood and John Green, and every one else who came in contact with the dying Rothstein testified that he hadn't breathed the name of the murderer.

One of the nurses—Mrs. Love—testified before the Surrogate that Rothstein was semi-comatose when Maurice Cantor, the lawyer, guided his left hand in the motions which resulted in the wavering mark by which the last and contested will was signed —the will that made Inez Norton, among others, a prospective heiress, and which greatly benefited many of Rothstein's friends, including Cantor. Miss Martha Goerdel was reported to have been out of town when that particular hearing before the Surrogate was held. But more were scheduled.

No blood stains were found in 349, but that is not to be marvelled at, as the sort of wound Rothstein suffered, bleeds internally. There was no evidence whatever pertaining to a shooting; there were empty glasses, cigarette stubs, and McManus's overcoat.

Nate Raymond said he was going to sue the estate for the $19,000 he lent Rothstein. He knows the $200,000 he won from Rothstein is gone for ever. Well, it looks as if the $19,000 was gone too, because Nate hasn't an I. O. U. or a "scratch" to show for a nickel.

Rothstein had a habit of talking to persons, with his right hand in his jacket pocket, and a finger pushed forward so that it looked as if he were threatening with a revolver. One of many theories is that he may have adopted this characteristic pose, and have been shot. But it's not such a good theory because the bullet went in from behind and ranged downward.

Another theory is that, given occasionally to very rough language indeed, Rothstein may have gone too far with a man who had been drinking too much, and who acted in blind rage.

Rothstein had hundreds of efficient enemies. He had backed gangs, and hired thugs, and financed "white goods" traffic, and bootleggers, and had had a finger in almost every profitable illegal pie in New York,—and not a few that affected the country—so that he hadn't long to live by the most optimistic computations.

Only a few weeks before his murder, an attempt to kidnap him had miscarried because the kidnappers got the wrong man.

On December 4, 1928, just a month after the shooting, George McManus Hyman ("Gillie" or "Gil") Biller, and our old friend John Doe, and his pal, Richard Roe, were indicted of the murder. McManus, under $100,000 bail, hasn't said a word. He only has asked for a higher quality of literature than that provided in jail. "Gillie" Biller, who was McManus's payoff man—the chap that went around paying McManus's bets—hadn't been located at this writing. John Doe and Richard Roe are whoever they may turn out to be. The District Attorney says he knows. And he may. They are supposed to be two other men who were in Room 349 on the fatal night.

The one important fact is that the King of Easy Money in America is dead, and the underworld for the moment is without a "Brain."

When Arnold Rothstein died shortly after 10 o'clock on November 6, 1928—election day—in the Polyclinic Hospital, he left behind him in the city and the country such a whirling tumult as the departure from this life of no similar individual ever had caused.

The erasure of Herman Rosenthal with hot lead had induced a notable turmoil in the city: it caused the gamblers to close their palaces of chance: it walked Police Lieutenant Charles Becker and the four gunmen into eternity by way of the "hot seat" at Sing Sing, and it lifted Charles S. Whitman from the District Attorney's office to the Governor's chair.

Rothstein's murder resulted not only in the natural search for the person, or persons responsible, but it also led to a final effort to turn the light on all of the late "Big Shot's" devious activities in the underworld.

As a result of a peep at Rothstein's private files, Federal agents grabbed millions of dollars of narcotic drugs, and uncovered a trail that led to Chicago, Boston, Detroit, Philadelphia, San Francisco, and every other city of any size in the country.

This trail also led to other countries, where are the fountain heads of the streams of cocaine and heroin and morphine which pour through underworld channels into the United States, and are diffused throughout its length and breadth.

The authorities were "hopeful" also of showing that Rothstein was the biggest fence, or receiver of stolen goods in the country.

Not only was it charged that he had been behind the big bond robberies, but it also was asserted that he had turned back $25,000,000 in bonds, in a bargain that allowed him to keep $2,500,000 as his share. As a matter of fact, there never was anything to show that more than about $5,000,000 in bonds had been stolen, and there was nothing but rumor to support any contention that any part of this had been recovered. Officials who certainly should know, still were looking for the bonds.

Rothstein had guaranteed bail to the amount of about $1,500,000. He had enormous sums loaned at interest on various below-the-surface enterprises.

His fortune was of the sort that it took an Arnold Rothstein himself to manage. He was the only person on earth who ever had run that sort of big business; and he was the only person who knew all of its ramifications. Court appointees couldn't be expected to employ the Rothstein methods of collection, even if they knew from whom to collect.

Chances are that no sane person living would have offered Rothstein five cents for his vast business. He had a monopoly because he alone had the knowledge, the genius, the courage and audacity, and the peculiar twist of character, to hold sway over the invisible empire of the underworld.

Rothstein used to ask newspaper writers if they were happy in their positions. He would tell them to let him know if they became dissatisfied and he would "fix them right." He would make the same sort of statements to policemen, and city officials.

His vanity was inordinate, but his career backed up his own estimate of his powers.

I don't remember a great deal from the Greek of my rather hectic college days but I have a picture yet of old Socrates about to imbibe a dish of poison. Crito asked him what his friends would do with him after he was dead. Said Socrates, perhaps not in these exact words, but to this general effect:

"You can do anything you want to with me—provided you can get hold of me."

The forces of the law never got hold of Arnold Rothstein. His family buried the earthly tenement of Arnold Rothstein in the ground, after Arnold Rothstein had departed for some locality, where at least we know Sing Sing and Leavenworth are not located.

Looked at from the point of view of his own world Arnold Rothstein's life was as much of a success as the successful lives of many great Emperors. He lived longer than Alexander, and certainly was responsible for fewer deaths and less human misery; and he didn't have to linger in exile as did Napoleon. A chap who tosses the ordinary rules of society over his left shoulder, and sets out to assault life in his own way, always is prepared for the natural dénouement.

Rothstein had been warned often enough that he might expect a lethal bullet. He had employed bodyguards for a long time. He had been told if he didn't retire he was likely to be ejected forcibly, not only from his business, but from life. However, he was a fatalist.

He told a friend once who remonstrated with him for carrying such huge sums of money:

"If this money in my pocket is destined to go into the hands of some gunman, no power on earth could prevent it. So, I'm not worrying."

He had the same feeling about himself. For long those who knew him wouldn't have wagered one dollar against ten that he would die a natural death, but Rothstein had absolute faith in his ability to get himself out of a hole.

It always seemed to me, and still does at this writing, that the fact that only one bullet was fired, indicated that the person responsible had not intended to kill, or even to press the trigger. I believe that the man with the revolver was threatening, and that Rothstein was joshing.

Rothstein walked a long way after he was hit. The underworld's method of murder by gun-fire is to empty all the guns available at the moment into the target. It is not customary for underworld slayers to stand idly by and watch a target stroll off with only one bullet as ballast. The fact that Rothstein declined to tell who shot him was no proof that the man who fired the shot knew he wouldn't tell.

I'm not a betting man myself, but a small wager now and then adds zest to life. I tried to bet with various persons who know their Broadway that no one ever would be convicted of the murder of Rothstein, and from the moment news of the shooting was known until now—the first of January—I haven't been able to get any takers. They all are willing to give odds that there won't be any convictions that

294

will hold water, anyhow, in a higher court. I always was willing to take a chance, and I'm going to leave in this book the prophecy that no one goes to the electric chair for Rothstein's death. If I'm wrong, it won't be the first time. And what's the use of being wrong unless one can be wrong in a big way?

The squabble over Rothstein's will failed to interest me as much as a glance over the personality of the man. Reports that his net estate was "only $1,500,000," or that it was minus nothing, or what, didn't seem very pulse-stirring. He always had controlled millions and millions of dollars, and that was an important item. The fact that the blond widow, Carolyn Rothstein, and Inez Norton, the blond charmer, actress and divorcee, were lined up on opposite sides of the will fight, was interesting—but nowhere near as interesting as the character of Rothstein himself.

Snapshots always are more interesting than studio portraits. They catch the subject off-guard, and while not so artistic, certainly are more realistic.

The earliest snapshot of Rothstein as a gambler would have been of his playing the game of stuss, still extremely popular on the East Side. I once made an investigation of those stuss games for *The World*. I knew before I began the investigation who controlled the upwards of 100 coffee houses in which they were maintained, and also who was back of the poolrooms in which East Side crap games were played, but proving it was a different matter. The man who ran them then, and runs them now, so far as I know, was an old friend of Rothstein, and of

Rosenthal, and is a power in politics. Stuss is a poor man's game. It is one of the methods by which he pays his contributions to easy money.

When Jim Corbett ran a café in Broadway more than twenty years ago, Rothstein often was seen there. He was just emerging at that time from the ordinary gambler class into the landed proprietor type. Among the patrons were Sam Bernard, and other actors.

In 1916 Rothstein was famous as the biggest gambler of them all. His reputation for readiness to bet on anything had been established. His purchase of a Cadillac runabout that spring was the occasion for a deal of joking by his intimates who, as all during his life, included most respectable members of society, who enjoyed betting on this or that, as a little fillip to the task of living.

"Ha! Ha!" said his friends, "you'll never drive that thing, Arnold."

"What'll you bet I don't drive it down to Belmont Park to-day?" was Rothstein's rejoinder.

Rothstein never had driven an automobile before in his life, although he owned several cars.

George Considine, proprietor of that famous rendezvous of the sporting fraternity, the old Hotel Metropole, Jack Connors, George Young Bauchle, the lawyer, and others, promptly offered to give him odds, even as high as 10 to 1, that he couldn't do it.

Rothstein took all the bets that were offered, which was his usual system, and then spent four feverish hours practising driving. After that, amid cheers and laughter, he started from Broadway—and in three hours of hairbreadth escapes, and stalled engines, and curses from other drivers, he arrived at Belmont Park, and collected. After he saw the Metropolitan Handicap run off, he walked back to the runabout, and drove back to Broadway, a feat which hadn't been included in the bargain.

When Rothstein arrived at his offices, which in later years were at 45 West Fifty-seventh Street, his first glance was at a sheet of paper on which had been written mysterious symbols. That paper revealed whether or not Rothstein's gambling and other regular enterprises had prospered the night before or not. If the news was good, Rothstein was most cheerful; if the news was depressing, he was extremely snappish with his employes, and put more than usual emphasis into the "God help you, if you don'ts" which he whipped into the telephone transmitter to delinquent promisers to pay.

Before him as he sat was a form on which were entered the details of business he wished to attend to that day. A receiver was clamped over one ear, leaving the other free to hear the words of the office workers. Rothstein didn't pay them too much, and he was a most exacting employer.

It was not unusual for him to apologize to some one for having sent a dunning letter, and to say that he would see that no more such letters were sent. Then he would turn to his secretary and say:

"Keep on sending letters like that until they pay up."

Rothstein always kept many safety deposit boxes

in many banks, and what the boxes, or his files held, is still a mystery.

Rothstein was a restless person, and one who enjoyed gay parties. He liked to sit around and buy wine for men and women acquaintances, although he drank none himself. He was a most amiable and amusing table companion, was extremely affable to chance acquaintances, and liked to give the impression that he knew everybody worth while.

A friend of Rothstein, now in a high position in the world, told me only recently:

"He certainly expected his friends to pay for his friendship. He'd put the pressure on right up to the limit."

In this connection there fits in his visit to Police Headquarters when George McLaughlin was Commissioner. McLaughlin ordered Rothstein thrown out. Instead of getting thrown out, Rothstein went to see a high official in the building, who promptly went to the Commissioner to plead for Rothstein who was after a permit to carry a revolver. McLaughlin, it is said, never placed the same amount of confidence in that official again. In the Police Department were many close friends of Rothstein.

Much was made of that sitting in the newspapers of that last big stud game, but it wasn't by any means an unusual game for Rothstein. Nicky Arnstein used to tell of a game in which he saw Rothstein wager $500,000 on the turn of one card.

It would be possible here to give a description of any one of several games in which Rothstein sat, but those games did not differ materially from the ordinary poker games with which most persons are familiar. The only difference was in the size of the stakes. One of the most tiresome persons in the world is the one who inflicts poker game details on his friends.

Any one who has bet a few dollars on a hand may try to imagine for himself the sensation of betting half a million dollars on a card. Rothstein's bets were so tremendous that accounts of them fall dead because of their very magnitude. It is hard for the ordinary individual, who has a few dollars in the bank, and a mortgage on his home, to grasp them.

Among those in the last stud game were Nate Raymond and Edward C. Thompson. The police and the newspaper promptly dubbed Raymond "Nigger," and Thompson "Titanic," because "when he lost he went down like the Titanic"—a total loss. Now, neither Nate nor Thompson ever had heard of these nicknames before, and they both were more embarrassed by them than by their arrests in connection with the shooting. Nate, a bridegroom, who had left his new motion picture actress wife in Hollywood to come East for a go at cards, was especially upset. Under $100,000 bail in the Tombs, he wailed to all and sundry that a fate that tacked the nickname of "Nigger" on a guy was indeed a cruel one.

It is that way with many of the trick names applied to members of the underworld and of the gambling brotherhood. Bright newspaper reporters, and detectives with romantic imaginations and a love of the picturesque, do much of this impromptu title bestowing, all in the line of the day's work.

Rothstein was a stickler for having money loaned returned to him exactly on the date set, but he made exceptions in the cases of some of his intimates, and of persons whom he trusted.

He backed some theatrical enterprises, and some pugilistic enterprises, and was the money bag behind many little shops in the Times Square district. His passion was lending—and collecting. He hated to be owed money for any reason.

On one occasion he said to "One Time Charlie" Freedman:

"You owe me a month's rent, Charlie."

Freedman, who was a tenant of Rothstein's, said:

"No, I'm all paid up, and I've got the canceled check to prove it."

"I'll bet you $500 to $25 you're wrong," Rothstein said. "I never made a mistake in my life."

"It's a bet," said Charlie.

Freedman later showed Rothstein the canceled check for $500. Rothstein said at first that it was a check he had cashed for Freedman, and he never did admit verbally that he had been wrong. He couldn't do that. But he credited Charlie with $500 on the books, and let the matter drop.

Rothstein hated the word "welsh," although it was used for his benefit very frequently by bookmakers and fellow gamblers, many of whom detested him.

"What are you going to do—welsh?" he was asked, about that last poker game a few days before his death.

"My God," he exclaimed, "don't use that word talking to me."

Now that Rothstein is dead, the biggest gambler left is "Nick, the Greek," of Chicago. "Nick, the Greek" could clean them all out in his home town, but he never could clean out Rothstein, though the desire to do so became the obsession of his life. "Nick" is left with no worlds to conquer now, and one may imagine him pining away for lack of real excitement—no place to drop a three or four hundred thousand dollar bankroll.

Rothstein also generally was believed to have a hand in the chain system of slot machines found in many localities, every slot machine being so arranged mechanically that no one has a chance against it.

The police long had considered Rothstein the backer of gambling houses all over the country in which are installed crooked roulette wheels—Cleveland, Chattanooga, Chicago and Los Angeles are some of the cities mentioned. A friend of mine from the latter place told me that the general impression was that Rothstein was the backer of the biggest gambling club in that city, and that there he had heard of the refusal of Rothstein to pay his losses in the last stud game. It also was said that "something might happen to Rothstein."

That isn't at all remarkable, however. That big stud game and Rothstein's refusal to pay was open gossip on Broadway for days before Rothstein was shot. Word of it probably had permeated to the furthest outposts of the underworld in all parts of the

301

globe. They knew of it just as well in Boston, in London, and in Paris, as they did in New York.

It was known that when he received threats over the telephone or in person that Rothstein always said:

"How will you get your money if I'm dead?"

And that's what the players in the stud game wanted to know after election day. They didn't even have the satisfaction of seeing any part of the small change of $6,000 which Rothstein had in his pocket when he was taken to hospital. Cantor took charge of that. One of Rothstein's favorite remarks was:

"The dubs who don't know how to make money are the ones that call me crooked. With me, it's brains. I can tell any man how to make money and make it straight. It takes brains, personality and opinion. I'll back my own judgment any time."

On the other hand, there is the tale of Rothstein's going into the noted barber shop run by "John, the Barber." He sat in a chair and after having had a haircut and shave he remarked that it was about time for a certain race to be run at some out-of-town track. Some one else said:

"The race has just about been run right now."

"Well," Rothstein said, "I'll bet you that such and such a horse [naming it] wins."

The bet was made and it was found that Rothstein's horse had won. The explanation commonly accepted was that another man who had come late into the shop, had informed Rothstein of the winner by a signal code. If this customer asked for a close shave, that meant one horse, if he asked for "once over, and light," that was another horse, and so on.

Another story of the same sort that was associated with Rothstein was that he was on his way to the Polo Grounds to see his favorite Giants play one day. One the way up, just at race time, he made a heavy bet with a friend, and later was found to have won it. Rothstein's enemies always insisted that he had planted a confederate at a vantage point along the route, and had caught the winner by prearranged signal before he made the bet.

One of Rothstein's boasts was that he never had paid more than $150 for income tax in any one year. Certainly, his income tax payments gave no indication of his immense income.

Rothstein's tentacles were everywhere. His grip on prominent men extended all the way from favors done in the way of letting bets ride, or of forgetting bets lost, through sums loaned, and merely friendly acts, to actual connivance in outwitting the law in greater or in less degrees.

Crap games, night clubs, bootlegging and "dope" smuggling all required capital. Rothstein had the capital, and he knew the underworld. A chap robbed your home, by the second story, if he were a second story worker, by a window on the ground floor, if he were that sort of thief, and got away with money and valuables. Then he went and played craps, probably, in one of the many games backed by Rothstein through agents.

Perhaps he was broke when he was arrested. Then, of course, he required a bondman, and money for a lawyer. Rothstein was in the bond business, and he had money to lend for such a legitimate purpose as hiring good counsel. So this thief got his liberty under bail and obtained a lawyer.

But he knew that the "Big Shot" had to be paid. And he only knew one profession. He couldn't make the several thousands of dollars he owed by selling newspapers, or laying bricks. He robbed another house, or held up another payroll messenger, or stuck up another speakeasy, or blackmailed, or badgered, or did what ever was his racket specialty, and got the money to pay his debts.

I don't believe that Rothstein ever laid out the plans for any individual rackets. That wasn't his reputation, even among those who hated him. But he backed the racketeers with his resources, and he knew what they were doing.

Rothstein had many encounters with gunmen, for whom he always expressed contempt. One gunman shoved a revolver into his stomach one day, and demanded $500.

"When you get $500 out of me you'll need it to pay your funeral expenses with," was Rothstein's reply. "Now think that over."

One chap who was Rothstein's bodyguard for five years, was asked why he had quit:

"Aw, he was too cheap," he said.

Ten dollars a day: that was Rothstein's pay for a gunman.

There's a chap in New York, however, we'll call Abraham, who thought that he had found a generous patron in the "Big Shot."

Abraham won $2,000 from Rothstein one day, and felt pretty good about it. He figured that if he put that with what he already had, he might be able to go into business for himself. While he was figuring Rothstein sent for him, and told him that he had located a "sucker," who had a plump roll of yellow backs. Abraham said he had no cash with him.

"Here is $2,000 I'll lend you," Rothstein said kindly. "You can pay me when you get this sucker's money."

Abraham lost the $2,000, and then he went out and got $12,000 which was all he had. And after that was gone he looked up Rothstein.

"You owe me $12,000," he said. "That sucker you dug up for me took your $2,000 and my $12,000."

"Why," Rothstein said, "I can't understand how that boob took a smart guy like you. But don't be foolish. That $2,000 I lent you was only a loan, and I will expect it back with interest. As for the $12,000, that was your money, as you have said— not mine."

"The majority of human beings," Rothstein said once, "are dubs and dumbbells. They've rotten judgment, and no brains, and when you've learned how to do things, and how to size people up, and have doped out methods of your own, they jump to the conclusion you're crooked.

"I knew my limitations when I was fifteen years old, and since that time I never played any game with a man I knew I couldn't beat."

In 1926, a "mysterious, disguised figure" was reported to have been seen in Cannes, France. This was supposed to have been Rothstein on a private holiday. The report which credited him with having won $6,000 at roulette, added that he decided the game was too slow, and suggested toying with a pair of dice. The Casino authorities requested him to go elsewhere after that. Whether or not the mysterious figure was Rothstein, the incident well might have occurred. There never was any such gambling in Monte Carlo, or in any of the other popular Continental resorts, as that in which Rothstein, "Nick, the Greek" and that crew indulged.

Those boys would stand down at the track on a sweet summer's day, and bet twenty or fifty thousand dollars on the bobbing noses of the horses as they came down the stretch.

They didn't want any limit, except their imaginations, when they rolled the dice.

Rothstein would cut the cards at $1,000 a cut any time anywhere.

The only barrier to Rothstein's playing for higher stakes was lack of some one else in the world to play with him. He sat on his throne in New York, and waited. They came, and went, but he always was on the job. It must be a lonesome world for that handsome daredevil, "Nick, the Greek." Nick would bet all he had, which is all any man can do. Rothstein had more. That was the only difference between those two sportsmen—in sport.

At the king business Rothstein stood alone.

NEW JERSEY

Hudson River

THE UNIVERSITY OF MICHIGAN

NX

AND

DATE DUE

DEC 1988

DEC 1 1989

SEP 12

MAR 09

1452302R0

Printed in Great Britain by
Amazon.co.uk, Ltd.,
Marston Gate.